WITHD

SERENITY IN CRISIS

ORTWIN DE GRAEF

Serenity in Crisis

A Preface
to Paul de Man,
1939–1960

UNIVERSITY OF NEBRASKA PRESS

LINCOLN & LONDON

© 1993 by the University of Nebraska Press
All rights reserved
Manufactured in the United States of America
The paper in this book meets
the minimum requirements of American National
Standard for Information
Sciences – Permanence of Paper for Printed Library
Materials, ANSI Z39.48-1984.
Library of Congress Cataloging in Publication Data
Graef, Ortwin de, 1963-
Serenity in crisis : a preface to Paul de Man, 1939-
1960 / Ortwin de Graef.
p. cm. – (Texts and contexts : v.4)
Includes bibliographical references and index.
ISBN 0-8032-1694-7
I. Title. II. Series.
PN75.D45G73 1993 801'.95'092 – dc20
92-14721 CIP

For Caroline

Contents

Preface, xi

A Note on Translations, xiii

List of Abbreviations, xv

PART ONE
Conditions of Truth, 3

Chapter 1
The Collaboratory, 5
*The Whole Truth, 7: Deduction, 11:
Induction, 16: Intuition, 21*

CHAPTER 2
Ambergris and Gudgeon, 27

Chapter 3
The Temptation of Irony, 29
*Inventory, 30: In Parenthesis, 36:
A Thing of the Past, 39*

PART TWO
Intention of the Dialectic, 45

Chapter 4
The Double Aspect: Two Roads
for Poetry, 49
Road 1, 51: Road 2, 62

Chapter 5
Evasion and Confrontation, 67
*The Existential Choice, 70: The Funda-
mental Dissymmetry, 80:
Foundations of the Dissymmetry, 87*

Chapter 6
Dialogue and Distortion, 109
*Knots of Resistance, 109: A Resistance
of History, 119: The Critical Choice, 133*

Chapter 7
The Critical Aspect: At Least Three
Roads for Criticism, 137
*The Single Aspect of Poetry and Recon-
ciliatory Criticism, 137:
The Single Aspect of Poetry and the
Future of Criticism, 145*

Chapter 8
Reversal of Priority, 155
*Unclaimed Garments, 157: Tempta-
tional Structure of the
Romantic Image, 163: The Question
after Serenity, 174*

Notes, 179

Bibliography, 211

Index, 227

. . . I never had an idea of my own. . . .
—Paul de Man

Preface

One of the most persistent criticisms of the work of Paul de Man is that it systematically effects a rejection of 'history,' 'reality,' 'experience,' 'politics,' 'humanity'—in short, the 'important issues'[1]—in favor of impersonal 'textual forces' or 'rhetorical mechanisms.' In an attempt to comprehensively address this criticism, I initially set out on a preliminary synopsis of de Man's writing before his pivotal 1969 essay, 'The Rhetoric of Temporality,' in which this 'programmatic (and utterly simplistic) substitution of technical rhetorical categories for existential categories'[2] is generally held to have definitively acquired shape, but I soon found myself unable to progress beyond local difficulties of interpretation and was forced to substitute the terms of these difficulties for those of explanatory summary.

Serenity in Crisis is the first of two books that try to perform this substitution. Its main concern is de Man's writing from the 1950s, but it starts out from a fairly detailed reading of one persistent problem in his wartime journalism, thus displacing the initial project into a further past, with all the complications this entails. This emphasis on the 1950s can easily be justified in observing that that phase of de Man's writing has up to now been either neglected or read only as background material written by the author of *Allegories of Reading,* but it is also motivated by a refusal to close off these texts by reading them *exclusively* as written by the author of 'The Jews in Contemporary Literature' (*Le Soir,* March 1941, 45).

Briefly, it is my contention that a pursuit of the issues developed in earlier interpretations of de Man's 'mature thought' and of his collaborationist or collaborative journalism may benefit from a consideration of the writing in between on its own terms, and it is on the basis of this contention—whose disturbingly banal and patently problematic nature I have tried to acknowledge, if not contain, throughout—that *Serenity in Crisis* presumes to its title as a preface to Paul de Man. As a preface, this book also participates in the production of what Wordsworth once called a 'tender fiction,'[3] in that it imposes a speaking face on a name and in doing so tries to develop a dialogue that is always in danger of being nothing other than a deluded monologue, performing what it eschews and celebrating what it fails to allow for: a reading of Paul de Man. But it is possible to resist this indifference.

My debts are what they always are. I am very grateful for the valuable comments on earlier versions of this book by Jonathan Culler, Sander L. Gilman, Samuel IJseling, Hendrik van Gorp, Ludo Verbeeck, Samuel Weber, and, especially, Herman Servotte. For their diverse remarks and contributions over the past years I am indebted to Michael Burri, Stefaan Cuypers, Patricia de Laet, Lisa Dolling, David Herman, Filip Huyghe, Bradley Jordan, Willem Lemmens, Dieter Lesage, Bart Philipsen, Jan Roelans, Tom Trezise, Dirk Vanderpoorten, and Luc Van Liedekerke, and particularly to Dirk De Schutter, Koenraad Geldof, and Hedwig Schwall. Conversations with Erik Leroy have frequently made all the difference. Special thanks are also due to Neil Hertz and Thomas Keenan and to Peter Brooks, Emory Elliot, Michael Holquist, Peter Hughes, Kris Humbeeck, José Lambert, Peter Steiner, Sanford Pinsker, and Gerald Prince for their generous invitations to speak on de Man at their respective institutions. To name everyone who has further helped my research would take up too much space, but I must mention Frida Vandervelden, de Man's daughter Patricia de Man, and Louis Dupré. If it had not been for the rare haven the Belgian National Fund for Scientific Research offers the humanities today, this book would never have been written; my gratitude to its scientific committee and to its permanent secretary José Traest is accordingly great. My colleagues at the Katholieke Universiteit Leuven know what I owe them, as do my parents and friends. Finally, thanks to Caroline: to her this book is dedicated.

Leuven, July 1991

A NOTE ON TRANSLATIONS

Most of Paul de Man's texts considered in this study were not originally written in English. Whenever possible I have made use of published English translations of these texts for the purpose of quotation. In some cases I have modified these translations for the sake of consistency. In other cases I have emended translations that were inaccurate or simply wrong. Both types of alterations are indicated as such in the text. When no English translations were available (as in the case of de Man's wartime journalism) I have supplied translations myself. Translations from secondary sources not available in English are also my own.

Abbreviations

References to de Man's wartime journalism identify the original source, the month and year of first publication (if not already specified), and the page number in the volume *Wartime Journalism*. References to de Man's later work are indicated by means of abbreviations for separate items and, if possible, for the collection in which these items are (re)published. To facilitate cross-reference to the Bibliography, the year under which an essay or article is listed is added after each entry. For the texts originally written in French or German, the title of the English translation is added in parentheses.

WARTIME JOURNALISM

BD	*Bibliographie Dechenne*
C	*Les Cahiers du Libre Examen*
HVL	*Het Vlaamsche Land*
J	*Jeudi*
LS	*Le Soir*

BOOKS

AR	*Allegories of Reading*
BI	*Blindness and Insight*
CW	*Critical Writings, 1953–1978*
RR	*The Rhetoric of Romanticism*
RT	*The Resistance to Theory*
WJ	*Wartime Journalism, 1939–1943*

'AD'   'Autobiography as De-Facement' (1979)

'AI'   Review of Harold Bloom's *The Anxiety of Influence* (1974)

'AT'   'Anthropomorphism and Trope in the Lyric' (1983)

'C'   Comments (1966)

'CC'   'The Crisis of Contemporary Criticism' (1967)

'DA'   'The Double Aspect of Symbolism' (1955)

'DF'   'Impasse de la critique formaliste' ('The Dead-End of Formalist Criticism') (1956)

'F'   'La critique thématique devant le thème de Faust' ('Thematic Criticism and the Theme of Faust') (1957)

'GL'   'Georg Lukács's *Theory of the Novel*' (1966)

'HE'   'Les exégèses de Hölderlin par Martin Heidegger' ('Heidegger's Exegeses of Hölderlin') (1955)

'HR'   'Heidegger Reconsidered' (1964)

'HRJ'   Introduction to *Toward an Aesthetics of Reception* (1982)

'HRT'   'Hölderlin and the Romantic Tradition' (1958)

'IG'   'The Inward Generation' (1955)

'INT II'   'An Interview with Paul de Man' (1983)

'IR'   'L'Image de Rousseau dans la poésie de Hölderlin' ('The Image of Rousseau in the Poetry of Hölderlin') (1965)

'IS'   'Structure intentionnelle de l'Image romantique' ('Intentional Structure of the Romantic Image') (1960)

'JL'   Introduction for Jacques Lacan (1975)

'KH'   'Keats and Hölderlin' (1956)

'MP'   'Modern Poetics: French and German' (1965)

'MR'   'Hypogram and Inscription' (1981)

'MT'   'Montaigne et la transcendence' ('Montaigne and Transcendence') (1953)

'PHD I'   Introduction to 'Mallarmé, Yeats and the Post-
             Romantic Predicament' (1960)
'PHD M'   Section on Mallarmé in 'Mallarmé . . .' (1960)
'PHD Y'   Section on Yeats in 'Mallarmé . . .' (1960)
'PN'   'Le néant poétique' ('Poetic Nothingness') (1955)
'PP'   'Le devenir, la poésie' ('Process and Poetry') (1956)
'PT'   'Patterns of Temporality in Hölderlin . . .' (1967)
'R'   'Proust et l'allégorie de la lecture' ('Reading
             [Proust]') (1972)
'RB'   'Roland Barthes and the Limits of Structuralism'
             (1972)
'RH'   'The Riddle of Hölderlin' (1970)
'RN'   'Nietzsche's Theory of Rhetoric' (1974)
'ROB'   'The Rhetoric of Blindness' (1971)
'ROT'   'The Rhetoric of Temporality' (1969)
'RP'   'The Return to Philology' (1982)
'RT'   'The Resistance to Theory' (1982)
'SL'   'Symbolic Landscape in Wordsworth and Yeats'
             (1962)
'SN'   'Situation du roman' ('Situation of the Novel')
             (1956)
'TP'   'Tentation de la permanence' ('The Temptation of
             Permanence') (1955)
'WB'   '"Conclusions": Walter Benjamin's *Task of the Trans-
             lator*' (1983)
'WBY'   'Image and Emblem in Yeats' (1960)

Part One

Conditions of Truth

—Here it is, this terrible maturity which made de Man, Mussolini, and so many others move from 'spoken international
socialism' to 'lived national socialism.' . . .—Maurice Merleau-
Ponty, 'Epilogue,' *The Adventures of the Dialectic*

I t is not ironic that Paul de Man, whose wary reading of the
power of narrative was and is exemplary, should have become
the protagonist of some of the most compelling academic
narratives of the past years. It just happened. Neither is it ironic
that these narratives are never really told, but are rather projected,
plotted, promised. That, too, happens. This happening is related
to the nature of relation, to narrative as the name of the impossible task to relate everything ('Only connect . . .'). Narrative must,
therefore it cannot: like Mrs. Gradgrind, we shall never hear the
last of it.

My narrative begins in America, in the first half of the 1950s,
when the central figure of this book began to write his impressive
essays on literature. But because it is a narrative, it must begin
elsewhere, on another continent, and at least fifteen years earlier,
with this central figure's involvement first against and then with
totalitarian ideology. My obedience to this wholly legitimate imperative is willfully limited: the only thing I propose to do is to
read a minimal amount of de Man's wartime journalism with the
single-minded intent to articulate it with the work to come, in the
first instance with his essays of the 1950s. I shall not document in

further detail the immediate historical, political, and institutional context of de Man's involvement with the collaboration, not because enough has been said about this already,[1] but because what I wish to add here demands a response to the historical occurrence of de Man's collaboration in another mode.

CHAPTER ONE

The Collaboratory

The application of a precise, unequivocal language, of a mathematical style of fact, adequate for the twentieth century, is to
be desired. . . . The journalistic conscience here involves a
maximal measure of descriptive accuracy.—Ernst Jünger, *The
Worker*, § 74

T he narrative Paul de Man tried to write from the late 1930s
       onward is that of the relation between what happens and
       what happens to be written: from the outset, it was a
metanarrative. To appreciate this point is to question at least two
possible accounts of his journalistic work under the German occupation: de Man's reviews were not the work of someone whose
true interest was in literature but who was required to occasionally
expound on the state of the world; neither were they the work of
a self-styled propagandist who used the literary review as a convenient excuse for the exposition of a contemporary ideology. To a
certain extent, they were both of these and neither: his observations on both literature and on what he often calls 'the events' are
powered by the assumption of an extraordinary confidence whose
principal source lies elsewhere.

De Man's early public life constitutes a remarkable frame for
this source. In July 1937 he passes the admission exam at the poly-
technic of the Free University of Brussels and subsequently enrolls
as a student of civil engineering. The following year he abandons
these studies and turns to chemistry, in which he receives a first

degree, *cum laude,* in October 1940. But he unexpectedly does not pursue this line and instead registers for a special complementary program in social sciences.[1] He does not sit his exams and soon after (November 1941) the Free University closes. Meanwhile, from March 1939 onward, he had been active as contributor to and later editor of publications of the left-liberal student organization Le Libre Examen, writing mainly on literature and in defense of a Belgian policy of neutrality in the face of the war. Under the German occupation, Le Libre Examen ceases its publications (May 1940) and in the Christmas 1940 issue of *Le Soir* de Man publishes the first of his contributions to the German-controlled press.[2]

No matter how contingent the decisions structuring this narrative may have been, they do form an instructive pattern: a reasonably successful student of science with an evident interest in literature and in ideological issues abandons a scientific career, inconclusively turns to social sciences, and ends up as literary reviewer. The pattern involves three practices—the discourse of natural science, of social science, and of literature—and it quasi-mechanically invites the hypothesis that it is in the contest of these faculties that de Man's early work comes to be written, in an awareness of the rivaling claims to truth represented by these three disciplines and their subdisciplines and in response to a demand to demarcate clearly their respective jurisdiction.[3] It may seem far-fetched to read such an ambitious and prestigious desire to police the disciplines in pieces of journalism which at first sight could so much more economically be explained as the hack work of a young opportunist, but as I shall try to show, this desire is arguably one of their main formative concerns. In the course of this demonstration, which will focus on only a very small number of texts in which this concern is most explicitly present and which will therefore only ever tell part of the story, the three disciplines or cultures function as forces in a heuristic fiction whose principal aim is to serve as a provisional grid for structuring de Man's own attempts to impose a grid on the discourses of truth.

The Whole Truth

A significant incidence of de Man's early concern for the conditions of truth is the January 1940 essay in which he tries to sketch a paradigm clash in literature: 'On what depends this abyss we sense between *The Forsyte Saga* and *Ulysses,* the same there is in France between *Le Démon du midi* and *Du côté de chez Swann,* or in Germany between *Buddenbrooks* and *Das Schloß*' (C, January 1940, 16).[4] The question does not have a mark: de Man has an answer. The difference dividing these pairs is that between 'simplification,' 'schematization,' or 'typecasting,' and a respect for, in Huxley's phrase, 'the Whole Truth.' The 'classical' novel has always been based on 'character *[caractère],*' a 'fairly simple concept, born from observation': human beings were thought to consist of a certain number of primary qualities and to 'differ from each other, a bit like recipes for cooking, through a more or less subtle mixture of ingredients. The task of the novelist consisted of the fabrication of these skillful mixtures, sufficiently complex to be plausible. He thus created *types,* which he placed before certain circumstances and submitted to certain events.' The 'new' novel, on the other hand, is marked by 'a more penetrating and more lucid attention for the observation of the human being. . . . The novelists have transformed themselves into ruthless psychologists, enemies of any simplification which would falsify the truth on human nature' (17). 'This new discipline,' as de Man calls it, is in fact 'perfectly revolutionary' and will destroy the 'solid edifice' of the nineteenth-century novel (based as this latter was on the 'manifest falsehood that man is an immutable and rigid composition') in order to replace it with an 'anarchic chaos.' Instead of merely narrating the story of types, the 'psychological novel' investigates the truth of man as an 'essentially mobile' being. It

7

thus brings to light the plurality of characters in one individual and exposes the differentiation between types as a 'superficial' discrimination. Yet, what a 'serious analysis' thus yields is not merely a desimplification but ultimately the disappearance of differences in the face of 'universally human factors' (17). The *telos* of the psychological novel is not the institution of anarchic chaos but the true determination of the universal motives of human action.

The evolution de Man sketches here unmistakably takes place under the aegis of truth, but it is important to grasp that the development is not simply one from untruth to truth. In fact, the conflict mimics a crucial contention within the social sciences: what is at stake is the rivalry between a certain sociology and a certain psychology, both of which pretend to scientific truth.[5] The difference involved is not a matter of intent—both disciplines are bent on the production of truth through 'observation' (16, 17)—but of focus: sociology projects its truth as the interaction of primary qualities with 'a determined social condition' and with 'diverse circumstances' (16), whereas psychology seeks to explain the truth of human behavior by sounding the murky depths of unstable personal motivation. De Man's preferences in this are clear; to him, psychology is the cardinal social science and researchers into 'the Whole Truth' *(la complète vérité)* must needs take recourse to it, lest they end up in the realm of what merely resembles truth *(vraisemblable)*.[6]

The consequences of this view for the specificity of literature are considerable, though de Man only obliquely acknowledges them. Given the primacy of truth as determination and explanation through observation (i.e., a model of truth rooted in natural science), literature figures only as skill and technique. The classical novelists fabricated their 'dosages savants' of standard ingredients; the modern novelist follows different procedures (interior monologue or rational analysis), but they remain merely representational techniques in the service of truth. As for the 'beauty of expression' (Huxley's 'harmonies savantes,' for instance), that is only a 'purely aesthetic' technique to avoid 'the boredom that threatens to emanate from these quasi-scientific expositions' (18). Both the sociological and the psychological novel require skill, but the prime criterion with which they should be judged is their ability to reproduce scientific truth, even if only in the mode of the 'as if.'

Despite its confident presentation, this model harbors a significant uncertainty, already apparent in its somewhat paradoxical double rejection of the consistency *within* types in favor of an unstable mixture of 'dissimilar characteristics' and of the differentiation *between* types in favor of 'universally human factors,' but more manifest in de Man's 'illustration' of his argument.

> The prototype, the one in whom nearly all the characteristics mentioned are almost excessively present, is James Joyce. In laboratories one sometimes displays phenomena developed up to monstrosity as an aid to understand normal facts. To some extent, Joyce fulfills this role in the field that occupies us. (17)

Thus Joyce is cast as a protagonist in a narrative, and as de Man's analogy makes clear, the method of this observation is a scientific one. Turning back to his earlier characterization of the sociological novelists, we see that the pattern is admirably consistent. The individual sociological novelists are themselves characters in a sociological narrative: he or she is a 'typical representative of the institutions, traditions, and manners' of his or her country, and like the novelist's characters, the sociological novelist functions with the predictability of 'an admirable machine' (16), producing sociological truth. The psychological novelist, on the other hand, is a character in a psychological narrative: he or she is 'moved by influences that are difficult to detect' (17), but the final analysis reveals that the psychological novelist's real motive is the production of 'la vérité entière.' Both approaches, whether they are the novelist's or the critic's, produce *types*. The difference between these productions is that between cooking and chemistry: sociological truth consists of types that, 'like recipes for cooking,' confirm the existing ideology (of taste); psychological truth consists of types that exaggerate in order to understand normality. Cooking is amateur chemistry, chemistry is critical cooking, but ultimately both are intent on the reproduction of the norm in the name of the type. The purpose of de Man's model is to demarcate the boundaries between the naïve universality of sociological simplification and the scientific universality resulting from psychological desimplification, but the language of typology renders these boundaries more blurred than the model can allow for.

Deduction

Some eighteen months later, in the course of a review of Gregorio Marañon's study of Tiberius, de Man reproduces another monstrous specimen. Marañon's intention, as summarized by de Man, is to define a particular 'psychological type,' the 'man of resentment,' and for this purpose he uses the 'relatively new' and 'extremely fertile method' of tracing the historical destiny of an individual placed before circumstances that are unusually 'neat *[netteté]*' (LS, June 1941, 107). The principal merit of this method is that it allows one to establish 'with particular precision' phenomena which otherwise are 'submerged in the complexity of influences' (107). We are back in the laboratory: 'It is thus that one proceeds in laboratories of physics and chemistry: one 'isolates' phenomena even in order to subsequently determine the resultant of the diverse actions one has observed separately. History allows us to produce similar 'isolations' in the field of human psychology.'[7]

Thus, the best way to analyze, for instance, the effect of the possession of power on an individual, is to observe the life of the great dictators of antiquity, 'who were equipped with absolute power,' and who hence present a purer case than can be found in the comportment of common, merely more or less powerful mortals, whose life 'does not allow us to adequately determine the laws of the problem in question, since the determining causes remain obscure.' The Roman emperor, then,

> realizes the ideal state which could serve as the crucial experiment *(expérience)*. And when one would have succeeded in deducing from the comparison of several similar historical cases a complete theory, this latter could serve, first to foresee similar

11

situations that would reproduce themselves for dictators of another period, and then to constitute a new chapter in general psychology. (107)

The main difference between this model and that of the psychological novel is the introduction of history and politics. The predominance of scientific truth remains unquestioned, but this truth is now not only valued for its participation in the whole truth, but also for its use, which, in fact, is an effect of its inscription in 'circumstances' susceptible of repetition before which the individual is placed (as was also the case in the sociological novel). This shift is underscored by de Man's explicitly personal suggestion of the example of absolute power (as distinct from Marañon's focus on the psychology of resentment), and it is hard not to read this swerve as a deliberate allusion to the contemporary situation, in which the effects of dictatorial power were all too evident. Yet, there is no actual judgment of dictatorship. Even while he obliquely praises Marañon for his political and moral opposition to anti-Republican forces in Spain, and moreover avoids the symptomatic gesture of Anatole de Monzie who, in his preface to the volume in question, underscores that, as opposed to the isolated Roman emperor, 'the modern dictator' remains in contact with 'the common people [le commun]' and thus safeguards the community,[8] de Man does not therefore pass judgment on dictatorial forces as such. Much as one might want to see this reticence as inspired by an uncomplicated fear to criticize the power behind the occupation or even as a laudable tacit refusal to legitimate modern dictatorship, it is at least equally possible to read it as a mark of reservation rigorously consistent with the scientific model of 'deductive' reasoning defended here. In the absence of the 'complete theory' that de Man projects as the outcome of this 'scheme,' there are no scientific grounds on which a balanced judgment can be based.

The problem, all too briefly put, is this: the use of the scientific truth to which de Man aspires is that it can lead to the production of an absolute objectivity which can serve as the foundation of rational judgment, but as long as this goal is not attained, such judgment must be suspended. This, in fact, is one of the major negative motives for de Man's collaboration: the absence of a scientific legitimation for the refusal to collaborate. What is primarily disconcerting in de Man's writing under the occupation is not his actually limited propagation of the values of the occupying power but rather his inability to effectively evaluate these and other values in terms other than those of what he takes to be scientific objectivity.[9] It should be clear that this by no means diminishes the extent of de Man's implication in the collaboration—perhaps even to the contrary. The important effect of this insight, rather, is that it allows us to address this collaboration along lines that are less overdetermined by the rhetoric of outright denunciation or circuitous exculpation than has often been the case up to now. That this brings us close to the very attitude of proclaimed objectivity to be analyzed is not merely an unpleasant side-effect: what is of vital importance is that we realize, no matter how vaguely, to what extent our position is *not* a priori comfortably different from that of de Man as a collaborator. Only on this condition can we pretend to think what *must* separate us from this position.[10]

I have suggested that de Man's adherence to an ideology of scientific truth prevented him from delivering judgment. Obviously, this is an untenable generalization: de Man frequently does judge, and even the absence of judgment is always a judgment of sorts. Still, the judgments we do find are almost invariably arrived at under the pretense of scientific truth, while the implicit or explicit absence of judgment is also almost always justified under the cover of this model. A striking example here is the juxtaposition of de Man's condemnation of the opponents of a politics of neutrality before the invasion of Belgium and his later parallel condemnation of those who abstain from collaborating under the occupation. In both cases, his judgment is straightforwardly justified as being derived from an appreciation of the matter at hand as 'a practical, concrete problem that cannot be dealt with except with lucidity and sang-froid' (J, November 1939, 9), as a question to be approached with 'a lucidity close to coldness which ensures that the reality is never deformed in favour of a defended thesis' (LS, June 1942, 253). Before the invasion, de Man's reality is that there is no valid ground to translate a condemnation of Hitler, which he characteristically presents as an institutional fact, into an active Belgian participation in the war. Such a translation would rely on the notion of an 'ideological war,' which he confidently rejects as being quite simply 'false' (10). With the occupation, reality changes, and so does de Man's judgment, but its principles are identical: collaboration is not an 'ideal desired by the whole of the people,' it is not a result of 'ideological considerations' but rather of the 'necessities inscribed in the facts'; abstention from collaboration is to be 'condemned not from the moral viewpoint, but from that of imperious reality' (253).

Instances of this type can be found throughout de Man's writing of the period. One more necessary example can suffice to reveal the horror and terror that this nonideological ideology can always irresponsibly sustain and condone: 'But the reality is different.' Vulgar anti-Semites are wrong because they fail to see the truth that 'the Jews' are far less influential in the field of European literature than they (themselves) pretend. Consequently, the truth is that 'a solution of the Jewish problem which would envisage the creation of a Jewish colony isolated from Europe, would not entail, for the literary life of the West, deplorable consequences' (LS, March 1941, 45). Period.

But this cannot suffice: the terror of this verdict cannot be exhausted. Its logic is that of a terrible prolepsis: the truth is that in de Man's 'reality' here, 'the Jews' have *already* ceased to exist; that, as Jews, they are only a name and a myth. In de Man's 'reality,' the 'specific characteristics of the Jewish spirit' are those of the psychological novelists, themselves mere mouthpieces of scientific truth: they are 'cerebral,' they have 'the capacity to assimilate doctrines whilst preserving a certain coldness in relation to them,' they possess 'qualities that seem very precious for the work of lucid analysis required by the novel.'[11] To the typifying scientific gaze, 'the Jews' as Jews (i.e., not as psychological novelists, or as French analysts) do not exist except as what is 'foreign' (see also HVL, August 1942, 323): in the labor of analysis, which consists of the isolation of types, they have already been isolated and generalized out of existence. Their 'specific characteristics' are nonspecific, the residue left of them after these characteristics have been isolated is strictly immaterial in the 'healthy' chemistry of European nations—except, of course, as the ('reassuringly' ineffectual) threat of a disease. We are back in the laboratory.

Induction

'... the affinities become interesting only when they bring about separations *[Scheidungen]*.'

'Does that sad word, which, unfortunately, we so often hear nowadays, also occur in natural science?' Charlotte cried.

'Certainly,' Eduard answered, 'It even used to be a significant title of honor for chemists that they were called 'artists of separation' *[Scheidekünstler]*.'

'Well, that is no longer customary,' Charlotte retorted, 'and all for the better. Unifying is a greater art, a greater merit. An artist of unification *[Einungskünstler]* would be welcome in every discipline throughout the world.'[12]

One could strive to arrange the 'Elective Affinities' in the norm of the literary traditions of all the great creative centres of Europe. We shall limit ourselves to examining the work in relation to the French and German artistic qualities: the synthesis of these two national temperaments, realized rarely and with difficulty, being already amply sufficient to prove its particular attraction. (LS, May 1942, 238)

For de Man, Goethe fulfills Charlotte's wish and thus becomes the 'universal genius' of 'Western civilization' (Goethe, 239). He is the cultural avatar of what is elsewhere programmatically defined as 'complementary nationalism,' the aim of which is 'to discover the national virtues, to cultivate and to honor them, but [also] to adapt them to those of the neighboring peoples, in order to thus attain, in summing up the particular gifts, a real unification of Western culture' (LS, April 1942, 226). But the dice are loaded. The 'spirit of the times' (227) is German (which, in the qualifications migrating through these articles, means 'mystical,' 'mythical,' 'mysterious,' 'metaphysical,' 'moral,' 'drunk'), not French ('clear,' 'lucid,' 'rational,' 'cold,' 'cerebral,' 'objective,' 'logical,' 'psychological'): the necessity inscribed in the historical facts is that it is the German people that is summoned 'to exercise a hegemony in Europe' (LS, October 1941, 158), and the new 'type' of man (159) bears a distinct German stamp. But the dice are at least doubly loaded: for the determination of this necessity as truth is the product of a spirit which in the logic of de Man's analysis is still primarily French. The point is not merely that de Man always pleads for a synthesis of diverse national types, nor that he emphatically underscores the necessity to maintain the French spirit in the face of the spirit of the age (LS, April 1942, 227), but ultimately that the authority of his decrees derives from his 'French' stance as the dispassionate, objective, scientific, nonideological, lucid, value-free observer of the chemistry of values. This is the scandal: de Man's observations on the ideological reality of his time are those of someone who has 'the capacity to assimilate doctrines whilst preserving a certain coldness in relation to them' (LS, March 1941, 45).

But this is not the whole truth. Alongside this positivistic scientific model, there emerges from de Man's wartime writing a different conception of truth which explicitly proposes to demarcate the limits of the laboratory. Among the first relatively clear instances of this modification is a sketch of the evolution of 'the study of man' in his March 1942 review of A. E. Brinckmann's *Geist der Nationen* (HVL, 300–301).[13] De Man starts out from a hypothetical analogy: just as 'pure science' can 'fix' the 'eternal movements of nature' in 'general laws' and can thus accurately predict future occurrences, so the scientific study of the individual and society makes us 'master of our historical future' (300). Such, in fact, was the rationale of the historicopsychological deductive method ascribed to Marañon. Yet, 'whether under the name of sociology, historical science, or social psychology,' research into 'human problems' has failed to establish this analogy, and de Man's explanation of this failure takes the shape of an exact translation into impossibility of the possibility conditions that he presented as attainable for Marañon's model: 'a clear delineation of the active forces . . . cannot be achieved' and one can never dispose of 'a sufficient amount of experiments' to allow for 'a clear and distinct observation' of the phenomenon to be explained, so that 'statistical laws—and those are the majority—' cannot be formulated (300). The isolation of the pure phenomenon is not feasible in the study of human beings, and the specific powers of prediction proper to the pure sciences, previously also projected as the goal of historical psychology, cannot be claimed for these disciplines. This observation, however, does not lead de Man to skepticism. Not only does the model of pure science still function as a motor for 'discipline of thought,' but the students of humankind have also gained their own specificity from the realization of their difference: 'Instead of continuing the sterile recording of facts, they have started to think inductively, and to derive general truths from . . . collection[s] of separate cases' (300). The move is one from the necessary (deductive) production of truth on the basis of analysis to the 'creative' (inductive) production of 'synthetic' truth. No more 'hair-splitting *[haarklieverij]*,' that hair-splitting which also marked the psychological novel (*coupeur de cheveux en quatre* [C, January 1940, 18]), but the 'accurate description' of 'the deep causes' of 'empirical truths' (HVL, March 1942, 300).

De Man's specific example here is art history—or rather, significantly, art-historical *science*. 'Pure' science no longer offers the primary frame of reference, but truth remains a scientific product. And although art can be a valid object for the study of human beings, the artist is not the 'appropriate person' to undertake such a study: the artist creates out of a 'fairly intuitive choice, made outside his objective consciousness,' in obedience to 'the laws of an evolution of style which is totally unknown to him. Hence the necessity of art-historical science' (300). Thus, de Man's methodological reflections not only qualify the analogy of the laboratory but, in their insistence on the scientific nature of extralaboratorial investigations, they also reemphasize the potential conflict of (objective) fact and (subjective) value that this analogy sought to control. A comparison of the justification of collaboration already referred to with the present (and in fact earlier) justification of complementary nationalism (the truth produced in *Geist der Nationen*) is illuminating in this respect.

Arguments in favor of collaboration should appeal to 'the necessities inscribed in the facts,' not to 'ideological considerations,' since collaboration is 'an irresistible necessity,' not an 'ideal desired by the whole of the people' (LS, July 1942, 253)—that much we knew. Yet, de Man feels the need to add that while those who have isolated this truth may now seem 'isolated,' they shall eventually receive their just rewards: 'Later, it will turn out that they were the precursors of a unanimous will *[unanime volonté]*' (253). That is to say: the net effect of a dissociation of fact from volition is the institution of fact as the object of the unanimous volition of the future. Isolated from mere ideals, fact becomes the sole ideal. In the case for complementary nationalism, the argument is differently arranged, but the outcome is the same. There used to be an awareness of the 'empirical truth' that Western art constituted 'a unity' consisting of subunits corresponding to the European nations, but 'the deeper causes of these phenomena' were not yet adequately charted (HVL, March 1942, 300). 'Now,' with the birth of 'a great stream of thought' out of 'the inclination to consider the national essence of a people as one of the foundations of all civilization,' the time is ripe for a determination of these causes. But while this determination—which yields the law of complementary nationalism in a European frame—is thus born out of an 'inclination,' it nonetheless turns out not to be 'the expression of an ideal wish, utopian and remote,' but rather 'a concrete truth, corroborated by a number of facts.' Produced in response to a desire, in the final analysis the object of desire is vindicated as 'a concrete truth,' and the ultimate voice of complementary nationalism is not one of 'exaltation and ecstasy *[ivresse]*' (LS, April 1942, 227) but instead radiates 'a sober faith' (HVL, March 1942, 300).

The process in both arguments is that of a purification which produces the coincidence of fact and value in truth, and in both cases the decisive element in this purification—the unchangeable catalyst—is fact. The power of fact isolates that in the matter of value which is also fact, removes it to the realm of truth, and rejects the residues (such as 'sentimental patriotism' (300), or 'narrow-minded regionalism' (301), or the 'will *[volonté]*' of some nations which seems to oppose the necessary movement of history [253]). Understood in this way, this new, inductive process of truth-production can fulfill the hypothetical promise of the earlier deductive scheme: it implicitly allows 'us' to become 'masters of our historical future,' which is why this labor is a necessary task for 'anyone who wishes to find his bearings in the present chaos' (253), an indispensable exercise 'for all those who, in the contemporary revolutions, try to find a firm guidance according to which they can direct their action and thought' (301). The laboratory has not so much been left behind as it has been redefined.

Intuition

One of the most striking features of this modified model is the extreme confidence with which it assumes the 'practical' effects of the truth it claims to produce, the feasibility of its attempt to 'ensure,' through the production of 'concrete truth,' 'the future of Western civilization, in all of its aspects' (301). There are, however, also some indices of strain. One of these indices, particularly important for our present purpose, involves the determination of the 'appropriate person' for the production of this workable truth.

We have already noted how in his review of Brinckmann, de Man explicitly denies artists the capacity for this production, and in fact this exclusion from the laboratory of, in particular, literature (*as* literature—that is, not as an object of investigation, as a mirror, or as a mere carrier of truth produced elsewhere) is one of the major themes in these articles, whether it is explicitly stated or negatively implied in a doctrine of the autonomy of literature. De Man's justifications for this exclusion are diverse and confused, but their general tenor is fairly clear: literature does not qualify as an agent of truth in its own right since it is insufficiently aware of its own constitution. The fundamental point is not that novelists and poets would not be able to address the appropriate subject matter, but rather that their approach is not sufficiently 'general and theoretical' (LS, November 1941, 163), that what literature produces may very well turn out to be true but that it is itself incapable of authorizing this truth as truth. Which is also why, when it is no longer considered as art, literature can be used 'to demonstrate anything *[n'importe quoi]*' (LS, December 1941, 171). The truth value of such a demonstration is not denied a priori but is radically independent from literature's own truth claim. Unless it has passed through the acid bath of the 'specialist' (163), unless what it may contain of truth has been isolated from its literariness, literature cannot participate in the production of the type of truth that allows for practical application.

Thus, typically, an author like Gerard Walschap can be said to have a 'message' that succeeds in restoring 'the links that unite us with certain forces of the instinct from which an artificial coldness has detached us,' and his work can be praised for 'carrying our whole being along [entraîne] in the frantic course of the passions it describes,' instead of merely satisfying our brain with the vain pleasure of 'a fine operation of the spirit' (LS, November 1941, 165). Yet, Walschap is not authorized to produce this message as truth himself, for his metastatements to that effect betray 'that inevitable lack of objectivity which always comes to light when an author transforms himself into a critic' (165). Whereas Walschap illegitimately transforms what message he has into 'a general truth,' the true critic is the one who objectively isolates this message and places it in its proper perspective—an exercise resembling 'mathematical' abstraction and remarkably close to the 'fine operation of the spirit' that this message itself would abandon. The true critic knows and controls this complication: 'If then this conception of criticism may not seem very brilliant or useful and may resemble a sterile exercise of the spirit, it nonetheless permits the establishment of a philosophy of literary history which is no less fertile than philosophy of history as such' (LS, December 1941, 169). The function of criticism is to accomplish what lies beyond the lawful power of the literary mind: to reproduce literature as truth by establishing its participation in the 'eternal cyclical laws of literature' and by processing its essential difference from the extraliterary realm of truth.

And the author cannot win. Louis Carette, for instance, also has a message—'the effects of total individualism have been entirely negative' (LS, March 1942, 204)—and as an author of psychological novels, he has two techniques at his disposal for the expression of this message, interior monologue and 'detached' 'objective observation' (205, i.e., the two methods already indicated in the first model we have reconstructed here). Carette chooses the second method, which entails that over the characters in his narrative there 'hovers a cold but omnipotent presence,' of a 'supreme lucidity that understands the (f)acts *[faits]* and gestures of the characters even in their most obscure recesses' (205). Yet, this detached objectivity does not produce truth: to the contrary, it is 'a power . . . which absolutely falsifies reality,' because it 'destroys the very basis of the aesthetics of the novel,' which should be 'like a living thing, that is to say, fundamentally mysterious, unpredictable, and above all undetermined, capricious. The distinctive feature *[le propre]* of the great novelists is to become prisoners of the destinies they describe and to let themselves be carried by them instead of commanding them' (205). Thus, it is the stance of total objectivity that prevents Carette's novel from being more than 'a superior witness account' and from rising to the level of 'the work of art properly speaking' (205). In other words: if it tries to become aware of its own constitution, which is the indispensable condition for the production of truth, the novel betrays the laws of literature. If the novelist tries to objectively produce what used to be called 'the Whole Truth'—a project previously recommended by de Man, but even then already recognized as distinct from aesthetic concerns—then the novelist 'opposes' the founding 'intention' of art. Literature lacks objectivity, and if it tries to remedy this lack it is no longer literature: the production of objective truth is none of its business.[14]

But there is yet another strand in de Man's wartime writing, a strand that is more or less clearly articulated only toward the end of 1942, and then only a very few times. The strongest instance here is the September 1942 article 'Literature and Sociology' (HVL, 331), in which de Man focuses on the presence of 'sociological insights' in German as opposed to French literature. Whereas the French typically analyze single individuals, German authors concentrate on 'the subtle links between the individual and the community,' and this to the advantage of both literature and sociology. De Man admits that it may seem paradoxical for a science to benefit from an 'artistic representation,' and that it may even seem 'a danger for real knowledge' to prefer 'a direct intuitive sensitivity over a logical deductive method,' but he immediately adds that such a conception derives from an illegitimate transfer of principles of the natural sciences onto sociological thought. The argument is familiar: the phenomena of sociology cannot be 'isolated' and the experiments cannot be repeated ('such practices can easily be carried out in the laboratory: in reality they cannot exist'), and on the basis of this argument some 'pessimistic or prejudiced minds' have ruled that sociology can never be a science and that we are consequently doomed to live in total 'arbitrariness.' The future course of events cannot be 'foreseen' and 'all attempts at organisation are useless since we cannot logically justify them anyway.' But, he continues, 'such a conclusion is too negative to be true and is moreover contradicted by the facts. So there has to be a possibility to discover sociological knowledge, not along purely rational, natural-scientific paths, but by other means.' The proof of this possibility can be found in 'modern German sociology' and in 'the traces it has left in literature.'

Yet, this is more than a matter of 'traces': literature is not only a carrier of 'sociological insights,' the literary sensitivity is now also recognized for the first time as a legitimate agent in the production of knowledge. De Man's crucial witness here is Ernst Jünger, who, 'tellingly,' is not only probably 'the greatest German man of letters of the moment,' but also 'the author of a most remarkable sociological study, *Der Arbeiter*' (HVL, 331). That this 'not only, but also' does not constitute a division between literature and sociology becomes clearer in a slightly later review, which explicitly affirms that 'reasoning reason is not the only means to attain a truth,' and that there is also 'a poetic comprehension which immediately grasps the lessons of the world, in the very contact with concrete things, objects, and beings' (LS, October 1942, 276).[15] And although this mode of knowledge is often denied 'scientific value' since it would lack 'the indispensable qualities of generality and objectivity,' it is 'nonetheless true that certain sciences make constant use of it, even without admitting as much.' De Man's prime witness is once again Jünger, but this time, significantly, not on the strength of *Der Arbeiter* but as the author of *Auf den Marmorklippen,* a novel that 'abounds in very fertile sociological ideas, even though it contains no abstract expositions and no demonstrations' (276).[16] This is that same *Marmorklippen* of which de Man only a few months earlier had written that its sole 'justification' lay in its being 'a product of the artistic imagination,' that it pertained to the realm of 'myth,' which 'cannot be translated into the language of everyday reality,' and which 'never teaches us anything concrete and never enriches our knowledge' (LS, March 1942, 216).[17]

De Man never tells us what precisely the 'fertile sociological ideas' he finds in Jünger's novel are. It is likely that they would be in keeping with the truth of complementary nationalism, Jünger being, alongside Goethe and Rilke, one of the prime representatives of the 'synthesis' of European culture (HVL, July 1942, 319), which is also to say that they would remain inscribed in the typology of nations, albeit that the authority of this typology would now no longer be primarily rooted in a 'French' frame of mind. One might also suspect that Jünger's/de Man's insights would be less than favorable to the contemporary regime,[18] but this suspicion would be seriously complicated by de Man's simultaneous praise for *Der Arbeiter,* which was and remains a totalitarian, if not therefore a national-socialist, treatise.[19] The only point we can legitimately emphasize in de Man's reading of Jünger toward the end of 1942 is that it bespeaks a crisis in the model of truth which dominates his wartime journalism, and that this crisis explicitly arrives in the shape of literature's claim to truth. De Man's conclusion in 'Literature and Sociology' indicates and evades this crisis:

> Here [in the case of Jünger] we clearly see how an intuitive spirit, who does not analyse problems systematically but senses them intuitively, obtains a result which also yields excellent effects in practice. And this leads us to one of the deepest prob-

lems of knowledge in general, a problem we cannot pose here. We only want to point out that if literature cannot be acknowledged as a scientific means of formation, it can still, from a sociological viewpoint, at the very least go together with theoretical research and, in many cases, open up horizons and offer possibilities which otherwise would never have been suspected. (HVL, September 1942, 331)

The truth produced by a literary sensitivity can yield excellent practical effects (what effects?), but why this is so is too fundamental a problem to be investigated—in a newspaper article. Literary intuition can complement theoretical, scientific truth, but both the possibility of this condition and the products of this new agent of truth remain unspecified. No conclusions are drawn from this conclusion: this is as far as this narrative of de Man's wartime writing goes.[20] It is appropriate that the first essay he publishes after the war should rephrase the question. In the interval, there is a crossing of the Atlantic and an allegory of ambergris.

CHAPTER TWO

Ambergris and
Gudgeon

There is perhaps no news item *[fait divers]*
which cannot give rise to profound thoughts.—
Maurice Merleau-Ponty, 'On News Items'

In 1945, the Antwerp publishing house Helicon published a Dutch translation of Melville's *Moby Dick*. The name of the translator is not mentioned, but all the available evidence suggests that it was Paul de Man's work.[1] The translation abridges the original, and there are only two translator's notes.[2] One is a simple explanation of the 'ominous' ring of the name of the landlord of 'The Spouter-Inn' ('Coffin, the English word for coffin').[3] The other note is a curious return to the newspaper and to the laboratory which hindsight can hardly avoid refracting into an allegory of valuable wreckage—I translate it here without further comment.

> In September 1945 one could read the following report in the newspapers: A warship of the American navy, the *Santiago Iglesia*, discovered at a few kilometres distance from the Azores a hulk which resembled a floating parachute.
>
> When the parachute was hauled aboard and turned over it proved to be a greyish, fragrant mass which the captain—who apparently had never read *Moby Dick*—kept on board as a curiosity.

27

Presently, chemists in a New Jersey laboratory discovered that this enigmatic wreck is nothing other than ambergris, a very rare waxy substance which is secreted by whales. Ambergris is worth approximately 9,000 francs per kilogram, for it is one of the ingredients in the production of numerous perfumes.

The officers and the crew of the *Santiago Iglesia* excitedly discuss their catch and try to calculate how much it will bring in for them. The value of the find is estimated at more than 10 million francs, a sum which the crew of the ship will have to divide between themselves.[4]

Among the 'Extracts (supplied by a sub-sub-librarian)' and deleted in 'de Man's' translation, there is a fragment that invites another allegory. It is taken from a passage in Montaigne (the subject of de Man's first postwar essay) which can be read as the wishful self-definition of a member of the 'intellectual elite' (HVL, May 1942, 307) who felt called upon to act as pilot for the European Leviathan:

> It is said that the whale never moves if it does not have in front of it a small fish resembling the sea-gudgeon, which for that reason is called the guide; the whale follows it, letting itself be commanded and turned as easily as the helm makes the ship turn; and, as a reward, whereas all other things, whether beast or vessel, that enter the horrible chaos of the mouth of this monster are immediately lost and swallowed up, this small fish retires into it in great security and sleeps there, and during its sleep the whale does not move; but as soon as it leaves, the whale starts to follow it ceaselessly; and when, by accident, it moves away from the whale, this latter roams here and there, often hurting itself on the rocks, like a vessel without a rudder. . . .[5]

Inside the whale, a gudgeon is easily deceived.

CHAPTER THREE

The Temptation of Irony

His time is exclusively the present; . . . have we sufficiently understood the extraordinary fact that Montaigne never refers to his previous declarations?—Paul de Man, 'Montaigne and Transcendence'

The dominant trait of this character . . . is the extreme proximity to the real. The Belgian seems essentially at ease in the material and sensible reality to which he spontaneously adheres. . . . Close to things, his natural time is the present.—René Micha and Alphonse de Waelhens, 'On the Character of the Belgians'

I n 1948, Paul de Man wrote a letter from New York to Georges Bataille in Paris. In a postscript he announces that he is planning a study on Alfred Kinsey's *Sexual Behavior in the Human Male*, which he would like to contribute to *Critique*. We are back in the laboratory.

I intend to discuss the question on the sociological level only, using the document as a very sensitive reagent for the study of a certain structure of American society. (So there is nothing to stop someone else from discussing the work on the ethical level.) [1]

To my knowledge, this projected experiment has left no traces. When five years later de Man finally does publish in *Critique*, he requires a different perspective.

Inventory

ontaigne et la transcendance,' published in 1953, is an
excessively finished essay (and therefore, perhaps, not
an essay) which, following a problematic but eminently compelling imperative, must be read as written in the aftermath of a disastrous ideological involvement and of an ambitious
epistemological project that came to complicate this involvement.
Under the guise of a review of Hugo Friedrich's *Montaigne,* the
essay proposes a wholesale revaluation of the author of the *Essais*
which reads like a response to the crisis adumbrated in de Man's
late wartime journalism and to the blueprint for the preservation
of European civilization surrounding that crisis.

De Man's starting point is 'the temptation to make rejection of
transcendence the axis of Montaigne's thought,' to make him 'a
subjectivist, the chronicler of pure immanence,' a tendency he finds
instantiated in the contemporary appropriation of Montaigne by
those 'who vaunt the proposition that existence precedes essence'
('MT' CW, 3).[2] There are grounds for summing up Montaigne in
such a 'neat and definitive formula,' de Man admits, but, as was
to be expected, 'we must take a closer look' (4). Such a look reveals that the 'special' connection between Montaigne and transcendence is closer and finer than one of mere contrast: in fact,
Montaigne has given us 'one of the fullest and profoundest de-
scriptions of the difficult problem of transcendence, the problem
of the ambiguity of our relations with our own being' (4).[3] The
dominant quality of these relations is that of an 'impatience with
our own limits,' an impatience that becomes manifest in 'the exercise of reason' ('epistemological'), in 'the attraction of an absolute
morality' ('ethical'), and in 'the creation of form' ('aesthetic'). The
remainder of the essay consists of a systematic reconstruction of

these 'three types of consideration,' in search of 'the complex central core' from which Montaigne's thought 'emanates like a spiral, continued to infinity' (4).

The 'central intuition' of Montaigne's first critique is that, stripped of 'the entire apparatus in which it decks itself out in order to present itself as a definitive absolute,' knowledge is only an object of a 'frail and arbitrary' 'human appetite': our 'rational faculties' are powered by 'an entirely subjective intentionality,' not by 'some persistent principle' of transcendent truth (5). This insight is not simply an expression of 'the commonplace that all knowledge is impelled by the desire to know.' Rather, it reveals an essential contradiction in the 'intentional structure' of knowing: the object of the subjective intention of knowing is the acquisition of objective knowledge, which entails the 'sacrifice' of 'cognitive consciousness.' The desire for knowledge 'seeks to destroy itself by dissolving in a world of fixed laws, in which subjectivity is ultimately suspended' (6). Montaigne shares this awareness of the self-destructive nature of knowing with many philosophers and poets (Mallarmé, Rimbaud, Goethe), but his originality resides in his categorical refusal to remain stuck in this 'impasse': 'If subjectivity interposes an impenetrable screen between the object and the spirit, the spirit will be exercised on the level of this very screen' (7).[4] In 'an amazing change of sign,' Montaigne has turned the recognition of 'the endless series of failures' which the subject of knowing necessarily suffers into a positive principle—'just when the spirit falls into the despair of its impotence, it regains all its suppleness and elasticity in perceiving this very impotence' (7). Having offered us an 'interminable' (and 'tiresome') list of all the reasons why reason cannot be trusted, Montaigne turns to his own experience of epistemological impotence and immediately we find him 'in his true and best manner: ironic and playful and eloquent, admirably perceptive and subtle.' With this self-descriptive turn, Montaigne also decisively abandons 'total immanence' and subjectivity: 'Montaigne speaking of the impossibility of knowing himself is entirely in transcendence.' His reflections on his own

inconsistency and on the impossibility of 'absolute truth' are themselves inconsistent and void of absolute truth, but they retain the
reflection of transcendence: 'The joys of the spirit are preserved
in a transcendence that exceeds rational transcendence by denying
it' (8).

De Man admits that such an attitude may seem facile, but only
in appearance—in fact, Montaigne's stance is a supremely 'heroic'
response to the situation de Man had a decade earlier tried to
control by evading it.

> We are forever condemned to live in the arbitrary; all attempts
> at organisation are useless, since we cannot logically justify them
> anyway. Man has succeeded in using, understanding, and even,
> to a certain extent, dominating the forces of nature—but he
> does not have the strength to order his own life, his relation to
> his fellow men. (HVL, September 1942, 331)

Such was the conclusion that de Man's implied foreknowledge of
the solution to 'one of the deepest problems of knowledge in general' had previously allowed him to reject as 'all too negative' (331).
Ten years later, the strength of his conviction no longer suffices to
suppress this negativity:

> The man who has admitted once and for all the impossibility
> of an abstractly formulable truth deprives himself of all the
> false security we find in the illusion of governing matter and
> ourselves. He deprives himself of any possibility of sudden ex-
> pansion, of any passion in which he commits himself entirely
> and forgets himself. He strips the spirit of that hope of con-
> tinuity that has inspired so many audacious constructions. He
> compels a withdrawal into the self, ironic, perpetually lucid and
> curious, and tolerates no cheating. He leaves himself strangely
> naked and vulnerable to the inevitable powers that assail him
> and with which he allows himself no identification. ('MT' CW, 8;
> translation modified)

In the light of our narrative, this passage becomes so overdetermined that decoding it as the masked memory of a failed project

that has become a menace is almost a ludicrous exercise. But the text is even more tacitly explicit (the oxymoron is the law of this discourse) when de Man turns to Montaigne's second critique.

The heroic nature of Montaigne's 'epistemological transcendence' resides in his rejection of 'that skeptical sloth that reposes in the ignorance of its knowledge' in favor of a constant self-renewal which is fueled by this ignorance. This is what makes him a major representative of what Hugo Friedrich calls 'moral phenomenology,' a tradition that de Man (not Friedrich) finds continued in the work of Husserl: 'Since Husserl, we have learned to find in this fundamental humility of the spirit, which cannot claim to legislate but only to describe, the best source of resistance to the aberrations of our time' (8).[5] The ethical conclusions to be drawn from Montaigne's thought put this resistance in perspective.

'The negation of an absolute knowledge implies the negation of a knowable good'—this is the fundamental premise. Yet, just as the spirit does not capitulate in the face of its own impotence, so the 'moral sense cannot dissolve into a pluralistic cynicism that would leave us in an impoverishing stagnation. The ethical gesture must continue' (9). For Montaigne, the basis of this gesture was, 'naturally,' the 'continuity of the taught orthodoxy,' and de Man is careful to save this 'ritualist conservatism' from its apparent conflict with the previous rejection of wishful principles of continuity: Montaigne's adherence to the orthodoxy is formal and flexible, it is merely 'what remains of morality when it is drained of absolutes, just as phenomenology is what remains of knowledge when it is drained of objective truth.' And just as Montaigne's epistemological attitude does not succumb to 'skeptical sloth,' so his ritualist ethics and historical relativism do not entail a complacent acceptance of the status quo. 'If the prevailing orthodoxy hardens, crystallizes into sharp points, becoming massive and opaque, wounding anyone who comes up against it; if it has no concern but to perpetuate itself as an institution and if its ritual becomes a police regulation, Montaigne will be the first to detest it, and it remains for us to imagine what rebellions he is capable of' (9).

De Man's comment on one such oppositional passage in Montaigne does not say enough, perhaps, but it says a great deal. It asks us to remember what was forgotten:

> Let these words be remembered when we would invoke a conservatism like Montaigne's to extenuate some injustice of our own. What orthodoxy, at the present time, can invoke the breadth and comprehension of postmedieval Christianity? The wretched myths that surround us are no sooner born than they degenerate into sclerotic bureaucracies. They must appeal to the most factitious loyalties—those of nationalism and race—in order to gain any vitality at all. Imagine Montaigne in such surroundings; no doubt he would be on the side of the rebels [révoltés]. (10; translation modified)

Yet, in the abeyance of ethical certainty, this necessary resistance—a resistance to myths idealized into necessity—cannot 'take itself seriously.' Montaigne's moral transcendence can only protest against 'stupidity [bêtise]'; beyond this protest, 'it is entertained and justified and content to make a patient inventory of the dangerous structures men have produced in hopes of achieving some sort of rule.' As in the epistemological realm, here too the last word is for the language of gentle 'respectful irony' and 'utter honesty,' for the 'connoisseur's' delight in the 'beauty' of the 'absurdity' he observes. The tone is set for Montaigne's third critique, and for his third impossible transcendence: 'form' (10).

In the final analysis, Montaigne's phenomenology is of a 'formal and aesthetic order,' which brings him closer to 'the poets' than to 'systematic minds,' even while he transcends even these in that, unlike Baudelaire, Mallarmé, or Proust, he assumes 'the failure of the aesthetic' (11) and recognizes as vain the attempt 'to give form to the subjective.' 'His time is exclusively the present': the past is forgotten, because detached from 'the subjectivity of the immediate,' and the future is only ever open. But this presence is not the presence of lived experience, it is only the present of 'a man who observes himself in the gratuitous and fundamentally useless act of writing.' In this writing of writing Montaigne transcends the final transcendence of form and abandons all intentions to accomplish the intention of aesthetic intentionality, the 'objectivization of consciousness,' preserving only its 'movement.' Situated 'beyond aesthetic value,' his third and final last word is once more 'tranquil irony.' And de Man adds, in a bold appropriation of the voice of the dead, 'It is with the same irony that he must regard our incessant efforts to grasp him' (11).

With this last sentence, we are in a position to appreciate—or at least suspect—the excessive finish of this essay. Far from being 'incessant,' de Man's efforts to grasp his Montaigne are final and decisive, bent on a massive capitulation to the temptation of recapitulative postapocalyptic irony. For all its insistence on movement and flexibility, the mechanical dialectic of the argument tries to install the dead calm of tranquil irony in an everlasting present. But this present is not the absolute present in which de Man situates Montaigne. Rather, it is the present in the perspective of the past he ascribes to Proust, Baudelaire, and Mallarmé: in commanding Montaigne's irony ('he must') the essay 'is actually written from the point of view of Death—of a man who is already dead' (11). It is almost impossible not to read it as an attempt 'to transform the chaos of [past] experience into a construction,' to establish it as 'fixed in the immobility of the irrevocable'—and indeed, as a desire to be allowed to content oneself with making a 'patient inventory of the dangerous structures men have produced in hopes of achieving some sort of rule' (11, 10). What is this anxious desire for tranquil irony, if not the product of a request to be permitted never to have to talk about the past again, never to have to judge it again, except as recognized past failure and stupidity? We shall never hear the last of it.

In Parenthesis

To speak from the point of view of death is to take the words out of its mouth. In the autumn of 1941, Hendrik de Man left Belgium for the Haute Savoie. During the first year of his retreat he regularly returned to Brussels; later, he increasingly kept to himself, going on solitary walks and reading and writing in his mountain hut. In 1944, he published a selection of diary fragments from this period, *Cahiers de ma montagne*. One of these notes recalls how during his last stay in a city, while walking home alone at night, he heard someone running up to him from behind: 'I immediately said to myself: "This is it, this is how they killed so-and-so and so-and-so"; and without even thinking of turning round . . . I awaited the shot without the slightest emotion.'[6] The 'assassin' turned out to be someone wanting to ask the way, but 'the experience had been interesting': it proved that even in moments of sudden alarm, he was not afraid of death but remained true to the tone of his reflections in tranquillity, 'very calm and very lucid, without the least anxious emotion.' The fragment ends as follows: 'For the rest, I would gladly say with Montaigne: "I would take care, if I can, that my death does not say anything that my life has not said first." Living well, that is all, the rest will come on top of it.'[7]

One of the principal attractions of this anticipatory appropriation of the voice of death in the 'lucid' resignation to *bien vivre* is that it can also perform the assumption of limitations in the seductive mode of the apology, and Hendrik de Man does not hesitate to develop this potential:

To those who are surprised at not finding, among these reflections, any mention of the great drama now playing in the world, I would respond with this other text by Montaigne:

'My God, what a great service wisdom renders those whose desires it regulates according to their capacities! there is no science more useful. According to one's abilities *[Selon qu'on peut]*, such was the refrain and the favorite saying of Socrates, a saying of great substance.'[8]

Appropriately, among those whose surprise Hendrik de Man here anticipates, there is one whose surprise from beyond the grave was already quoted: 'In the *Mémoires d'Outre-Tombe,* Chateaubriand writes: ". . . I was surprised that Montaigne could write with such sprightliness in a castle he could not walk round without running the risk of being kidnapped by gangs of *ligueurs* or of protestants."'[9] Caught between the resistance and the German secret police as he claimed he was,[10] Hendrik de Man could not have chosen a better model to justify his retreat. But the attempt to speak as if one were already dead is not exhausted in justificatory assumptions of humility. The assumption of humility is the assumption of a limit and as such pretends to a position beyond that limit, in the realm of superior observation: 'But let no one think that I try to flee the war as one flees a spectacle one does not want to see and forget. In coming here, I have not distanced myself so as to see less, I have elevated myself so as to see better.'[11] This transformation of distance into superiority is as old as the hills (or the Cave): the moment the cliché of the *theatrum mundi* is introduced, someone is bound to forget that, in Bacon's phrase, 'it is reserved only for God and angels to be lookers-on,' and to lay claims to a loge in which to stage the cliché of splendid isolation in the composed mode of the inventory.

We could still extend this narrative inventory of Montaigne's presence in Hendrik de Man's *Cahiers,* in an attempt to at least prepare the last of it. The limit model of the matter of such a narrative is the encyclopedia, even if it is only the *Petit Larousse,* the only reference book in the library of de Man's 'hermitage.' It is no coincidence that the 'lesson in modesty' he draws from the recognition of his 'abyss of ignorance' in the face of this book should be cast in the language of death: 'What a marvel that one can contain, in a volume that is so compact, more matter of knowledge than a human brain can accumulate in the course of a lifetime!' But the encyclopedia is not only written from the point of view of death, the 'disproportion between its dimensions . . . and the importance of its invisible content' also gives it the metaphorical power to kill: 'I felt a lightly anxious respect, like that which can be inspired by a carton of explosives, which looks like a little packet of jelly but can unleash an almost volcanic eruption.'[12]

One more entry: about 1945, a German philosopher walking along an imaginary path through the fields began to develop an incomparably more intricate thought on the possibilities of composure, calmness, and distance. In 1952, the *Petit Larousse* ordained that it was the last thing he ever did and killed him in parentheses:

HEIDEGGER (Martin) German philosopher, born in Messkirch (1889–1945); one of the founders of existentialist philosophy.[13]

A Thing of the Past

B ut there is another finish here. Paul de Man's 'Montaigne et la transcendance' not only looks back upon the past, it also looks back upon the future. In a very important sense, it closes off the central argument of the writings to come. It is situated in the aftermath of its own aftermath, in a future which, however, fortunately, never quite becomes present. To put it less perversely—but it is the same thing—de Man's subsequent writings address the very same question that his Montaigne has already dissolved into irony. They do so in a renewed encounter with the poets to whom Montaigne is said to be close even while he leaves them behind. It is significant that these poets should also form the single most crucial exception to the mechanical dialectic of the essay: in his first critique, Montaigne comes close to but decisively transcends 'skeptical sloth'; in his second critique, Montaigne comes close to but decisively transcends 'pluralist cynicism'; but in his third critique, Montaigne is close to and decisively transcends what is nevertheless still acknowledged as 'the very respectable symbolist aestheticism.' The essays that de Man was to write in the years to come are a powerful attempt to come to terms with this hitch in the dialectic.

In one more sense, these writings, to which we can now begin to turn, are an attempt to understand why the tranquil irony of aesthetic transcendence celebrated here is also always in danger, through the relay of irony, of turning into a disastrous forgetting of the sole principle of moral transcendence—the opposition to stupidity—thus defusing the capacity to resist 'the aberrations of our time.' In the face of the miserable myths of nation and race, 'no doubt' Montaigne would be on the side of resistance. But his 'respectful irony' can only perform this mastering of doubt in 'a formal and aesthetic order,' which does not 'take itself seriously.' 'Doubt leads to form,' de Man quotes Friedrich's quotation from Paul Valéry, and there is 'no doubt' that this form is the locus of a lucid and ironical opposition to ideological aberration ('MT' CW, 10). Or is there? For de Man had already been where he sees his Montaigne before he failed to resist what this irony seeks to ward off. We must indiscreetly remember the private words he wrote to a friend in January 1939:

> If, for a certain time already, I have abandoned the hope to lean on some theory or doctrine to overcome the anxiety of doubt, I also no longer count on an individual to prove the fixity of the inner orientation. Or, more simply, at this moment I can do without this individual; more than that, he embarrasses and troubles me. Which is to say, quite pretentiously, that I am capable of enduring, of braving doubt, contenting myself solely with elementary (that is to say, material, aesthetic, and cerebral) pleasures. I am ready to admit that this state is probably only ephemeral and that it requires an adequate setting (Monthouet!) to maintain itself—but, on the other hand, I know full well that it is the state that suits me best and in which I am most happy, more than at the moments when I was most convinced or most in love.[14]

The least one can say is that when the occupation changed the 'adequate setting [décor],' the adequacy of this aesthetic recuperation of doubt into form as a principle of resistance was indeed cast into doubt. But under the cover of the ideology of necessity and fact, the memory of this 'ephemeral' state lingered, and sometimes shone through, as in the January 1942 article in which de Man proudly reports on the private conversation he had with Valéry.

> Everything is subject to reflection for an attentive spirit who does not allow himself to consent without any verification to the ready-made formulas that language puts at his disposal. This continual necessity to reverify, to cast into doubt, to make reser-

vations, is an inevitable characteristic of any thought that sees itself as rigorous. (LS, 182)

Having sketched the 'incessant struggle' against the limitations of language in which symbolism engaged in its search for appropriate form, de Man rehearses the lesson to be drawn from this experience, which 'for us' is already 'a thing of the past':

It is that, especially in his private conversation, one feels in this writer a concern, not without anxiety, for the safeguarding of what is called the values of the spirit. His generation, he explained, witnessed a crisis the moment it found itself deprived of the principal points of support on which it had habitually based itself: science, religion, etc. But it managed to win its salvation in that it found a value which allowed it to concentrate its spiritual appetites. This value was art. For us, the same problem poses itself, but in a much more anguishing way. For instead of choosing values, we have preferred to hide this inner void behind a facade of factitious satisfactions and sterile occupations which mechanized civilization takes it upon itself to furnish us with in abundance. From this is born that nervous tension of the modern world, that grimacing and warped character of our life, the only remaining dynamism of which is that of an automatic agitation. One cannot without disastrous consequences lose all respect for certain forms of human intelligence which can only be exercized in calm and serenity. This respect Paul Valéry has preserved, and it remains the principal element in his preoccupations and acts. And this suffices to give this man, who some have tried to depict as frivolous and careless, a boundless gravity when he speaks of certain aspects of contemporary life. It proves that he remains in the service of what is best in man. It is also what gives his personality an irresistible and captivating attraction. (182)

Ten years later, Montaigne is made to draw the final lesson from this memory (which is also a memory of Monthouet): like the 'nous' with which de Man ranks himself under the occupation, Montaigne looks on the values of symbolism as on a thing of the past, but his calm and serenity, rather than being marked by 'boundless gravity,' radiate a 'tranquil irony,' a 'respectful irony' which recognizes the 'ultimate absurdity' of humankind's 'dangerous constructions' even while it delights 'in the spectacle of their beauty' ('MT' CW, 10). An irony that is all too close to what de Man, in July 1942, singled out as the principal attraction of the 1939–40 diary of Ernst Jünger: his 'conception of the world which, even in contact with the cruelest of realities, manages to preserve a smiling serenity of admirable loftiness' (BD, 361). Such is the conception of someone who has managed to transform the war into a 'drama of which he is a witness prior to being an actor in it'—the phrase is taken from the celebration of this same diary in the final pages of Hendrik de Man's *Cahiers de ma montagne,* and it should not come as a surprise that its author should also ground the 'surprising similarity' of Jünger's thoughts to his own by expressing the desire to have expressed them 'in his place,'[15] just like in his mountain retreat near Mont Blanc—where 'Power dwells apart in its tranquillity / Remote, serene and inaccessible'—the governing desire is to take the place from which the *Essais* were written: ' "Our war can change forms, multiply and diversify into new parties as much as it likes; as for me, I do not budge *[pour moy, je ne bouge]*." '[16]

This is the argument: it is as a critique of the finishing closure of this retreat into postapocalyptic serenity that Paul de Man's return to the poets that Montaigne has left behind must be read. One privileged performance of this imperative in the course of this return occurs in the shape of a question that demands to be cut out of its context here. The question addresses the validity of the tranquilizing effects of the inventory. Its target is the temptation of irony in the voice previously envied in Jünger and Montaigne, the voice which has acquired that 'even and balanced tone that transposes what are often terrible words into an atmosphere of serenity': an atmosphere of serenity 'of which one can ask oneself whether it has really been *earned*' ('PP' CW, 65; translation modified). The place where this question is opened is the crisis of poetry in what follows.

Part Two

Intention of the Dialectic

... on a road that is from the first no road, but has
immediate being at its centre. ...
—Hegel, 'Preface' to *Phenomenology of Spirit*

I n 1966, speaking on 'The Crisis of Contemporary Criticism,'
de Man ordained that 'we can speak of crisis when a 'separation' takes place, by self-reflection, between what, in literature, is in conformity with the original intent and what has irrevo-
cably fallen away from this source' ('CC' BI, 8). Even when put in its
immediate context, it is not unlikely that this arcane and apodictic
definition left some of his listeners puzzled.[1] The statement calls
for an extensive gloss, and the fact that, to a large extent, the essays
de Man had been writing up to this point effectively consisted of
just such a glossary may well have been lost on his audience.

In a first, slanted, move toward the reconstruction of the perspective that this dictum requires, I now propose to read the essays
de Man wrote during the 1950s, most of them in French, most
of them also published in France. This linguistic and geographi-
cal determination is not unimportant: it leads the way to a certain
context of thought, or universe of discourse, in which these early
attempts promiscuously, but also uncomfortably, resonate. These
resonances are sometimes identified by de Man himself, but more
often than not they are unacknowledged echoes of disseminated
voices, distant or near.[2] Like most original thinkers, de Man is also
a thinking magpie, and one of the purposes of this book is to in-

45

dicate some of the possible sites of his frequent visits, without, however, therefore adding one more item to the already depressingly long list of contemporary capitulations to the genealogical temptation.[3] Put more precisely: it is by no means the pretension of the present study to uncover all these early writings' resonance chambers as if they were so many self-explanatory sources—sometimes not even the most immediately obvious or challenging ones will be mentioned, while those contexts that are highlighted will rarely, if ever, be articulated exhaustively. The general 'method' of the present study is stubbornly single-minded: my primary concern is always with de Man's text, not with some more or less phantasmatic description of the (primal) critical 'scene.' However (and this hardly needs to be repeated), as there is nothing in a text that is not also implicated in its outside, this 'scene' will repeatedly come to disturb our willful concentration. My remarks on the discursive context of de Man's writing, then, should be received as offered in a spirit of recognition and perhaps even imitation of such disturbance, and they should consequently not be expected to establish a reading presenting itself as accomplished or even entirely legitimate. Which, in turn, is not to say that one can seriously give oneself *carte blanche* in these matters: to allow for disturbance, even to imitate its occurrence, is not the same as to generalize possible illegitimacy into a legitimate method.

The intertextual density of these essays also entails that their arguments are developed, often simultaneously, on different and frequently not altogether compatible levels of thought. The contradictions and paradoxes resulting from this contribute considerably to the intellectual and critical challenge that de Man's writings pose for the reader, but they also make it a very cumbersome task to present and to gloss the arguments that they do contain in such a way as not to merely mimic in more explicit terms their unavowed mutual incompatibilities. At the same time, however, these incompatibilities are constitutive features of de Man's thought here and cannot be simply discarded in the name of the true thought that would explain the work to come. A further complication of this situation is the fact that de Man's notoriously confident and sometimes peremptory tone informs his discourse on each of these different levels of argumentation, thus rendering exceptionally difficult not only the detection of the possible and actual contradictions between different notions simultaneously held, but also the decision as to which notion, if any, should properly receive pride of place. At the limit, of course, this decision has already been made (for us) and it would be a foolish and presumptuous imposture to claim to be writing from a position of splendid ignorance of de Man's later thought. Yet, as an exercise in reading, assuming the simulacrum of such an imposture may prove to be helpful.

One more preliminary remark is in order. It might be objected that the following reading, which properly deals with a handful of apparently outdated essays only, is too long for what it delivers, which is ultimately not much more than a confirmation of de Man's own judgment, in 1982, that these early texts are the work of 'someone most uncomfortably stuck in ontologism.' But he immediately added that 'maybe they can still have some use as "das warnend ängstig Lied" to those tempted to go the same way.'[4] Pedestrians such as ourselves, perhaps.

CHAPTER FOUR

The Double Aspect:
Two Roads for Poetry

Is the 'distinction' between 'consciousness' and 'Thing' sufficient for tackling the ontological problematic in a primordial
manner?—Heidegger, *Sein und Zeit*, § 83

A convenient point of entry in de Man's poetics in the
1950s is 'The Double Aspect of Symbolism,' a text probably written between 1954 and 1956 and certainly among
the first of de Man's writings in English. It is not a particularly
outstanding text, but it has the advantage of sketching one strand
of de Man's thought in a way that invites a critical line of reasoning
germane to his other writings of the period.

The essay revolves around what de Man would later call a 'binary
polarity of classical banality' ('RN' AR, 107): the poet's 'acute awareness of an essential separation between his own being and the
being of whatever is not himself: the world of natural objects, of
other human beings, society, or God.' ('DA,' 6). Adding a reactive
dynamics to this observation, he continues that the poet 'lives in a
world that has been split and in which his consciousness is pitted,
as it were, against its object in an attempt to seize something which
it is unable to reach' (6). This conflict is then immediately incor-
porated in the implied narrative of a 'no longer,' in an apparently
rather naïve assumption of a prelapsarian but unnamed time in
which this separation did not yet hold sway. What must instantly

interest us is de Man's transcription of this situation 'in terms of poetic language': the poet 'is no longer close enough to things to name them as they are,' his language, which is 'an agent of consciousness,' his word, or even 'the logos,' 'no longer coincides with the universe but merely reaches out for it in a language which is unable to *be* what it *names*—which, in other words, is *merely* a symbol' (6). This predicament (the description of which, to use a phrase de Man would later apply to Georg Lukács's presentation of this same situation, is 'eloquent but not strikingly original' ['GL' BI, 54]) appears to give rise to two possible, diametrically opposed attitudes: answering 'the first and natural impulse . . . to use poetical language as a means to restore the lost unity' through a principle of *identification* ('DA,' 7), or trying to establish a different and 'true' unity by means of a principle of linguistic *mediation* (13).

In most of the essays he wrote in this period, de Man traces the windings of these 'alternate roads' of poetry, and the following pages try to follow him in this cartographical undertaking, largely by taking the surface of the map as it is laid out in 'The Double Aspect of Symbolism' as an exemplary instance. It will soon become clear that the superficially dichotomous aspect of this map of poetry is fundamentally deceptive, but since this ambiguity is not consistently controlled in de Man's thought at this stage, our attempt to follow this thought through in its encounter with the problems that constitute it cannot begin to reflect upon the deceptive nature of this dichotomy without first having recognized, however briefly, its initial schematics. Hence: two roads for poetry.

Road 1

The first road that de Man's map offers the poet confronted with his own awareness of the essential separation between himself and what can be rigorously called 'the rest,' is, as noted earlier, that which promises a return to the 'lost unity.' His vehicle on this journey home is the symbol, which functions as 'a key to reenter this world of unity from which he has been exiled' ('DA,' 7). One of the poets who is deemed to have exemplarily trodden this path, and in whose company de Man purports to travel here, is Baudelaire.

To illustrate his point, de Man reads an extraordinary restorative power in a line from 'Le Cygne'—'Et mes chers souvenirs sont plus lourds que des rocs' (And my precious memories are heavier than stones)—through which Baudelaire succeeds in 'conferring upon a purely mental consciousness, by means of a mere act of symbolic language, the very quality which one feels to be the essence of matter: weight and opacity, eternal stability, whatever contrasts most with the fleeting transparency of a subjective awareness such as "memories"' (7). Through this figure, moreover, the 'infinite distance' of the essential separation 'is crossed at lightning speed, and unity is restored, not merely among the diversity of natural objects, but also among the spiritual and the material world' (7). The pattern of this argument is simple enough—it is, in fact, identical to that of the most orthodox readings of, in particular, Baudelaire's 'Correspondances,'[1] which comfortably take for granted the 'ténébreuse et profonde unité' (a phrase de Man also quotes) that one is alleged to recover on one's passage through the 'forêts de symboles.' Despite (or because of) this simplicity, however, this reading as it is pursued here already points up a difficulty that begins to undercut its self-assurance. This difficulty triggers some odd movements and contradictions in de Man's text, most markedly so in his treatment of 'the inner tensions and hesitations' (9) that he himself seeks to uncover in the travels of the poets of the first persuasion, and a reading of these confused moves may help us to better understand what is really at stake, both in the poetical project deployed on the first road and in de Man's interpretation of its intent.

✳

A first oddity already occurs in de Man's tacit assimilation of the effect of 'Le Cygne,' one of Baudelaire's more intensely morbid poems, to the foundation of unity professed in 'Correspondances.' Baudelaire's 'belief in the fundamental unity of being,' which is accessible only by 'an act of the imagination' discovering 'the hidden roads . . . to a world of recovered one-ness' (7), can be quite intuitively projected onto the transport of senses and spirit chanted in the latter poem, but it is not as readily evident how it would apply to a poem of unchanging melancholy such as 'Le Cygne.' Nevertheless, de Man's choice of textual example is by no means a mere coincidence (or, more accurately, should not be read as such): the fact that it displays the same (albeit inversely actualized) figural crossing that allows the 'vivants pilliers' in 'Correspondances' to let forth their 'confuses paroles,' and that it valorizes this pattern in a markedly different fashion, is a crucial strategical point in his argument, insofar as it prepares—all of this implicitly—the 'supreme paradox' (10) in Baudelaire's project that de Man intends to bring to light.

For a fundamental complication 'puts in question' Baudelaire's (and other similarly inspired poets') 'adherence to what can rightly be called a creed' (9). This creed or belief demands of them that they 'name the unity to which they aspire . . . as if it were a region that one would naturally inhabit.' This unity, still according to this creed, 'is not merely an intent, a future state towards which one moves without knowing it, but an actuality of which, in certain privileged moments, language can state and hold the true experience' (9). It is important to underscore that de Man appears to take seriously—or, more accurately, to acknowledge as conceptually valid—the stated intent of this creed: it is not an intent, and that which it intends to name is indeed something that is (always) already there to be named, and which can indeed be named by those who succeed in clearing away the debris that has come to obscure it since the Fall. De Man assumes as correct and adequate the contention he ascribes to Baudelaire that 'the symbol achieves identity between all things,' and concludes from this, quite logically, that if this is indeed the case, the poet, in naming this identity, 'in fact never names anything but the universal One of which the 'minute particulars' are only immediately accessible emanations.'[2] And it is here that arises a venerable metaphysical difficulty, for 'as readers of Plato's *Parmenides* well know, it is a particularly vexing problem to develop the apparently simple statement that the One *is*' (9). And since it is precisely such a development the poet is in fact said (by himself, but also by de Man at this point) to succeed in bringing about through his naming, it comes as no surprise that this name carries a heavy metaphysical burden.

De Man's matter-of-fact assertion that the *Parmenides* shows the problem of unity to be a very vexing one is unproblematic; but his subsequent laconic statement of that problem cannot sustain critical scrutiny for very long: 'The ontological status of the One,' he writes, 'is ambiguous, and it is impossible to state unity of being except in terms of not-being' (9). While this statement is certainly contained in the aporetic metaphysical perplexities that Parmenides stages, it is, even on a very first level, manifestly insufficient as a rendering of the true ramifications of the problem, and this because it implicitly assumes the possibility of stating the unity of being—which is precisely what is at stake and has to be demonstrated. That is to say, while it can be argued, metaphysically speaking, that the unity of being cannot be expressed except if one also takes into account not-being, this does not entail that, in order to actually express the unity of being, it would somehow suffice to employ 'terms of not-being.' Nor do the lucubrations in the *Parmenides* support this. De Man's statement is in fact a crude distortion of the problem in that it promotes an indispensable requirement for the thought of the unity of being to the status of a sufficient requirement to fulfill this thought, and one finds it difficult not to suspect that his reference to the authority of the *Parmenides* here is a fairly basic rhetorical ploy introduced to cover up a certain inconsistency in his argument, rather than a recognition of genuine reliance on this dialogue.

Our primary concern here is not to flesh out this metaphysical conundrum, which in itself would necessitate taking recourse to, at the very least, Hegel and Heidegger.[3] For our present purpose, it is more urgent to note the role the distortion of this problem plays in de Man's larger argument. We saw that he was led to introduce this difficulty largely in response to the programmatic concern with the recovery and actual naming of the 'complex but undivided' totality to which Baudelaire pleads allegiance, and the conclusion de Man draws from his statement of the problem bears this out:

> It is impossible to state unity of being except in terms of not-being. This metaphysical problem has a direct equivalence in the thematic evolution of all the poets of the Baudelairean type: inevitably, they come to express unity in terms of death. The only human experience which offers a symbolical correspondence with unity is that of death, and we should not be surprised to find Baudelaire invoking death as the pilot on his voyage towards recovered unity. (9)

One certainly wishes that de Man had stated this point in a rather less sweeping manner, with a good deal more argumentative explicitness and less reliance on theses supposedly established elsewhere. The structure implicit in the argument is clear enough, but it can hardly be said to have been argued for: to name the crucial flaw, it is by no means evident how 'the human experience of death' (itself far from being a self-explanatory notion) can be said to be the direct thematic equivalent of the metaphysical 'category' of not-being; de Man merely *states* that such is the case, and even then only by implication, as if it were a matter of course. And, a fortiori, one may consequently well wonder how it can be said that Baudelaire manages to express *unity* in terms of death. The reasons for these somewhat specious moves, however, are perhaps less difficult to grasp. Because he has set himself the desperate task to demonstrate the actuality of the object of Baudelaire's professed concern, de Man is obligated to produce an identifiable textual mention of the name of that actuality (i.e., unity); but since he is at the same time properly suspicious of even the conceptual possibility of such an actuality, he chooses for the name of this unity the negatively valorized theme of the 'human experience of death,' pretending, as he does so, to legitimate this choice of death as the ultimate and ineluctable name of unity by means of a metaphysical argument.

Obviously, this is not to say that death is not in fact an overriding concern in, for instance, Baudelaire's poetry—the point is only that de Man's interpretation of this theme as the actual name of the (actual) unity of being is insufficiently founded, that the metaphysical justification and interpretation of this thematics in Baudelaire's poetry (and) in de Man's argument is ultimately deficient. Fortunately, however, the same text already supplies us with the makings of a very different sort of argument which is altogether more promising, if not therefore wholly convincing.

The most immediately important feature of this 'second' argument—which is in fact incompatible with the 'first'—is that it is no longer directly dependent upon the stated beliefs of the 'poets of the Baudelairean type,' and thus frees itself from the spurious thematic arguments required for the previous interpretation. Instead, it bases itself on the poetological structure of the 'Baudelairean' symbols, and this is where the second purpose of de Man's choice of textual example is revealed. Not only is the line from 'Le Cygne,' especially when put in its context, sufficiently morbid to pave the way for the theme of death that was already hovering in the wings, it also, and certainly more powerfully, prepares for the problem of the 'intrinsic superiority of natural being over consciousness' (13) that is sketchily developed further on in the essay and which forms one of the foundational difficulties of de Man's early thought.

The emphasis in the 'second' argument, then, is not on any supposed naming of unity as an actuality, but on the poetical act of ascribing the features of matter—especially eternity and stability—to that which is by virtue of its very essence at the furthest possible remove from such features: consciousness. This can only mean, so the argument goes, that, in effect, this sort of figure does *not* establish a 'true unity' (13): 'the kind of unity to which Baudelaire aspires is in fact the annihilation of consciousness absorbed, as it were, by the power of being in which it searches to drown itself' (12).

Thus, we notice that death is now no longer inscribed in Baudelaire's poetry, as de Man reads it, as a mere *theme* (albeit a particularly tenacious one) that would offer a symbolic correspondence with unity through its equivalence to not-being, but as the 'death,' or the sacrifice, of consciousness as it is stabilized into the *figure* of the natural object. 'Death,' in other words, is not only a possible thematic expression of an inherent flaw in the project of naming unity, but it is an ineluctable consequence of a *structural* feature of the figures employed in this project, irrespective of the explicit valorizations attached to particular instantiations of these figures, because these figures divest consciousness of its essential temporality of becoming in favor of a permanence of being. On the basis of this insight de Man can conclude that Baudelaire's poetry 'can be called a poetry of being,' as opposed to a poetry of becoming (14). Rather than naming a unity of being, which would rigorously have to include becoming as well, the Baudelairean symbol is now said to establish a sacrificial and nonreciprocal identification between consciousness and the natural object: the essential separation, far from being overcome, is actually foreclosed through the abolition of one of the separata in its identification with (or absorption in) the other (this latter, in addition, having been reduced from whatever is not the poet's own consciousness—i.e., 'the world of natural objects, of other human beings, society, or God' [6]—to 'natural being' pure and simple).

✱

Even though it will force us to run ahead in our narrative, it is imperative to note at this juncture that the structure of this poetics as sketched by de Man already betrays a barely veiled hierarchization of the initial dichotomy. Not only is there an essential separation between consciousness and natural being, but this separation is also immediately implicitly thought as a valorized opposition, with natural being conceived of as intrinsically superior to consciousness. In itself, such a hierarchization of posited opposites is hardly surprising: as has been tirelessly and by now classically demonstrated by Derrida, it forms one of the founding gestures of metaphysics, and one could almost be excused for reading its occurrence in de Man's text as a relatively unimportant (be it not therefore any the less questionable) received presupposition. A closer inspection, however, reveals that this particular movement in de Man's thought bespeaks a radical riddle which migrates throughout his entire early work.

In a certain sense, this pattern effects a considerable swerve from the fundamental ontology projected by Heidegger in *Sein und Zeit*. To grasp this, one should first register that what de Man here calls 'intrinsic superiority' in fact amounts to an *ontological* superiority. Although he does not yet employ this qualification (he will do so later on), the narrative sketched here suggests—at least in one of its main strands—that what is ultimately at stake is indeed the question of the proximity to Being, and that the entity whose being is closest to Being is the natural object. It is on the basis of this suggestion that Baudelaire's project is described as driven not merely by the desire for unity with natural being but quite specifically by 'a desire for direct, unmediated contact with *Being*' ('DA,' 12; emphasis added). It is in the natural object, intrinsically superior to consciousness, that an unmediated contact with Being can be projected, and while de Man argues that such a *contact* is ultimately inconceivable, he does not conclude from this that the designation of natural being as the *locus* onto which such a contact is to be projected (irrespective of the actual accomplishment of such projection) is in error. It is the stability and permanence deemed characteristic of the natural object that allows its mode of being to be thought of as closer to Being than is the mode-of-being-as-becoming ascribed to consciousness, and while Baudelaire's project is said to fail because the identification in which it would culminate would fail to accommodate the movement of becoming which should also figure in a true unity of being, this failure is still thought of as an absorption in, precisely, 'the power of being.'

Thus, although this formal hierarchy can be said to echo Heidegger's call for a distinction in ontological priority between *Dasein* and what is not *daseinsmäßig*, it must also be understood as a crucial distortion of this echo in that it reduces Being to the permanent and stable being that is opposed to becoming (a reduction, in other words, to the presentness of the kind, or measure, of being which to Heidegger is emphatically not in privileged proximity to Being), and in that it consequently relegates consciousness (itself already a distortion of *Dasein*) to an ontological realm more distant from Being than that in which natural being has its being. In this strand of de Man's thought, Being is to be found—i.e., not to be found—in the immediacy of natural being from which consciousness is barred by the essential separation, and it is because of this bar that natural being is intrinsically (ontologically) superior to alienated consciousness. Consciousness, then, is marked by an eternal instability, and the mark of this instability is its inability to claim for itself a privileged proximity to Being.[4]

Yet, at the same time there is in de Man's thought another strand that appears to locate Being precisely in the bar, in the separation itself, which would mean—and this would be much closer to Heidegger and less prone to run into the particular type of ontico-ontological confusion courted in the opposite strand—that it is in consciousness's thoughtful and authentic acknowledgment of this bar that a maximum proximity to Being can be ensured. This raises the further problem that the acquisition of such proximity could stabilize consciousness out of its constitutive instability, which seriously complicates this already highly intricate maze. But for the moment it is sufficient to briefly identify some of the governing folds and turns of de Man's map, and we can return to its surface aspect.

✱

The schematics of de Man's interpretation of the first type of poetry instantiated by Baudelaire remain largely the same throughout most of the essays he wrote in this period (although, as we shall see, the position of this scheme in his larger argument is subject to some radical modification). Thus, for instance, in 'Process and Poetry' (1956), he speaks of 'poetic eternalism' ('PP' CW, 65) and its attendant 'metatemporal poetics,' and writes that 'an eternalistic poetry, such as Baudelaire's, sacrifices consciousness to a certain extent,' but 'does preserve a sensible materiality,'[5] or, again, that the 'poetic attitude' of the 'poetry of substance' maintains 'the sensible object at the expense of consciousness' (71). Similarly, in 'The Temptation of Permanence' (1955), this poetics of being is characterized as pertaining to a certain kind of 'thoughts . . . that are susceptible to leading to the death of the spirit by way of the temptation of permanence' ('TP' CW, 31).

As this last example makes clear, the important advantage of this reading of the 'Baudelairean' symbol is that it can contain and account for the undeniable presence of the theme of death in this poetry, without however falling prey to the dubious argumentation the 'initial' axiological-thematic reading of this isotopy displayed. The 'supreme paradox' that 'the most powerful of all human desires, the desire for unity, should have to be stated in terms deriving from the most dreaded of all experiences, that of death,' which introduces 'an almost unbearable tension in a poetry which set out to be all quietness and appeasement' ('DA,' 11)— this is the conclusion reached in the thematic reading—is far from being leveled by this second, more figural reading, but it is no longer overtly impaired by the dubitable status of such precritically valorized concepts as, precisely, 'the human experience of death,' or by the critic's uneasy allegiance to the notion of unity of being as 'an actuality of which, in certain privileged moments, language can state and hold the true experience' (9). To be sure, the 'human experience of death' continues to haunt de Man's readings of the 'poetry of being,' but it does this no longer primarily as the name of an actuality of unity, but rather as the projection of the annihilation of consciousness in its aspiration to coincide with the ontologically superior natural object in order to thus acquire the characteristic qualities of substance—stability, eternity, materiality, metatemporality, and being (read restrictively as opposed to becoming). Death, then, is indeed only 'la mort *de l'esprit*,' as the unactualized consequence of a project inscribed in the figural crossing of properties of matter onto mind, and its presence in poetry of the Baudelairean type is no longer a contingent effect of an actual instantiation of its semantic register.

Now, if this is an adequate account of the schematics of the first road, it should be registered that, precisely because of its schematicity, this pattern also invites a number of schematic objections. First, the chiasmic crossing, of which a figure such as 'memories that are heavier than stones' actualizes only one direction (matter onto mind), is not allowed to develop fully. Although de Man does refer to 'Correspondances,' the poem in which the opposite direction is canonically manifested, he does not pursue this problem of the double aspect of the chiasmus yet, and it will in fact continue to riddle his readings in most of the work to come. Second, and we have already touched upon this objection, de Man does not justify his reformulation of the 'essential separation' between consciousness and everything else into a separation between consciousness and the 'intrinsically superior *natural being*' ('DA,' 13).

Still, our principal concern for the time being is to trace the schematics of de Man's own plotting of the trajectory of the first road, and we shall only be able to confront objections such as the two just mentioned (both of which testify to the inconsistency in de Man's ontology hinted at before) when we begin to insert these schematics in the larger poetics he is trying to develop here. Before we continue our scan of de Man's rudimentary map and turn to the second road, however, one more schematic remark (this time not an objection) may be in order. What should perhaps be retained from the preceding discussion is that the two, contradictory readings of the 'supreme paradox' de Man offers here actually stage the conflict between an 'existential' and a 'rhetorical' reading, which, as a complex and unresolved problem, is crucial to an understanding of his work. It should be evident that this conflict does not develop as a pure opposition between two entirely different readings: both interpretations are fundamentally hybrid constructs that almost simultaneously employ 'rhetorical' and 'existential' arguments. The point is only that the respective balance and modality of these two interpretations are markedly different, and that the discrepancy in the larger argument that ensues from their simultaneity indicates the outlines of a problem whose development deserves to be attentively traced.

Road 2

Given the previous description of Baudelaire's way, the 'alternate road' ('DA,' 11) that poetry can take will come as no surprise: what is aspired to by the poets of being, de Man's Virgil on the second road, Mallarmé, will seek to avoid. Having begun his poetical career with a brief trip on the road of being, aspiring 'with all his strength to an ideal condition "anywhere out of this world,"' the symbol of which is '*l'azur*, the blue sky of the natural universe,' Mallarmé soon changes his mind: the sky turns into 'a highly ambiguous symbol which still haunts the poet but from which he now tries, with even greater effort, to escape,' and 'as the poetry develops we see that the union with natural being, Baudelaire's highest hope, becomes for Mallarmé man's greatest—and unavoidable—misfortune and that, instead, his entire poetic effort goes to avoid direct identification between consciousness and the natural object' (11–12). For Baudelaire union with natural being was rife with ambiguity too, mainly because it turned out to spell the projected death of consciousness in its identification with the natural object rather than a true unification, but in de Man's narrative, the Baudelairean poets are willing to pay this price. Mallarmé, on the contrary, rejects such 'desire for direct, unmediated contact with Being' and opts instead for a principle of mediation that leaves him 'on the side of consciousness and *against* natural being' (12). Mallarmé's swan's song is entirely different from the song of correspondence, transport, and death of the spirit that de Man had read into Baudelaire's 'Cygne,' and it is in sounding this 'cygne d'autrefois' that the second road takes shape.[6]

The poetic act . . . is for [Mallarmé] an act by means of which natural being is made accessible to consciousness. Consciousness attempts to think through the essential otherness of the object, to transform this otherness into a cognitive knowledge stated in language. Poetry is not an identification with the object but a reflection on the object, in which consciousness moves out towards the object, attempts to penetrate it and then, like a reflected ray of light, returns to the mind, enriched by its knowledge of the outside world. And it is by means of this process of thinking the other that the mind learns to know itself. (12)

If the poet could really embark on this instant (Hegelian) odyssey and succeed in bringing it full circle, if the poet could really send out rays of consciousness that would penetrate the object (of desire, no doubt) and then return to the mind, such would be a formidable feat indeed, and de Man, at least initially, seems to hold this to be the case. 'The Mallarmean symbol,' he writes, is 'a mediation between the subject on the one side and nature on the other in which both keep their separate identities, but in which a third entity, language, contains within itself their latent opposition' (12–13). The 'common structure' of these symbols, which are 'altogether different' from Baudelaire's identifications, would be that of a fluctuating back and forth between mind and matter, in an oscillation that is poetically transcribed in presentations of the object 'in the process of metamorphosis into another object or, more frequently still, in the process of dissolving into nothing.' Thus, 'Mallarmé's things act out, as it were, the movement of the human mind as it grows in consciousness of its own self.' The symbolic object acquires a highly ambiguous status in that it is still an object but also a transparent entity emptied of material substance 'as the mind takes possession of it,' and this is reflected in the third entity, language, which is treated both as an object ('considerable attention is given to its objective qualities of sound, visual appearance, and form') and as an entity subject to 'the necessities of cognitive consciousness' (13). But there is a limit to this project: 'At the limit, if language *were* able to be a perfect mediation and to contain within itself the essence of natural being as well as that of the subjective consciousness, it would succeed in establishing a true unity, . . . the balanced unity in which, in Hegel's words, "the concept expresses the object and the object the concept"' (13; emphasis added; see also 'PN' CW, 21; and 'PHD M,' 67). As the subjunctive suggests, language is not able to be this perfect mediation and, as was the case with Baudelaire, the poetic intention gets to be recognized *as* an intention only—the sole but, as we shall see, all-important difference being that, unlike Baudelaire, Mallarmé is fully conscious of the failure of his project to attain full actualization. As de Man writes, 'Language does not succeed in this task and . . . the poet knows it. The intrinsic superiority of natural being is such that all attempts to master it are doomed at the outset' (13).

Thus, rather than to succeed in mastering natural being by making it fully 'accessible to consciousness' in a 'true unity,' Mallarmé's project would appear to end up as a symmetrical counterpart to Baudelaire's. Whereas the latter develops a poetics that would result in a sacrifice of consciousness, Mallarmé's enterprise would result in a sacrifice of the object. As de Man puts it in another essay that also stages a confrontation between both poets, Mallarmé's 'poetry of becoming,'[7] even while it allows for 'an extremely acute form of self-consciousness,' can only acquire this clarity 'by a necessary sacrifice of the sensible object.' Beginning 'from an experience of alienation or separation . . . , it tries to suspend it by safeguarding the movement of consciousness at the expense of the object, to save consciousness by killing the object' ('PP' CW, 70–71). But just as was the case with Baudelaire's sacrifice of consciousness, Mallarmé's sacrifice of the object is never quite completed. Just as Baudelaire's aspiration to unity got relayed as an intention to abolish consciousness, which, if carried through, would mean death, so Mallarmé's project seems to slip into an unfulfilled intention to destroy natural being in order to achieve 'the total accomplishment of the spirit,' which, de Man tells us, would also be 'total annihilation,' the 'cosmic death of all things' of which Mallarmé's *Un Coup de Dés* purports to be a 'symbolical evocation' ('DA,' 14). And what is important is that both these failures ultimately preserve the ontological superiority of natural being over consciousness. Baudelaire's project fails because of the impossibility for consciousness to actually attain the intrinsically superior natural object, whereas Mallarmé's project fails because this ontological superiority shelters the natural object from its destruction as intended by consciousness. The fundamental pattern thus seems to be that of a perfect symmetry between the respective dynamics of the two roads, powered and checked as they both are by the same unavoidable principle of the superiority of natural being.

Seems to be: for this apparent symmetry is singularly misleading and by no means adequately renders the full thrust of de Man's argument, although it is he himself who has introduced the symmetry—*as* symmetry—in the first place. In order to understand this puzzling pattern of symmetries and ultimately superior dissymmetries, we must first investigate more explicitly the overriding evaluative concern of de Man's somewhat deceitful presentation of the 'alternate roads' between which poets can choose. In the course of this investigation, we shall also be able to complete the presentation of the second road which we have so abruptly (but in accordance with the abrupt dissolution of de Man's own pretense to offer two viable 'alternatives') broken off here.

CHAPTER FIVE

Evasion and Confrontation

Yet it would be erroneous to believe that the inevitable pathway
through Hegel means that one has no choice but to accept the
Hegelian solution.—Rodolphe Gasché, *The Tain of the Mirror*

To address the pervasive judgmental concern of the conflict of poetic attitudes that de Man stages, we may briefly
circle back to our earlier suggestion that his narrative appears to be in complicity with what he himself would later call
'a highly familiar set of historical fallacies' ('AI' BI, 272), among
which looms large that of the prelapsarian age before the 'essential
separation.' De Man's text is very much aware, albeit confusedly,
of the difficulties such a historical scheme raises, even while it cannot therefore bring itself to completely abandon it. The underlying
question of such historicizations—in this case, 'Where did the
separation we are now aware of come from and where is it going
to lead?'—indeed stubbornly worries the essays he wrote in this
period.

In the short but very ambitious 1955 article 'The Inward Generation,' for instance, de Man asserts that the 'awareness of a deep
separation between man's inner consciousness and the totality of
what is not himself had certainly existed before 1800, but it becomes predominant around that time' ('IG' CW, 14–15), whereas
in 'The Double Aspect of Symbolism,' which was written at about
the same time, he displays a much more articulately suspicious
attitude:

We could question incessantly and vainly why, how, and even when this separation came about. One is tempted to look for specific facts, historical events, or sociological determinations which caused it as a certain virus causes a disease. But in trying to think in such a mechanistically historical way, the problem becomes more and more elusive and vanishes in a series of endless circular reasonings in which it becomes impossible to distinguish cause from effect. ('DA,' 6)

He then adds that rather than to fall prey to such an 'all-too simplistic historicism' (which in fact is the diagnostic historicism of the [sociological] laboratory), we had better investigate *how* the, in this case 'symbolist,' poets dealt with 'a problem which may well be at the root of all human consciousness,' thus having the cake he had just eaten (or vice versa), at least to a certain extent. And elsewhere, he even erases the hypothetical framing of this reading (which he also associates with Hegel [6, n. 9] and goes so far as to speak of 'an experience of alienation or separation that *is* universal' ('PP' CW, 71; emphasis added).

Still, in the final analysis it would appear that de Man is indeed not primarily concerned with a historical identification of the origin of the essential separation, and whenever he does seem to relegate 'this origin' to some specific period in time, this gesture turns out to be more in the interest of creating an enabling narrative frame for the argument than a serious contribution to traditional historiography. More immediately important to de Man is that the *awareness* of this separation was prominent in Romanticism, and that it is still of primordial urgency 'now,' which then leads him to reflect on its future, which is to say that the problem does remain intimately linked up with the *question* of history. And it is here that his valorization of the two roads acquires its full significance—a significance by no means restricted to poetry alone.

It would not be an overstatement to say that one of the principal (if not the sole) concerns of the poetics de Man tries to develop, is to offer a plea for an 'authentic' attitude toward time. That this authentic attitude has to be sought on the side of a 'poetry of be-coming' rather than on that of a 'poetry of (permanent) being' comes as no surprise, and the question in which de Man, in 'The Inward Generation,' concisely formulates his problem is overtly rhetorical. 'When are we being deceived: is it when we try to think within a context of death and rebirth, failure and its transcendence, nothingness and being—or is it when we abandon ourselves to a stream of passive permanence?' ('IG' CW, 13). The answer in-deed appears to be already decided upon, but the reasons de Man adduces for that decision are subject to some decisive modifica-tions—so decisive, in fact, that they feed back into the question and question its status as rhetoric(al).

The Existential Choice

THE CAPITULATION OF THE SPIRIT

An important point of departure for the reasons de Man develops against the acceptance of the 'stream of passive permanence' is a fairly vague intuition that centers on a conception of a certain ('natural') apotropaic economy capable of governing the human mind. The underlying argument is roughly genealogical and hence derives its impetus largely from a negative logic which, in addition, is positively reinforced by a good deal of existential pathos. De Man presents this argument first (and perhaps ultimately always foremost), not in response to a certain poetry, but in response to a contemporary 'state of mind' (which includes and makes use of a poetics) that he intends to debunk. This is conspicuously the case in 'The Inward Generation,' where he takes issue with 'the general symptom which, for the sake of convenience, we can refer to as "conservatism"' ('IG' CW, 13), a mode of thought that can be properly understood as arising from a 'resistance' to the now familiar 'awareness of a deep separation' (14). As this general awareness not only gives rise to 'an entire set of problems' relative to human existence (including 'most matters of contemporary history, literature, and to a large extent, ethics and theology'), but also puts considerable obstacles in the way of dealing with these problems, it is no wonder that a powerful resistance to this awareness and, more crucially, to the 'inward meditation' (15) that develops it, gets to be voiced, often in the format of systems that are passed off as solutions to the said problems. Ultimately, however, such systems merely appeal to 'a temptation that exists in all of us: a desire for serenity which tries to forget and repress the original anxiety' (15) and which is typical of what he elsewhere refers to as 'our age of fatigue' ('TP' CW, 31). We must remember, de Man writes, that the inward meditation is the activity of 'what Hegel called the *unhappy* consciousness,' and

> since this consciousness is, per definition, painful and hard to bear, the temptation always exists to give up our awareness of ourselves and to fall back on something which would not be conscious, namely nothingness. This is the most insidious and persistent form of nihilism. Because our consciousness, at present, is an unhappy one, nihilism appears generally in the misleading shape of a refreshing relief. It seems to contain a promise of serenity, because it keeps us from facing the issues in which our being is at stake. ('IG' CW, 15)

Who would dare admit, after such a passage, to belong to those who would offer 'concrete systems of organization as substitutes' for the inward meditation of the unhappy consciousness? Fortunately, de Man's critique of this cowardly 'capitulation of the spirit' to the temptation of permanence ('TP' CW, 32), is not exhausted in the performance of reactive pathos (though it always benefits from the considerable authority such pathos produces). Immediately after the preceding passage, we find a first indication for a more argumentative approach of the matter in de Man's suggestion that the type of nihilism in question 'preferably takes on the form of anti-historicism,' which is proof of its strategical acuteness, as 'the conceptualization of history has been, together with poetry, the main access kept open to the difficult and necessary question of being' ('IG' CW, 15). This raises the question of how exactly 'modern conservatism' (or 'modern nihilism,' or 'nihilistic conservatism' [16; see also 'DA,' 11]) tries to obscure what de Man does not hesitate to call 'the ontological question' ('IG' CW, 15). In other words, how does it mount its attack on history; or—to put it inversely—how *should* the ontological question and the question of history and poetry be approached?

De Man's answer to this question can best be discussed through an example (which he uses twice), but before we turn to that discussion, the obvious perhaps ought to be registered. The critique of the nihilist spirit of the age that is under way here cannot not invoke the complicated call for 'concrete systems of organization' in de Man's wartime writing, while the suspicion of the promise of serenity in this critique must necessarily also recall the deployment of the isotopy of serenity in his readings of both Jünger and Montaigne. The texts in which this critique is voiced are themselves unmistakably marked by an urgent appreciation of the pertinence of the memory of the Second World War in general,[1] and nothing can stop this generality from breaking down into the components of de Man's particular past. Yet, no attempt to sound the precise measure of this retrospective modulation can dispense with a patient reading of the argument insofar as it does *not* present itself as primarily (or therapeutically) determined by this past. It is such a reading that is to be undertaken here—the past shall impose itself again soon enough, which is never to say that it can ever be postponed.

✳

In a central scene in André Malraux's *The Walnut Trees of Altenbourg* de Man detects an image which, he suggests, admirably sums up the obfuscation of history upon which Malraux would later found his studies in the history of art. After a debate on the question of 'whether one can isolate a permanent fact *[donnée]* . . . on which the notion of man can be founded,'[2] which had ended, in de Man's reading, in the formulation of a choice between 'a discontinuous, conscious, but always fragile and backsliding historical improvisation, and the utter lifelessness of an inanimate thing— as symbolized in a mere log of wood' ('IG' CW, 16), the protagonist receives 'the revelation of the permanence of man by seeing the ancient trees of the ancestral manor' ('TP' CW, 31). The seductive power of this image, de Man argues, its capacity to figure as a third alternative dislodging the debilitating choice between mute lifelessness and conscious but fatally unstable life, derives from the opposition it stages between two 'movements': the movement of history and the movement of natural growth ('the inexorable power of generation' ['IG' CW, 16]). The revelation of permanence offered by the tree is based on the 'fact' that 'its being remains identical with itself, and its movement is only the extension of what already is and what will always be' ('TP' CW, 32).[3] This stands in marked contrast to the movement of history, which is a movement of becoming:

> A consciously created *being,* whether it be a work of art or a historical fact in general, is unstable in its being, and it negates itself to be reborn in another *being.* The two are separated by the abyss of a negation (in organic language: a death), and the passage from one to the other is essentially discontinuous. (32, translation modified)

The burden of de Man's critique resides precisely in the phrase in parentheses, which translates the negations and discontinuities of history into organic and literal death. As a result of this sleight of hand, the movement of consciousness, which is that of history as becoming, is fundamentally misunderstood, and it is around this misunderstanding that Malraux's conception of art modeled on natural growth, which forms the proper target of de Man's criticism, revolves.

The argument, roughly, runs as follows. Because Malraux conceives of the discontinuities of history as organic, literal, death ('in the biological sense of the term,' 32), and because such an organic death is essentially 'the destiny of man,' historical consciousness, insofar as it is necessarily marked by discontinuity, must, for Malraux, be seen as an acceptance of this destiny, which is to say that it would be fundamentally passive. Having introduced this new term (passivity), Malraux can then, almost automatically, introduce its traditional counterpart, activity, in his argument and bring this to bear on the concept he champions, to wit, 'the quintessential free act that is the act of artistic creation.' And thus de Man can conclude that, for Malraux, art, 'in opposing itself to destiny (or to death), opposes itself in fact to becoming and to history,' which allows de Man to forcefully drive his (preestablished) point home:

Art as antidestiny is antihistorical; its movement will certainly no longer be a discontinuous vibration, but it will be like the slow and certain growth of a tree. The spirit at once complies in this affirmation, where it finds repose. To reflect on art thus conceived would be to espouse the unassailable and solid security of the walnut tree, and, as time is eliminated by a grounded future, to rise splendidly toward a sky that one will not be long in reaching. . . . This is to yield to the temptation of permanence, for art so considered is in reality only a sediment without life. (32)

We should underscore here that this entire passage is presented in a hypothetical mode (except for the final sentence) and speaks not of art but of conceptions of art said to be so many instances of capitulation. We shall return to the import of this hypothetics later on—for the moment it suffices to point out that it is part and parcel of de Man's ideological and psycho-economic polemic. When he designates 'the precise spot where the spirit capitulates' (Malraux's refusal to actually think the negations that make for the discontinuities of consciousness and history), the point is precisely that this 'spot' is the place in which 'nihilist conservatives' like Malraux *wish* to come to rest (32). Theirs is the ideology of the 'prostration of the spirit' (31) where the encounter with the negations in history has fostered a desperate 'nationalistic conservatism' (33)[4] that attempts to establish 'a suprahistorical continuity' and effectively ends up as nothing but a vast exercise in 'watch[ing] over a dead thing' (33). Such is the 'antihistoricism' of those who are unable to resist the temptation of permanence, the presence-unto-itself they find revealed in a nonconscious and nonbecoming, all too becoming, natural being: 'The virtue of the walnut trees is that they negate the nothingness of man.'[5]

In another essay written at about the same time de Man rehearses his harangue, now focused more explicitly on the poetics (not the poetry) attendant upon this antihistorical aesthetics of permanence. This poetics, he asserts, confers upon poetry 'a power of eternity that makes it either distinct from or superior to a process of becoming' ('PP' CW, 64). Poetry is seen as the re-deeming memory of an ideal state from which we have separated ourselves by our own volition, but which, through this memory, we might be able to recover. The apparent temporal destiny this view seems to present is, for de Man, indeed only apparent, since poetry, as 'a recollection of original being,' always remains 'above' temporal movement. 'This kind of metatemporality,' he continues, 'coincides at bottom with a belief that poetry founds Being im-mediately,' which is a reassuring thought as it entails that 'no mat-ter how strong the pull exercised by a historical process that would assimilate poetry to its own movement, it is always possible for poetry to elude this pull since it is not bound to it essentially, and to return to the immediate self-presence that is also an immedi-ate presence to Being' (64–65). De Man then quickly develops a critique of this conception of becoming as it is formulated by Nietzsche ('the direct ancestor' of eternalist poetics) in the con-clusion to the second *Untimely Meditation*. As de Man sees it, it is only because Nietzsche reduces becoming and history to the status of objects of 'scientific observation' that he can then ridi-cule them and oppose to them 'the eternalizing powers of Art and Religion,'[6] and a similar misconception lies at the roots of contem-porary movements of thought that would reject becoming after having identified it with 'technology or a certain political activism' (66). The argument is structurally identical to the critique of Mal-raux's great-rooted blossomer: permanence or eternity are favored over becoming—which is incorrectly understood—by those who are unable, or unwilling, to face the real problem of history. 'It is in its protest against the present historical reality, in a categori-cal refusal of participation, that poetic eternalism draws its most powerful forces' (65).

De Man's next and inevitable question must then be what a proper understanding of history and becoming, and of poetry, *would* consist of, and he answers the challenge quite promptly—the grounds, after all, had been prepared.

If an improper understanding of history is based upon a refusal to differentiate between organic death on the one hand, and the negations that make for the discontinuities in the becoming of history on the other, a true attitude toward history will have to found itself in just such a differentiation. And this, de Man submits, is only possible if one recognizes the movement of consciousness as a dialectic. In this dialectic, the negations of history are not perceived as exterior negations in the manner of 'death pure and simple,' but as 'an integral part of the life of the spirit.' 'Death,' in other words, is no longer simply death, but also the moment of 'a renewal, difficult and uncertain, but possible' ('TP' CW, 32).

The strong voice behind this doctrine of the two deaths cannot be mistaken. The governing utterance is Hegel's, for instance in the introduction to the *Phenomenology* (§ 8), where a distinction is drawn between the death of natural life, which is wholly external to the life of natural being, and the self-reflexive activity of consciousness, which constitutes a kind of death that does affect the being of consciousness. A leading voice in the choir relaying this utterance—certainly for de Man—is Jean Hyppolite, who succinctly scans these deaths as follows: 'Whereas in nature death is an external negation, spirit carries death within itself and gives it positive meaning.'[7] That this death of the spirit is diametrically opposed to the 'death of the spirit' as conceived (often unwittingly) by 'antihistoricists' like Malraux and Baudelaire should be clear. And once this death is properly thought, history can no longer be a passive destiny, or a movement of growth, but consciously becomes the creation of what de Man calls, in a crucial, but highly problematic phrase, 'that intention of the absolute,' which is itself the only ('real') permanence (as opposed to the inauthentic permanence illegitimately borrowed from the growth of natural being). 'The only permanence is that intention of the absolute that creates history, and the lesson of the past consists in the recognized repetition of this intention, beyond its successive defeats, the remnants of which cover the surface of our earth' ('TP' CW, 32–33).

This view has grave consequences for the conception of poetry, which is not only 'an integral part' of the dialectical movement of consciousness ('PP' CW, 65; just as discontinuity was previously asserted to be 'an integral part of the life of the spirit,' 'TP' CW, 32), but which is also, and more importantly, the very *expression* of this dialectic, as the language of history itself:

> Far from being antihistorical, the poetical act (in the general sense that includes all the arts) is the quintessential historical act: that through which we become conscious of the divided character of our being, and consequently, of the necessity of accomplishing it, of making it within time, instead of undergoing it in eternity. (33; translation modified)

Far from being the eternalizing power it is for Nietzsche, poetry is 'the *logos* of becoming,' which constantly negates the eternal as an immediate given and transforms it into an intention: becoming is recognized not as an object of science but as 'a consciousness of the eternal as intention and not as existent *[étant]*' ('PP' CW, 66–67). Thus, rather than to conserve the permanence an eternalist poetics desires to secure by being the 'recollection of original being,' poetry, as true consciousness, conserves an intention toward 'the absolute' by constantly and increasingly consciously repeating the intention, 'beyond the failure to found itself as eternal truth' (67). It does not found the immediacy of Being, but envisages it, through 'a risky process of successive mediations and stages of consciousness' (64), and in doing so honors the true truth of Being. 'To conserve being in its truth is to conserve the incessant struggle that constitutes it, and it is consequently to think in a necessarily insurrectionary *[révolté]* mode' ('TP' CW, 32).

The passage to existential pathos in this thesis brings de Man close to affirming that it is in performing its antagonism to eternalism that consciousness can develop and claim for itself an ontological superiority over natural being. Yet, he abstains from articulating such an affirmation and retains the notion of natural being's privileged proximity to Being (itself still thought as immediacy), even while, paradoxically, the truth of Being can only be authentically preserved in consciousness and is betrayed the moment this preservation lapses into the inauthentic aspiration to the status of natural being. Again, the difference of this thought with what it resembles in Heidegger bears emphasizing. De Man subscribes to the division between an authentic and an inauthentic interpretation of Being as, more than for instance, it is construed from Heidegger's work by Alphonse de Waelhens, but he is unwilling to pair this division to the further (but for de Waelhens's Heidegger more fundamental) claim that *Dasein,* precisely in its authentic refusal to think itself according to the model of the object, 'projects on the obscure backdrop of brute beings *[existants bruts]* a view that illuminates them *in giving them being.*'[8] The analytical ground of this unwillingness is that in de Man's ontology the 'existants bruts' hardly stand in need of more being than they already have; the more interesting dynamics of this difference from Heidegger will emerge later on. For the time being, what must interest us is the a priori positioning of an essential existential choice between authenticity and inauthenticity which informs this model—a choice that everyone has to make, but which is most conspicuously urgent for the poet.

We know that this choice is what divides Mallarmé from Baudelaire, and we know where de Man's sympathies lie. But fortunately matters are not as simple as that, and de Man is the first to upset his own set-up by referring us back to the poets:

> Thus, we are led to distinguish two kinds of poetic attitude: the first would be that of a poetry of becoming, maintaining itself as consciousness at the expense of the sensible object, whereas the other would be a poetry of substance, maintaining the sensible object at the expense of consciousness.

Quite clearly, though, this schema is oversimplistic. The problem of poetry and becoming does not present itself in the form of a choice between two equally possible directions. ('PP' CW, 71)

The Fundamental Dissymmetry

Just as Baudelaire's aspiration to unity gets relayed as an intention to abolish consciousness which, if carried out, would mean death, so Mallarmé's project seems to slip into an intention to destroy natural being in order to achieve 'the total accomplishment of the spirit' which would also be a 'total annihilation.' This is where we abruptly abandoned our description of de Man's map of poetry—on a supposedly established symmetry of choice, which we then put in a larger context of existential judgment. But beyond the obvious affective (pathetic) dissymmetry inscribed in this existential choice, de Man's poetics also displays a more fundamental imbalance, which can be thought of as the original intrinsic supplement of the extrinsic imposition of this choice.

The bare outline of this dissymmetry is not difficult to draw. Its organizing principle is the concept of the failing intention central to de Man's presentation of the two poetic attitudes, and the heart of the matter is the difference between these two failures. The poet of permanence tries to establish a unity that would be a supratemporal reign of immediate presence, but he can only conceive of this reign by intending the sacrifice of consciousness in its identification with the stability of natural being. Ultimately, the question whether the poem actually reaches this ideal state of permanence-unto-(Being-present-unto)-itself, and the ulterior question posed by the observation that the poet's intention toward this state proves to be an intention pointing in the direction of the death of consciousness, are of no major concern to an eternalist poetics, which is at liberty to satisfy itself in a complacent performance of serenity even in the face of the abysmal death prefigured in the poetry it claims as its object (or, more accurately, as the objective subject of its theses). But, as we know, the question is whether this 'atmosphere of serenity,' which is supposed to contain the failure of the poet of permanence, 'has really been *earned*' ('PP' CW, 65). The question is, evidently, yet again rhetorical. For the failure of permanence to be actually founded—in terms of poetical intent, the failure of the intention to sacrifice consciousness— leaves the poet with a radically problematic residual.

A first recognition of this residual occurs in de Man's commentary on a prose poem from *Spleen de Paris*: 'an eternalistic poetry, such as Baudelaire's, sacrifices consciousness *to a certain extent,* since it gives up trying to account for its own necessity to be and, in agreement with Nietzsche, succeeds in *partly* forgetting what it is' ('PP' CW, 71; emphasis added). The salient point is the *incompleteness* of the sacrifice, not merely because it points up a failure, nor only because it can convey the necessity of that failure, but decisively because it underscores that that necessity is a rigorously *logical* consequence of the intention itself, which that intention in its constitutive nonlogic cannot contain. At first sight this thesis may seem little more than a willful paradox, as intentions are not commonsensically supposed to contain their failures in the first place, but a simile may help to render the problem more accessible. Like the proverbial man lifting himself up by his own bootstraps, the intention of the poet of permanence intends to lift itself up by itself—the difference being that in this case not only do the subject and the object coincide, but also both these and the action, that is, the sacrificial intent of lifting (or *aufheben*). The intention intends, as intention, to abolish itself *as intention* (i.e., not merely by attaining a goal postulated as the external object of the intention as a process), for it intends to abolish that by which it can only intend (consciousness) in identifying it to natural, nonintending being. And as this is logically impossible on the level of an intention, the failure of the intention to abolish consciousness and consequently itself is a nonintentional necessity of that intention. As such, this failure is not merely a contingency but a complete devastation of the intention, precisely because the latter does remain an intention. The intention is hoisted back into intentionality by dint of its own anti-intentional intent.

If one has no taste for paradox (willful or not), such reasonings are not very likely to hold much water, but before we turn to a slightly less laborious (and ultimately more convincing) way to argue this difficulty, we must consider the opposite intention of the poets of becoming as it can, in turn, be described on the present (roughly pre-Husserlian) level of argumentation.[9]

What, then, is the intention of the poet of becoming? This is where the crux, as kernel and as stumbling block, of de Man's thought as he tries to trace it in these essays, has to be situated. The poet of becoming responds to the awareness of separation by trying to establish a perfect mediation which, however, is relayed as an intention to sacrifice natural being. And if this intention were to be fully actualized, this would lead to a 'total accomplishment of the spirit' which would also be a 'total annihilation.' But this entails a puzzling contradiction, for the sacrifice of the natural object is intended to preserve the *movement*, the *becoming* of consciousness, that is to say, its existence as intention. And an accomplishment is not an intention. This would mean that the intention of the poet of becoming has for its object (as target) something which is not becoming. The poet of permanence may intend something that is logically impossible, but the poet of becoming appears to sink even deeper in inconsequentiality in that he intends something (accomplishment) while at the same time intending something else (becoming) which is logically incompatible with this 'other' intention. The projected outcome of the poetry of being is compatible with the self-definition of this project, and this tautology holds even though this project must necessarily fail; but the projected outcome of the poetry of becoming would in fact, insofar as it is an accomplished state, betray the movement of consciousness the project is meant to preserve. This would mean that the failure of the intention of the poet of becoming is not only inevitable but in fact intentional. Not, however, in the banal sense of a mere perverse intention to fail (which is structurally identical to an intention to accomplish something), but in the rather more difficult sense of an intention to accomplish something which at the same time consciously contains its own failure in its intentional structure, so that what remains after this failure is not a residual so radically problematic as to demolish the self-definition of the project, but rather a trace that was already intentionally inscribed in the intention. To keep up, somewhat fancifully perhaps, our simile: this intention tries to lift itself up as intention while at the same time consciously cutting its bootstraps. This might result in a visual scene of an intention bending over backward until it falls over—a scene which, incidentally, de Man shall have to say more about later on (see 'ROT' BI, 213).

For the moment, it is imperative that we recognize that this paradox is indeed the crux of de Man's poetics of becoming. It governs his reading of Mallarmé's project as that of the tragic, because *consciously* failing,[10] progression of the spirit, as a progression toward something that not only cannot be reached but which the progression, insofar as it is essentially only ever progression, does not 'want' to reach. A phrase such as the 'intention of the absolute,' which de Man uses to designate the only true permanence of the movement of becoming ('TP' CW, 32), *simultaneously* has to be read as the 'absolute intention,' and it is this simultaneity that accounts for many of the contradictory statements of the intention of the poetry of becoming we come across in these texts. Thus, for instance, the following description of Mallarmé's development as a succession of destructive but 'not altogether meaningless' failures, which, surprisingly, uses the very (and very Wordsworthian) metaphor for which Malraux was so severely castigated:

The growth of the spirit is a tragic growth, which implies ever-increasing pain and destruction, but it nevertheless is a movement of becoming that marks a kind of progression. The failures are not just an alignment of identical absurdities; each one is enriched by the knowledge of the one that precedes it and the spirit grows by reflecting upon its successive aberrations. ('DA,' 14)

The question remains exactly what kind of progression this is, as the metaphor of growth seems to smuggle in again the idea of perfect unity and presence-unto-itself which would effectively suspend the movement of becoming. The same difficulty transpires when we wed de Man's description of the poetical act as the privileged effort through which we gain consciousness both of 'the divided nature of our being' and—and even 'consequently'—of 'the necessity to accomplish it' ('TP' CW, 33), to his simultaneous assertion that 'it is in the essence of becoming not to posit itself as eternal, we cannot count on a poetry of becoming as though it would necessarily find accomplishment' ('PP' CW, 74–75).

The Covering Cherub hovering over these (partial) paradoxes is perhaps most acutely identified in the following passage:

> There are two ways of meeting the challenge this experience [of separation] presents to the spirit: one is defensive, the other confronts the problem. This second way attempts to save both life and consciousness in *a new synthesis that Hegel had the audacity to name but that less imprudent spirits limited themselves to foreseeing*. ('PN' CW, 28; emphasis added)

Hegel, then, audaciously named the intended synthesis—and we know this name to be that of the Absolute Spirit, the total accomplishment of the spirit. The continuation of the preceding passage on the growth of the poet's mind identifies this problem as the problem of naming and necessity—of language—that it is:

> At the limit, the total accomplishment of the spirit will also be a total annihilation, but this event, of which *Un Coup de Dés* tries to be a symbolical evocation, remains in the future as long as there remains a language able to express it. This language is the poetic work, and we see how Mallarmé's entire enterprise is centered, not on unity like Baudelaire's, but on *the incessant movement of becoming* by means of which language *grows* to new

dimensions of precision, universality, and clarity. ('DA,' 14; emphasis added)

As the persistence of the metaphor of growth already indicates, the problem may well be identified (named) here, but this definition is not (yet) consistently worked through. What remains after—or, more accurately, in—the (intentional) failure of the poet of becoming is indeed language, but at the same time language is still said to partake of the movement of natural being, like the ignominious walnut tree in Malraux's ancestral park, and thus still seems to move toward, or even in, a realm beyond becoming, toward, we cannot but suspect, the Absolute that Hegel was imprudent, and impudent, enough to name.

But precisely because of this confusion—which, in the deceptively simple terms used by Hegel in his 1807 'Selbstanzeige der Phänomenologie,' is the confusion that arises from the tension between the becoming of 'das werdende Wissen' and the being of 'die letzte Wahrheit'[11]—the passage also allows us to see why de Man has to say that the scheme through which he develops this metapoetics is 'clearly oversimplistic,' and why he must come to admit that the problem of poetry and becoming cannot be distilled down to the 'choice between two equally possible directions' he himself had imposed upon it ('PP' CW, 71). For indeed, the dialectic of consciousness borrowed from a certain Hegel and put at the service of the poet of becoming fails to consistently account for the problem of language as a becoming which does not culminate into a being but instead preserves separation; and this because the suspicion has not been adequately laid to rest that the difference between, on the one hand, the synthesis Hegel names, and, on the other hand, the idealist reconciliation which is itself in complicity with the poetics of permanence, is not as self-evident as the proposition that one can choose between them would have us believe. De Man is certainly right to state, in an essay we shall study more closely in the next section, that 'to assimilate the notion of Absolute Spirit with idealist reconciliation is to simplify all the way into

nonsense' ('HE' BI, 265; translation modified), but this mere assertion of scorn for Schelling *cum suis* does not control the profound
problem of the relation between Hegel's audacious name and the
separation it is supposed to observe rather than surmount.

But for all its confusion—and this is important—de Man's
argument does not espouse the strategy he had only a few years
earlier celebrated as the exemplary response to what will have
been recalled as literally the same predicament in which he here
places Mallarmé: the painful resistance to the temptation of permanence is at no stage anaesthetized in the superior postapocalyptic
serenity of the ironical inventory. Like Montaigne, Mallarmé is
continuously and consciously moved by the essentially contradictory nature of intentionality, but the despair of this contradiction
is not contained in the tranquil irony that can content itself in
looking back on the tragic failure of consciousness as on an unresolved thing of the past. If Hegel audaciously names the finale
of this tragedy and Montaigne takes ironic delight in the ultimate
absurdity of such audacity, Mallarmé remains caught in a realm
where both named transcendence and the serene recognition of
its impossibility are radically suspended. Such is the crisis de Man,
inconclusively, tries to think as the essence of poetry.

Foundations of the Dissymmetry

THE SIGN OF FAILURE

I n a central transitional passage in 'Le devenir, la poésie,' de Man admirably formulates the problem of the choice he has developed before and continues to explore. The passage offers an accessible intimation of the double aspect of this problem: the choice is not only a problem for those who have to choose, it is also itself a problem, insofar as it is postulated as a choice—by de Man, by us.

> If the eternal is an intention, and poetic language is the sign of this intention's failure, will it then be possible to rest content with such knowledge, that is, to equate poetry with a universal becoming satisfied in the certitude of its own accomplishment, even if such accomplishment be apocalyptic? To judge from the unfolding of those poetic oeuvres that have gone furthest in reflecting on the process of becoming, this is by no means the case. On the contrary, the poetry of Hölderlin, Keats, or Mallarmé remains exceedingly tormented and uncertain, constantly experimental and unsatisfied with itself. There are, however, in addition to them, poets who categorically reject the idea of becoming, without for all that leaving any doubt about the authenticity of their poetic vocation. Poetic becoming, then, seems to leave suspended certain essential tensions. ('PP' CW, 67–68)

Poetic language is the sign of the failure of the intention toward the eternal. It is imperative that we underscore that this is the case for both 'types' of poetry, the difference being, again, that only the poet of becoming knows it. But what does he know? (And— but we have not yet arrived there—who is he?)

He knows that this language is the sign of the failure of the

87

intention whose failure he also intends. But why does he have to intend this failure, or, more problematically still, why does he intend the eternal which he knows he cannot reach, which indeed he does not intend to reach? The becoming that is preserved by his failure is, de Man tells us, 'the knowledge of a nonknowledge' (67), but he cannot settle down in this knowledge. He recognizes that poetry has a 'necessarily temporal character,' but he cannot completely assume that recognition as a last word, and always returns to his 'intention of taking up again a lost struggle' ('TP' CW, 33; translation modified). As does the poet of permanence. But this latter only sees, blindly, that the battle is lost, not that the battle cannot but be lost. He knows that he has failed, but he does not acknowledge that he *had* to fail and that his language is the sign of that failure. His is a nonknowledge of (the) knowledge (of nonknowledge), a nonknowledge of an eternity still deemed to be knowable as a being. Yet, the poet of permanence—there is no doubt about that—still is an authentic poet, even though his categorical rejection of the notion of becoming would appear to place him in the fulsome company of the cowardly modern conservative nihilists.

To account for this complication, de Man, as we already indicated, begins to upset his dichotomous discretional model. 'A genuine poetics has to be able to include this oscillation in a vision of the whole that would account for its passionate, and sometimes even tragic, character' ('PP' CW, 71). Such a true poetics, de Man continues, can be found in the late poems and theoretical essays of Hölderlin, and especially in his commentary on his Sophocles translations, where the notorious distinction between 'etwas treffen' and 'sich fassen' is developed. This is de Man's version of Hölderlin's attempt:

> These commentaries express the distinction between a poetry
> of becoming and a poetry of the sensible as a dialectic of inten-
> tions and desires. For the poet capable of self-consciousness, the
> enthusiasm for becoming soon transforms itself into a nostalgia

for the object, and his language, more and more animated by the desire to recapture a lost plenitude, becomes almost haunted by a preoccupation with the sensible. For the poet capable of attaining the object, on the contrary, it is the power of spirit that appears as the most desirable goal, and his language becomes the language of self-consciousness. (71) [12]

The significant difference between this description and the previous map of 'alternate roads' is that now we have a dialectical view of the opposition between a poetry of becoming and a poetry of substance within one poetics. Indeed, the present dialectic should not be collapsed with the dialectic of consciousness sketched before; whereas this latter properly belonged to the second road only, and ran its course between substance and becoming as such, the former ostensibly develops in two different ways—following one structural pattern—between two types of poetry inside the poetry of two types of poets, as it were. The obvious question, then, must be who these two types of poets are, since it will be clear that the distinction can no longer be simply that between, say, Baudelaire and Mallarmé, as that is precisely what had to be revised in a more encompassing conception.

De Man's answer takes for its point of departure the 'historical symbolism' that Hölderlin uses 'to illustrate his thought' ('as Hegel often does'). In the third paragraph of the 'Anmerkungen zur Antigonä,' but in de Man's words, Hölderlin 'defines the Hellenic world as one in which language is capable of reaching the sensible object immediately, whereas in the occidental world, it grasps itself only insofar as it is spirit, that is, as distinction and mediation' ('PP' cw, 71–72). De Man then combines this history with the scheme it illustrates, which renders the pattern, in Hölderlin's own terms, that the main tendency in the representations of the Greek 'is to be able to grasp oneself [sich fassen zu können], since that is where their weakness lay,' while 'the main tendency in the representational modes of our time is to be able to strike something [etwas treffen zu können], to have fate, since the lack of destiny, the dusmoron, is our weakness'[13]—the *dusmoron* is, in de Man's reading, the absence of 'sensible substance.' The 'Haupttendenz,' then, is an intention toward the opposite of what is proper to each type of poet respectively—or, in de Man's remarkably confident interpretation, near the end of 'The Double Aspect of Symbolism,' the main tendency obeys the law that 'it is in the nature of men to prefer to state their desire for that which they do not have rather than dare to be what they really can be' ('DA,' 16). This already points to the final and decisive turn of Hölderlin's hypotheory, the much-debated notion of the 'vaterländische Umkehr,' a renunciation of the desire for that which is not proper to us and a return to our own strength, turning the tables on Byron and beginning to think on what we are—or can be. De Man writes,

> Here we come face to face with an attempt to go beyond the idea of becoming without at the same time falling back into its antithesis, which is the eternal. For Hölderlin, the ultimate truth of poetry resides neither in the eternal nor in the temporal, but in the turning back through which a poetry of the sensible tears itself away from its need to become self-consciousness, or a poetry of becoming tears itself away from its desire to get back to the object.
>
> The power of this vision has its source in the renunciation that is at its center, and is expressed in the profoundly original idea that what is inborn appears to us as what is most difficult, whereas the spirit complies and feels comfortable in what is foreign to it. ('PP' CW, 72; translation modified)

Now, de Man is properly suspicious of 'an overliteral historical application of this notion,'[14] but this does not prevent him from using the scheme to rephrase some of the questions his thought on the 'Western' poets Baudelaire and Mallarmé had encountered. The main gesture here is that what was initially merely postulated as the intrinsic (ontological) superiority of the natural object is now explicitly restated as (and thus retained in) the promotion to universal law of an observation that is, perhaps suspiciously, close to the old saw that the grass on the other side of the hill is invariably greener—a similarity which, incidentally, is in keeping with the isotopy of authentic aridity so liberally in evidence in these texts. Thus, de Man can now say of a poetry like Baudelaire's that it follows a call that is 'a form neither of weakness nor of hypocrisy in Western poetry, but rather its profoundest necessity.' 'Such poetry,' de Man remarks, 'must go out of its way in trying to imprint, on its true face, the mask of the eternal, precisely in the sense that Nietzsche defines the highest will to power as the attempt 'to imprint on the process of becoming the character of being,' where being is conceived as the eternal' (73). And thus we can also put in a broader perspective an earlier passage, devoted to the repeated failures of Mallarmé, which affirms that

> as opposed to consciousness and to poetry, there exists a world where the perception of the real has not passed through the mediation of reflection, the world of a spontaneous contact with things, within a single sphere of unity. The more conscious we become, the more desirable and precious this world appears— and the more impossible to achieve. ('PN' CW, 23; translation emended)

This by no means entails that we have gone beyond the model of the choice. We have merely refined it, with de Man, in order to better understand the dissymmetry of his earlier (and persistent) presentation of this choice. The 'vaterländische Umkehr' is indeed still a task for which one has to choose—*against* the profound necessity of Western poetry even, and *against* Nietzsche's 'highest will to power.' But the grounds on which de Man defends this choice are gradually being argued with less suspiciously pathetic overdetermination. Which, in turn, and again, is not to deny that this entire poetics remains deeply entrenched in existential deliberation: 'What is required for us to be ourselves is to accept the death of things and to turn back toward the process of becoming, which we have in fact not yet begun to think. The poetry of becoming remains entirely to be done' ('PP' CW, 74;

translation emended). Moreover, we can by no means be certain that we shall ever truly succeed in this task. As 'an act of consciousness and an asceticism of thought, the process of becoming appears as a task whose law is that of an incessantly heightened concentration and rigor, but which finds in the past no guarantee that it will be possible for it to come into being' (75). The conclusion to this same essay, which echoes the slightly less forbidding finale of 'The Double Aspect of Symbolism' almost verbatim and tentatively opposes at least a hint of promise, and perhaps even salvation, to the categorical rejection of both promise and salvation earlier on in both essays, demonstrates that the difficulties of de Man's scheme are far from being resolved: 'It seems, then, that no matter how we view the turning back that Hölderlin demands, all that it promises is aridity, barrenness, and deprivation. Perhaps this is because, at least in its beginnings, such is the climate of our truth' (75). This at least leaves open the possibility that 'our' truth will sometime, beyond 'its beginnings,' blossom forth (again)—in a movement of growth toward, perhaps, the Absolute that Hegel dared to name. Even though de Man explicitly warns against 'the temptation to think the turning back toward becoming in eschatological terms,' he has to add immediately, quasi-automatically, but not therefore necessarily unwittingly, that 'the work of its accomplishment can begin only with a loss of hope, for we have to give up, as though it were something foreign, whatever it is we are striving toward' (74). And he *has* to do this because the teleological moment—even if it be in the form of a quasi-teleology toward a *telos* left undefined—is inherent in the very model of the choice that fundamentally governs this presentation. The choice may no longer be one between two equally possible roads, and what was previously a possibility may now well be contained within a poetics of a more encompassing grasp, but the dialectic of this poetics still remains caught in the existential model of apriorisms from which it appeared to promise an escape.

But there is another way in which this problem can be thought through in de Man's texts, a way less prone to lead us stumbling

over metaphors of drought into wastelands that pathetically invoke
the greener pastures forever forbidden.

THE CAUSE OF FAILURE

'If the eternal is an intention, and poetic language the sign of this
intention's failure . . .': such was the double hypothesis that served
de Man as a point of departure for the development of the alternative choice model superseding his initial version of this model.
But, to jump to our conclusion, what if language were not the sign
of this failure to accomplish the opposite of what the return to becoming requires, but, on the contrary, its cause? Both propositions
are simultaneously asserted, with varying degrees of emphasis and
accuracy, in de Man's text, and it is here that we fully confront,
head-on but still hesitantly, the ultimate foundation of the dissymmetry we have been trying to grasp all along: the necessity of
naming and, more generally, mediation.

Thus, for instance, in the passage where de Man characterizes
poetry as the '*logos* of becoming' which negates the eternal as being
and transforms it into an intention, it is said that this transformation results from a recognition of 'the necessity of *naming* the
eternal by means of an entity—language—that is immediately adequate to neither eternal being nor temporal being-there [*être-la*]'
'PP' CW, 67; translation modified). Those poets who have understood this necessity of the third entity, then, have 'resigned themselves to the transformation of the eternal into the temporal and
[have] recognized the necessarily temporal character of poetry'
(67). The difference between this necessity and the necessity of
the law according to which human beings 'naturally' desire what
is not their own should not be underestimated: for if poetry, as
language, is *necessarily* temporal, the dubious dialectic of preexis-
tent desires and renunciations is no longer necessary to establish
the problem of poetry and becoming. The fact that de Man still
explicitly pledges allegiance to this dialectic, with all the existential overtones it entails, does not in itself invalidate the possibility

for this 'new' necessity to move, so to speak, beyond the model of the choice of the poet. Turning to a central development in de Man's quarrel with Heidegger's readings of Hölderlin,[15] in which this point is most forcefully stated, may allow us to appreciate the singular importance of this shift in terminology and, but it is the same thing, thought.

✱

'But what remains, is founded by the poets. . . .' It is Heidegger's reading of this troublesome final verse of 'Andenken'—as rendered by de Man—that de Man takes special exception to. *Was bleibet aber stiften die Dichter* . . . , which Heidegger takes to mean: the poet founds the immediate presence of being by naming it' ('HE BI, 252). Why does Hölderlin's line signify this for Heidegger? Because he needs a witness, 'someone of whom he can say that he has named the immediate presence of Being' (252). And why does he need a witness? Simply because he needs proof that the truth of Being that has been forgotten in (the long dark night of) Western metaphysical oblivion, indeed actually exists, has existed, and/or may come to exist once more: 'The experience of Being must be sayable; in fact it is in language that it is preserved' (253). Someone has to have had this experience *and* has to have preserved it: 'One such person is enough, but there must be one. For then, the truth, which is the presence of the present, has entered the work that is language. Language—Hölderlin's language—is the immediate presence of Being' (253).

But why precisely Hölderlin? Why does Heidegger choose Hölderlin (rather than, say, Rilke) as his quasi-scriptural authority, as his indispensable witness? The answer arrives in the (italicized) shape of what Derrida has called 'de Manian provocation.'[16] '*It is the fact that Hölderlin says exactly the opposite of what Heidegger makes him say*' (254–55). That is to say, while Heidegger violently misstates Hölderlin's thought, he does deserve credit for having misstated precisely 'the central "concern" of Hölderlin's work,' rather than some other, subordinate point. Hölderlin is Heidegger's witness elect because he indeed focuses on Heidegger's own central question, to wit, 'how can one not only speak *of* Being, but say Being itself?' (256). Poetry is itself 'the experience of this question'—not, however, as Heidegger would have it, the experience of its solution. On the contrary, for Hölderlin (meaning: in its essence), poetry is the assertion that the experience of this solution is precisely the one, 'among all others, that is totally forbidden to man' (255).

Why, then, is this experience forbidden to man? Why can Heidegger be said to be 'falsifying' the purport of Hölderlin's poetics when he uncovers the poet as he who names the presence of the present, who establishes the desired *parousia* in his language? De Man concentrates his critique on Heidegger's *Erlaüterung* of two short passages from the unfinished *Feiertags*-hymn. The first passage, which completes the extended comparison initiated by the poem's first lines, runs as follows:

> So stehn sie unter günstiger Witterung
> Sie die kein Meister allein, die wunderbar
> Allgegenwartig erziehet in leichtem Umfangen
> Die Mächtige, die göttlichschöne Natur.
>
> [Thus they stand under balmy skies
> Those whom no master alone, whom wondrously
> All-present educates in a light embrace
> The powerful, the divinely beautiful nature.] (257)

Grossly and quite literally, what these verses state is that the poets are those who stand under favorable skies, and are 'educated' not by one master alone, but by powerful and divinely beautiful nature, who keeps them in a gentle embrace. Contrary to a suggestion made by Derrida,[17] de Man has no quarrel with the identification Heidegger establishes (always according to de Man) between nature and (the immediate unity of) Being (256), but he does object to Heidegger's further suggestion that the poet would, in some special way, 'belong *[zugehören]*' and 'correspond *[entsprechen]*'[18] to that Being. The only relation between the poet and

nature/Being the passage in fact allows for is a relation of educa-
tion *(Erziehung, Bildung),* which is to say that the poet is he who
accepts nature as his *guide,* 'instead of submitting to some institution that accepts and perpetuates the separation between man
and Being' (258). This refusal to submit oneself to a master who
would unquestioningly perpetuate the separation, however, does
not therefore entail a union with the 'other' *Meister,* nature. 'To
accept someone as one's master, far from signifying that one identifies with him and that one belongs to him, means rather that
there is, and continues to be *[demeure],* an unbridgeable gap.'[19]
And de Man concludes, 'In any case, the passage . . . does not
say that the poet dwells *[demeure]* in the parousia, but only that
it is the principle of his becoming, in the same way as the absolute is the principle of the becoming of consciousness in Hegel's
Phenomenology' (258).

The argument is familiar to us: that which would overcome
the separation, namely, the experience of actually dwelling in the
immediacy of Being as in something to which one belongs, is an
object of desire, a state that can be intended and actually motivates
intention itself, but not therefore something that can be definitively attained or recovered, let alone be *preserved.* And, as if this
were still necessary, the reference to Hegel makes it quite clear
that this stage of de Man's argument does not move beyond our
earlier dialectic, thus leaving us well within the complications this
dialectic generates.

Nor does the first movement of de Man's discussion of the second passage to which Heidegger takes recourse (in order to name
the poet as the one who names the presence of the present) offer
us anything decisively different. The lines occur in the third stanza,
which for Heidegger 'carries everything.'[20]

> Jetzt aber tagts! Ich harrt und sah es kommen
> Und was ich sah, das Heilige sei mein Wort.
>
> [But now day breaks! I waited and I saw it coming
> And what I saw, the Holy be my word.] (257)

De Man is ready to grant that this passage presents us with the poet as the 'faithful disciple of Being,' privileged because called upon to see the Holy, the *parousia* of Being (258), but the real problem is not the status of this perception, but the question whether it can be preserved—as language, whether the 'Jetzt' of Hölderlin's statement (de Man speaks of 'the lightning of the *Jetzt*,' which is 'the absolute temporal present') *can* be retained in the 'Wort.' Before this 'now,' there is 'only' *das Ahnen,* the vigil, but what (of Being) can be preserved after the lightning of the absolute present? 'If one could say it,' de Man writes, 'it would be founded because the word has durability and founds the moment in a spatial presence where one could dwell *[demeurer],*' and to accomplish this is the 'supreme goal' and the 'ultimate desire' of the poet—witness the precatory mode of Hölderlin's verse. But this praying mode, the subjunctive *sei* itself, already underscores that such accomplishment does not take place—or, if ever (which is doubtful), that it has not *yet* taken place: 'It is not because he has seen Being that the poet is, therefore, capable of naming it; his word prays for the parousia, it does not establish it' (258).

It is at this moment that de Man's argument suddenly gathers momentum and appears at last to shed its implication in a poorly articulated dialectic which cannot quite decide whether it is going to culminate in a synthetic name or no:

It cannot establish it for as soon as the word is uttered, it destroys the immediate and discovers that instead of stating Being, it can only state mediation. For man the presence of Being is always in becoming, and Being necessarily appears under a non-simple form. In its moment of highest achievement, language manages to mediate between the two dimensions we distinguish in Being. It does this by attempting to name them and by seeking to grasp and arbitrate their difference and their opposition. But it cannot reunite them. Their unity is ineffable and cannot be said, because it is language itself that introduces the distinction. Propelled by the appeal of parousia, it seeks to establish the absolute presence of immediate Being, but can do no more than pray or struggle, never found. (259)

Rather than being the sign of the failure to found the eternal, the immediacy of Being, the presence of the present, or whatever circumscription one prefers, language is now explicitly designated as the cause of this failure, and this new perspective brings with it some enabling repercussions for the problematics we outlined earlier. To appreciate these adequately, we must look more closely at the category of mediation as it is being introduced here.

✳

'If the word mediation has any meaning, it is that what mediation ends up with is never identical to one of the two elements in presence to the exclusion of the other; it is a third entity that contains them both' (260). These 'two elements' are the two poles separated by the essential separation from which de Man set out (here called 'Being' and 'the consciousness of Being' (262) and the 'third entity' is language (see also 'PP' CW, 67; 'DA,' 13), but this also means that language, as the 'product' of mediation, does not coincide with consciousness, and neither is it simply a 'product' of consciousness, which would then coincide with mediation. On the contrary, language is said to be not merely the product of mediation but mediation itself, and this insofar as it, language, 'itself introduces the distinction'—a distinction, moreover, which, as a product, it is still said to 'contain.' The root of this difficulty (if we can still use such metaphors, which of course we can) resides in the fact that, in an as yet unspecified way, language has itself become an 'agent.' It is no longer the sign of a certain failure of the poet's intention, but (also) the process which itself causes this failure. What is more, it causes this failure against the prayer of the poet who uses it (language). But it also 'contains' this failure in that it preserves the mediation between the two elements which the prayer hoped to unite in the immediacy of 'das Heilige' finally named.

This is a difficult but necessary proposition. It states that what is contained in the mediate is the immediate itself, as the mark of an indispensable absence. Indispensable, because the immediate itself 'contains the possibility of the mediation of the mediate because it permits it in its being' ('HE' BI, 260). Language cannot but mediate, which is to say that it negates the immediate, but because it does precisely that, or, to put it more rigorously, because such negation is the very essence of language (an essence the possibility condition of which is itself contained, as the possibility condition of language, in a realm radically exterior to it, in the immediate), language cannot but preserve the immediate as the object it cannot name in its immediacy even while it *must* intend it in order to exist at all. Language negates the immediate in that it affirms its being (absent). Language, differently still, and in a more complicated sense of the verb, 'contains' the immediate in that it prevents this immediate from overwhelming mediation itself, in that it checks (cannot but check) the power of the immediate which, if unchecked or uncontained, would effectively spirit language out of existence. The crucial point being that language does indeed exist—irrespective of the poet's prayer, because of the poet's prayer. 'However impossible language may have been, it was there.'[21]

Thus, de Man can say, and we return to our initial poets, that 'the truth of Baudelaire's poem . . . is in direct contradiction to the existence of the work' ('PP' CW, 70), and that the 'total accomplishment of the spirit' which appeared to be the intention of Mallarmé's poetry 'remains in the future as long as there remains a language able to express it' ('DA,' 14). What remains is indeed, in both cases, language, as an instance coinciding neither with natural being, nor yet with the intention of the poet. The ultimate foundation of the dissymmetry of the choice gradually emerges. It was, of course, present from the beginning: there never was such a thing as a choice, there was only ever the law. 'Already' in 'The Double Aspect,' apparently speaking of Mallarmé, de Man stated that 'the poet's only but irrevocable commitment is to language' (12). 'Now,' apparently speaking of Hölderlin, he rephrases this commitment in legal terms that spell out its implications: 'When he states the law, the poet does not say Being . . . but, rather, the impossibility of naming anything but an order that, in its essence, is distinct from immediate Being' ('HE' BI, 261). And the poet is *the* poet, Baudelaire as well as Mallarmé—in short: Hölderlin.

But we are running ahead: strictly speaking, de Man has not (yet) reached this singular and apparently perverse conclusion which would seem to collapse all poets in *the* poet (Hölderlin, 'for instance'). Which is also to say that the model of the choice still prevails, as is only to be expected since (it should perhaps be repeated) the various types or levels of argument we have tried to trace are constantly interwoven throughout the texts under scrutiny here. In other words: while the law of language we have just articulated seems to be able to resolve some of the complications we have encountered, the simultaneity of the presentation of this law and the sketch of the choice model leading up to these complications ultimately bars de Man's readings from surmounting these complications. In itself, the concept of language as an agent can indeed be made to account for the fact that the poetic intention to overcome the separation is both ineluctable as an intention and impossible to accomplish, that it is a battle in which one cannot help but engage but which also cannot be decided. Mediation is a necessary (original) supplement for the immediate, and vice versa, so that if there is language, there 'is' (the absence of) immediacy, itself the possibility condition of the mediation of language—'it is by virtue of the separation that it causes that the word prevents the struggle reaching conclusion. It transfers the struggle within itself, which is why it is ever-renewed mediation' (259–60). This would also mean that we can now better understand the notion of the intention that contains (intends) its own failure, for if the preceding theses are correct, we are now confronted with an intention which is itself the law of language and no longer needs to be relegated exclusively to the consciousness of the poet: language, to use a term we shall deal with more extensively in a later section, has itself an intentional structure, and this structure is that of the essential ambiguity of mediation, which simultaneously negates and acknowledges its own condition of possibility. In 'The Double Aspect of Symbolism' de Man wrote that language 'is on the side of the subject (or the poet)' by dint of its being 'an agent of consciousness' ('DA,' 6). The suggestion we presently confront appears to radically modify this: language is, no doubt, an agent of consciousness—but there are reasons to suspect that, here too, the well-worn screw of the double aspect of the 'of' can be given a turn.

Yet, to articulate this suspicion onto the *difference* in intention (or consciousness) between particular poets (such as Baudelaire and Mallarmé) which de Man also asserted, and still seems to want to uphold, is rather more difficult. In fact, such is the task he will be struggling with for many years to come. In the present essays, we find further testimony of this difficulty in a number of vexing complementary contradictions that can serve as illustrations of the extent to which a thought that proposes to engage fundamental questions may find itself compelled to sustain blatant inconsistency in order to maintain (or increase) its momentum.

A first minimal instance of this is the characterization of Hölderlin's and Mallarmé's poetry as being at the same time a choice against 'a poetry of prayer and salvation' ('DA,' 16) and 'a mediated and conscious prayer that achieves self-consciousness in its failure' ('HE' BI, 263). The problem remains the same: how can we tell a prayer such as Hölderlin's, which prays for what it knows to be absolutely, juridically impossible, from a prayer such as Baudelaire's, which is not performed in the knowledge of this law? It should be added that de Man is aware of this difficulty insofar as he identifies it as a typical paradox in symbolist—and Romantic—poetry ('DA,' 5); yet he does not succeed in adequately facing it insofar as it tears his own thought asunder. The same difficulty transpires with respect to the notion of hope. The turn to becoming should not be thought 'in eschatological terms,' as it 'can begin only with a loss of hope'; it should not be thought 'prophetic,' since we can never project it as something which 'would necessarily find accomplishment' ('PP' CW, 74). Yet, Mallarmé's poetic act, which enacts this turn, is said to be the sole remaining indication of 'a possible future birth, because it perpetuates *something* that transcends the antithetical notions of mediation and immediacy,' without, however, therefore being able to 'name' it: for 'short of rediscovering the true meaning of the verb "to name,"' such naming 'would be to destroy the hope that remains' ('PN' CW, 27). If that which remains *(qui demeure, was bleibet)* is named (or founded), the hope that remains is destroyed, but at the same time all hope has to be sacrificed—which would mean that the poet indeed has to name that which remains—presumably, however, in accordance with 'the true meaning of the verb "to name,"' which would, in turn, mean that he would *not* sacrifice all hope; that he would, perhaps, be so bold as to prophetically name what Hegel hailed as the Absolute Spirit, what Nietzsche called for in the radically innocent voice of Zarathustra, or what Heidegger was so imprudent as to merely call Being ('IG' CW, 13); that, like Baudelaire, he would keep alive 'a form of hope, the hope that if being were ever to return in the form of a direct revelation that would not be deadly, the poet would have prepared its return by his prayer and would be the only man ready to receive it on earth' ('DA,' 15). If, on the other hand, he were to name that which remains in a way that differs from true naming, he would in effect destroy all hope—but untrue naming can hardly be the goal of the 'mediated and conscious prayer that achieves self-consciousness in its failure' true poetry is asserted to be. And so on.

And so on indeed: we are left yet again with a sacrifice. Hölderlin's hymn expresses 'the impossibility of the desired identification between language and the sacred,' and this expression marks a progression in the poet's experience of his mediate relation to the Holy, in that Being is now recognized only in its 'indirect action,' that is, 'history' (as opposed to the 'immediate manifestation of Being' an eternalist poetics would have us read in its poetry). But this renunciation of the sacred is itself, still, a *sacri*-fice, an imposition of the sacred, which can always also be an imposture, an usurpation:

The poet . . . assumes the superhuman task of ensuring, through his own person, the mediation between Being and the consciousness of Being, its law founded in the Word. This supreme act is also a supreme sacrifice, for the restoration of Being to consciousness is effected at the cost of necessarily denying its ineffable all-presence and the no less necessary acquisition of the finite and alienated character of being-there *[être-là]*. The poet knows this necessity, but to those who have not reached this stage of consciousness, it appears in the guise of sorrow. By interiorizing the sorrow, the poet assumes it . . . and through his total sacrifice, which goes beyond death, gives it the value of an example and a warning. . . . ('HE' BI, 261–62)

And once again, this interior suffering is a dialectic, Hegelian death; first thought of as human suffering, then put on the transcendent plane of the death of (a) God, which it is 'the poet's task . . . to interiorize, to "think-of,"' in an effort of *Andenken* which, however, de Man admits to be too vast for 'this hymn' and which he projects, without demonstration, into Hölderlin's 'ulterior Christian Hymns.' And all the time we must realize that these warnings *(das warnend ängstige Lied)*, this exemplary suffering, this supreme sacrifice, are not eschatological, are not prophetic, do not establish the Holy. For such is the law founded in the verb of mediation—indeed, 'for Hölderlin, religious experience is also a mediation,' and this turn to the realm of religion as mediation aligns his development to that of, predictably now, 'the unhappy consciousness.'[22] The name of the Absolute Spirit and the problem of the law of mediation's being a law of language as such are once more left suspended.

Still, de Man is by no means unaware of the difficulty that this suspension entails. Further along in the essay, he takes Beda Allemann to task for having read Hegel and Hölderlin as if he was reading the young Schelling by emphasizing the idea of reconciliation as characteristic of all idealist thought. On the contrary, de Man asserts, in the most essential intention of Hegel's work, we find a philosophy of essential separation, and the Absolute Spirit consequently cannot be subsumed under the label of reconciliation. And he continues that

> Hegel's and Hölderlin's thought are remarkably parallel on this point; their difference lies deeper since it requires so dissimilar a tone and a vocation in spite of the noticeable similarity of thought. If one wanted to make use of this nearly miraculous happenstance to really shed light on the relations of philosophy and the poetic, it would be better not to start with the setting-up of differences that do not exist when the analogies are so much more fruitful. (265)

Which is all very well, but one is tempted to add that there are differences that do exist—such as, for instance, the difference that de Man himself points out, and to which we have already referred repeatedly: the 'new synthesis that Hegel had the audacity to name but that less imprudent spirits [such as Mallarmé, such as Hölderlin] limited themselves to foreseeing' ('PN' CW, 28)—without, however, these latter therefore becoming prophets.

At this stage, it may be useful to recite one of Hegel's more powerful oracular pronunciations of this name. One does not need to have read the *Phenomenology* to be able to reproduce a substantial list of such namings—a quick glance at the foreword suffices, as Hegel was well aware—and there is no merit whatever in such reproduction if it pretends to the status of a critique of Hegel on the basis of a supposed self-evident wrongness it would want to read in the passages quoted. Nor does it suffice to know this to exempt oneself from charges of intellectual laziness. But that is not the point. My only purpose here is to draw out a passage that poses the problem this name must necessarily be for the poetics de Man is trying to align to Hegel's dialectic. I have chosen an obvious instance, the finale of the final chapter, 'Das absolute Wissen,' which is doubly interesting in that it not only stages one of the more problematic sightings of the Absolute Spirit,[23] but also ends (and with it the entire *Phenomenology* as it is published) on two, interestingly modified, lines of poetry:

The *goal*, Absolute Knowing, or Spirit that knows itself as Spirit, has for its path the recollection of the Spirits as they are in themselves and as they accomplish the organization of their realm. Their preservation, regarded from the side of their free existence appearing in the form of contingency, is History; but regarded from the side of their [philosophically] comprehended organization, it is the Science of Knowing in the sphere of appearance: the two together, comprehended History, form alike the inwardizing and the Calvary of absolute Spirit, the actuality, truth, and certainty of his throne, without which he would be lifeless and alone. Only

> from the chalice of this realm of spirits
> foams forth for Him his own infinitude.[24]

Everything hinges on the question of whether this moment spells 'The End' or 'To be continued'—or, more radically, on the question of whether this moment should in fact be at all conceived of as a moment in a teleological script.[25] At times de Man comes close to actually stating this problem in so many words, as in the 1956 essay on Keats and Hölderlin where, speaking of the 'ideal of unity' as it appears in Hölderlin's *Empedokles,* he writes that

> instead of being a static condition that can be reached as one reaches a certain point in space, unity is seen as a dialectical motion between two antithetical poles. Unity *[Versöhnung]* is no longer a solution but only an infinitesimal moment in a process. Hölderlin calls this process 'Übermaß der Innigkeit,' the movement by which man rises to a new level of synthesis by going to the extreme of the opposites among which he lives ('KH' CW, 53)

and adds, in a footnote, that the metaphysical definition of these 'antithetical poles' is more essential to Hölderlin's thought than the dialectic itself, 'which, unlike his school companion Hegel, he sees as an ontological *donnée* rather than as an intellectual act.' The point, which de Man does not develop, could then be that precisely because he does not conceive of the dialectic as an intellectual act, the poet (Hölderlin) cannot *name* a synthesis for the antithetics he considers as 'given,' that he cannot discursively claim access to a 'comprehended History' which would be the throne of *Versöhnung* that the Absolute Spirit of his school companion takes possession of.[26]

However this may be, de Man stops short of further clarifying the issue and thus abandons his text to a proliferation of questions typically centering around Hegel's name. Perhaps one more instance can mark the point for the moment. Given de Man's categorical statement that the word, as mediation, can ever only separate, and is itself the agent of separation, a statement he wishes to subsume under the name of a properly understood Hegel, how then are we to account for his thesis in 'The Double Aspect' that 'if language were able to be a perfect mediation and to contain within itself the essence of natural being as well as that of subjective consciousness, it would succeed in establishing a true unity, . . . the balanced unity in which, in Hegel's words, "the concept expresses the object and the object the concept"' ('DA,' 13)? A problem made all the more difficult by his immediately subsequent assertion that language, of course, cannot do this, cannot perform Hegel's words, and that the poet (Mallarmé) knows this to be the case.

It would appear, then, provisionally, that our 'discovery' of the foundation of the dissymmetry in de Man's road map of poetry does not get us much further. We now suspect that there is only one road 'really,' but we are left in the dark as to what exactly is the task set to those—Baudelaire as well as Mallarmé—who, insofar as they are poets, are made to travel this road. Do they hope or have they given up hope; do they pray or do they not pray; do they foresee, or foresay, or forsake a synthesis or not; and, ultimately, can they still be said to differ from each other, as a result of a choice (in which case their one road would be paved with good or bad intentions respectively), as a result of a necessity, as a result of an impersonal law—or can they still be said to differ at all? In short, what can it mean for poetry to be 'an essentially open and free act' ('HE' BI, 263) which is at the same time absolutely subject to an incontrovertible law, and how can we recognize the workings of this paradox in any given individual poem or poet? Expanding the initial metaphysical conceit—and alluding to de Man's explosion of it much later in his work (see 'WB' RT, 80)—we could say that we are left with only one trajectory, as in the Tour de France, and that we do not know what the *Aufgabe* on this trajectory consists of, that we are locked *sur place*, left only with the knowledge that Hölderlin (as behooves a good Romantic) is wearing yellow. But, as in the Tour, standstill invites *démarrage*—and in order to find out whether we can indeed force some sort of breakaway with Paul de Man, even if only up to a certain point, a new turn to Heidegger, whom we have silently left behind, may be necessary here.

CHAPTER SIX

Dialogue and Distortion

And we would undoubtedly recover the concept of history in its
true sense if we were to get used to forming it after the example
of the arts and of language.—Maurice Merleau-Ponty, 'Indirect
Language and the Voices of Silence'

Knots of Resistance

In 'The Temptation of Permanence' (1955) de Man develops
one of his most consistent reflections on Heidegger's thought
on history. For Heidegger, he asserts, 'history is the concrete
manifestation of the very movement of being, movement whose
fundamental ambiguity is the origin of the historicity of our destiny' ('TP' CW, 34). To illustrate this 'conviction,' 'which is found
from *Being and Time* to the most recent texts,' de Man quotes a
passage from Heidegger's 1952 essay 'Moira':

> 'If we authorize ourselves to speak of a history of being, we must
> first remember that being designates the presence of the present,
> that is to say, division *[Zwiefalt]*. It is only by beginning with
> this thought that we can ask ourselves the significance of the
> term 'history.' It designates the destiny of the division. It is the
> revelatory process by which unveiled presence persists and in
> which present things appear.'[1]

This idea of Being as division (in Heidegger's words: 'Sein besagt:
Anwesen des Anwesenden: Zwiefalt'; in de Man's words, 'l'étre

désigne la présence du présent, c'est-à-dire division [Zwiefalt]') is, according to de Man here, a constant in Heidegger's work, and one way to follow this thought through is to trace the evolution of this notion.[2] In order to do so, for his own 'very limited purposes,' he refers to another text, 'The Origin of the Work of Art,' which dates from 1936 (some fifteen years previous to 'Moira,' a fact de Man does not mention). We are not here concerned with the details of Heidegger's argument (which revolves around the relation between earth and world), nor yet with those of de Man's treatment of his argument—for our limited purposes, it suffices to trace the conspicuous skeleton of this treatment.[3]

De Man first approvingly cites a passage in which he finds Heidegger 'clearly describing' the division of Being as a battle or struggle (combat, Streit), as, in fact, 'becoming in the Hegelian sense' (34). The continuation of Heidegger's argument, however, leaves him dissatisfied, as it seems to consist of a denial of the dialectic of this becoming by means of the (re)introduction of the concept of 'der einige Umriß,' which gathers the opposition in a unity, 'and that in a manner apparently permanent' (35). This 'unifying contour' is for Heidegger the work of art and, more in particular (Hölderlin's) poetry. De Man proposes to demonstrate the fallacy of this view by indicating how in '". . . Dichterisch wohnet der Mensch,"' which is roughly contemporaneous to 'Moira,' Heidegger goes out of his way to marshal Hölderlin's poetry in support of a 'serene idea of dwelling' (37), against this poetry's project of 'defiance and struggle.'[4] Upon which he appears to clinch the matter by concluding that in another text of the period ('Bauen Wohnen Denken'), 'Heidegger promises explicitly the transcendence of division and speaks more overtly than in his earlier work of the necessity to learn to think the simplicity of the earth (Einfalt, by opposition to Zwiefalt): the earth, the sky, mortal man, and God thought in their unity' (37).

Yet, at this juncture de Man retraces his steps. Instead of taking it as read that Heidegger has now definitively betrayed his 'earlier work' in a thought identifying the poetic word to the thing as a 'true gathering,' as opposed to division and 'mediation,' de Man marks a decisive warning:

> If therefore one agreed to make the identification that Heidegger suggests—*that is not to say he makes it himself*—and if one agreed to think the construction of the thing as similar in its being to poetic construction, one would have in fact succumbed to the temptation of permanence. (38)[5]

The criticism previously leveled at Heidegger is now restated in the form of a problem in and for his work which constitutes a strategically tied 'knot of resistance' with which one must come to terms in order to attain 'the truth' of his thought. Thus, while it may be the case that Heidegger's work increasingly opens up to a genuflection in the face of the temptation inscribed in this knot, the point of an attentive reading will have to be a resistance, *with* Heidegger, to this seductive betrayal of the movement of becoming (the true 'movement of being') for a thinking of the earth not unlike Malraux's. Rather than polemically presenting his remarks as 'the general sketch of a critical commentary on the work of Heidegger,' then, de Man insists that they merely point up 'a fundamental tension . . . that makes the originality of Heidegger's contribution and that constitutes the center of a possible critical dialogue' (39). It is as a preparation for this dialogue that his warnings here should be received.[6]

> One of the ways of approaching this problem would be to consider the effort of Heidegger as an attempt to sublate *[aufheben]* the antinomy between Hegelian historicism and Kantian eternalism by conserving what is essential in each. The critique of the work would then be an examination of the validity of this attempt. But here at the very most it is a question of putting one on guard against the possibility of letting oneself be seduced by promises of permanence that these texts suggest, and which can support the spirit in a state of beatitude that properly speaking is a lethargy. (39)

Heidegger, then, is now shown to be struggling with exactly the same problem with which we have seen de Man himself struggling. What here appears as an effort to 'synthesize,' after a fashion, Hegel and Kant, is, in our reading of de Man, an effort to escape from the synthesis (as a suggestion of eternity as being) already inscribed in the Hegelian system itself, without, however, therefore having to abandon the dialectical movement that (possibly) culminates in this synthesis, and it is no coincidence that the bare outline of Heidegger's effort here is (also) formally identical to what de Man admires in Hölderlin's renunciatory vision of going 'beyond the idea of becoming without at the same time falling back into its antithesis, which is the eternal' ('PP' CW, 72). But although establishing this formal correspondence between these two (or three) projects may foster the illusion of substantial understanding by exemplification, a closer investigation shows how this pattern complicates more than it elucidates.

For what does it mean to try to sublate the antinomy between Hegel's historicism and Kant's eternalism? A possible point of entry here is the recognition of part of Hegel's ambition as itself already an attempt to sublate Kant's rigorous distinction between *phenomenon* and *noumenon* by focusing on the origin of the *noumenon* in its mediation *(Vermittlung)* through the *phenomenon*. Insofar as it is itself posited by consciousness as a 'permanent *beyond [das bleibende Jenseits]*' 'above the vanishing *present* world' of appearance *(über dem verschwindenden Diesseits),* the thing-in-itself is always also the product of thought, and far from being only ever the knowable counterpart of what in the object is in itself necessarily unknowable, the *phenomenon* appears as the essence and fulfillment *(Erfüllung)* of this object.[7] Retranslated to de Man's terms, this difference between Kant and Hegel could be shaped into the following scenario. Kant's insistence on the radical split between the knowing subject and the object it can only know as it appears corresponds to de Man's 'eternal separation' and is further developed as an argument for 'the intrinsic superiority of natural being': the *noumenon* is fatally beyond the pale of consciousness and in a familiar twist of thought this radical exteriority is then read as proof of an ontological superiority. This state of affairs, so the argument would run, could then indeed be adduced as support for a certain eternalism: the eternal unknowability of the object can be valorized as a token of enviable stability and permanence which could then power the desire to attain such stability for consciousness itself.[8] Hegel's counterproposal, on the other hand, would function as a prop for the thought of consciousness's necessary and eternal becoming as mediation. The problem with this 'historicist' alternative, however, would be that if this mediation is indeed the fulfillment for consciousness of the essence of the object, this at once creates the projection of a final fulfillment that would put a radical stop to the process of mediation itself. After the denunciation of the unassailable exteriority/superiority of the object as an empty delusion, the movement of consciousness, if allowed to run its full course, would terminate (determine) the otherness of the object and would definitively come to rest by dint of the disappearance of the material for negation fueling its production of appearance.

The question is fundamentally this: when Hegel states that the goal of knowledge is the station where 'the concept expresses the object, and the object the concept,' and that the 'progress' toward this goal is 'unhalting,'[9] should we then emphasize the goal as something knowledge shall reach, or the progress as an open movement which *never* comes to a stop? Similarly, when he defines experience *(Erfahrung)* as the '*dialectical* movement which consciousness exercises on itself and which affects both its knowledge and its object' and from which '*the new true object issues*,'[10] should we then understand that there will always be another new true object (and thus never really one) or that at a given moment consciousness will generate the ultimate and unsublatable new true object (no longer an object) and will thus have reached the absolute end of experience? De Man's implicit answers to these questions are appropriately hesitant. On the one hand, the strength of his conviction that natural being is invariably intrinsically superior to consciousness does not allow him to conceive of Hegel's *Erfahrung* as a movement with (as distinct from toward) a determinate end; but on the other hand he is also aware that the Absolute Spirit *can* be read as a definitive terminus at the end of the road of experience, and while he typically shies away from this apocalyptic possibility,[11] it does continue to haunt his thought—for instance in his undeveloped hint at Hegel's imprudence, or in his tentative suggestion that there might be some point in trying to match him with Kant, retaining what is essential to each while lifting it up to a level on which the movement of consciousness can be thought as an incessant becoming (Hegel) rendered incessant precisely by consciousness's inability to fully sublate natural being (Kant).

The question remains how this excessively formal scheme can be brought to bear on de Man's plotting of Heidegger's 'effort.' An equally excessively formal answer could mechanically take shape as follows: Heidegger's categorical rejection in *Sein und Zeit* of a conception of *Dasein* on the model of the object ensures an opposition to the temptation of permanence (as does Hegel's rejection of the Kantian split), yet his concomitant promotion of *Dasein* to the status of ontological priority may entail the apocalyptic accomplishment of *Dasein* at the expense of a genuine appreciation of the Being of what is stated to be ontologically inferior to it (a consequence which, unlikely as it must seem, would align his project to Hegel's ontology of spirit).[12] Heidegger's subsequent shift away from the analytics of *Dasein* toward the question of Being could then be construed as an attempt to ward off this possible culmination (in a turn toward Kant, as it were), but this attempt would then also have to be recognized as a possible invitation to espouse the movement of capitulation in the face of the Being of beings other than *Dasein,* in a religious resignation from the task of consciousness under the aegis of the gathering of Being beyond the separation (Heidegger's turn to practical reason, as it were).[13]

Whether or not this dubious exercise in philosophical crossbreeding in the possibly irresponsible mode of the 'as if' can adequately stake out the grounds for de Man's unfulfilled promise (that 'there would be much to say' about Heidegger's 'ambiguous' rejection of Hegel and Kant, 'HE' BI, 252) is perhaps less important than its reenactment of the confusion of tongues riddling the conversation of Being and Becoming in these texts. The pattern indeed complicates more than it elucidates, but it will have succeeded if it has brought out the principal concern motivating de Man's elusive evocation of other voices: the necessity of a vigilant resistance to the temptation of permanence inscribed in the very language that causes the separation soliciting this temptation. The conclusion to 'The Temptation of Permanence' spells this out in terms that may have gained clarity now:

> For a thinker who calls himself *dürftig*—poor, bare—the language of Heidegger has a movement so captivating that it carries one along and tends to hide discontinuities. To what extent is this seduction willed? One would need a study far more extended to decide this question. The seduction is effective inasmuch as it requires a great vigilance to resist it. Perhaps that is its aim, for this vigilance is the very weapon of the struggle of being. ('TP' CW, 39; translation modified)

It is Heidegger's *language*, then, especially in his 'more recent' work, which is of a nature to invite foreclosure of a true critical dialogue in that it covers up discontinuities and points of resistance by means of seductive figures 'borrowed from the life of the earth' (38). And the point is important, for this is precisely the difficulty of Hölderlin—for Heidegger. Indeed, in 'Exegeses' it is said of Hölderlin's poetry that 'the abundance and the beauty of the images, the richness and the diversity of the rhymes carry one along *[entraînent]*' ('HE' BI, 247; translation modified), just as here it is said of Heidegger's language that it 'has a movement so captivating that it carries one along *[entraîne]*.' This implies that the cornerstone of de Man's critique of Heidegger's readings of Hölderlin—'there is never any critical dialogue' (254)—need not be in any simple contradiction with his statement in the same text that Heidegger does enter into a 'dialogue' with Hölderlin inasmuch as he recognizes what is the poet's 'central "concern"' (255). The structure, rather, is that of a serial chain where one variable (absence or presence of critical dialogue) governs the entire system. If de Man entertains a critical dialogue with Heidegger, he recognizes Heidegger's recognition of a central problem in Hölderlin and thus acknowledges the operation of a critical dialogue between the philosopher and the poet; if, on the other hand, de Man enters into an encounter with Heidegger which is not a critical dialogue proper, but rather a dismissive 'passive audition' of Heidegger's enthralled 'passive audition' (254) of Hölderlin's compelling language, he reduces a problem in Heidegger to the status of an erroneous choice which consists of a blind adherence to the notion that Hölderlin actually states the foundation of, the immediacy of Being, and which thus obstructs the possible critical dialogue between both discourses.[14] The irony of this system, then, is that de Man can only accuse Heidegger of the mistake of being swept up by Hölderlin's compelling language when he himself commits that same mistake in the performance of an accusation which depends on a negative compulsion emanating from Heidegger's language.

This consistent inconsistency is also discernible in de Man's approvingly quoting Heidegger's definition of Being as 'presence of the present' ('TP' CW, 34) as proof of the philosopher's deep insight into the division of Being—the point being that in 'Exegeses' he uses the very same phrase to say exactly the opposite: Heidegger 'begins to distort [Hölderlin's] meaning when he . . . show[s] the poet as naming the presence of the present' ('HE' BI, 256–57), where 'la présence du présent' is now clearly understood not as division (for to name division is what Hölderlin, for de Man, is admirably forced to do) but as the immediate itself.

Now, as this phrasing may already suggest, this would appear to imply that de Man (ab)uses Heidegger in a way similar to that in which the latter (ab)uses Hölderlin: Heidegger says, albeit not exactly, the opposite of what de Man makes him say. Frivolous and unduly mechanical[15] though it may seem, there are grounds for this thesis, provided one stresses an added qualification: that is to say, Heidegger *sometimes* says nearly (at times indeed even exactly) the opposite of what de Man makes him say.[16] And while this similarity is often complicated in the sense that de Man asserts as the law of inevitable mediation what Heidegger admits to be a possible inevitability, the point remains that, at least in 'Exegeses,' de Man ultimately refuses to grant this affinity (let alone this possible influence) and makes Heidegger speak a law whose ideal purport is diametrically opposed to that of the possibility actually also adumbrated in Heidegger's commentaries. In other words, de Man does not acknowledge that those of Heidegger's statements that indeed speak this, to de Man unacceptable, law—and such statements do occur—must be understood as being taken up in the much less confident movement of the entire interpretation. Which is to say that—again, in this particular essay—de Man does not observe the rule of dialogue that he himself laid down at the end of 'The Temptation of Permanence.'

The main reason for this neglect is yet again the problem of the choice, but there is one major difference between the present manifestation of this problem and its previous instantiations. Indeed, what is striking in the treatment of the choice as we encounter it here is that de Man explicitly tries to come to terms with the question of whether this choice should properly be located on the level of the production or on that of the interpretation of poetry. Previously, this question was left suspended in the sense that both answers were held simultaneously without this simultaneity being accounted for—at present, the balance decisively shifts and the problem of the choice is (at least for the time being) firmly established as a matter of criticism and, consequently, reading. What de Man objects to in Heidegger is not so much his philosophy but the way this philosophy is liable to be deprived of its acumen to the extent that it bows to the seductive power of poetry—sometimes even the poetry of its own language, as is the case in 'Bauen Wohnen Denken,' which, to de Man's mind, 'is rather more a hymn than an exposition' ('TP' CW, 37). And to succumb to this power is, for de Man, not to read (or rather understand) poetry at all.[17] It is, then, perhaps no coincidence that those texts of Heidegger that de Man singles out for disapproval are texts on poetry—on Hölderlin—whereas those of Heidegger's essays that do not as explicitly engage with poetry are treated with considerably more courtesy. This also agrees with the pseudochronology introduced in 'The Temptation of Permanence,' where de Man approves of a 1952 text on Parmenides, marks his distance from a 1936 text on the work of art, crucially disagrees with a 1951 text on 'In lieblicher Bläue,' and ends up by suggesting that this apparent 'evolution' in Heidegger is more and more in danger of leading him (and others) astray. In addition, it may explain why a phrase like *Anwesen des Anwesenden* in the 1952 essay 'Moira' can be accepted insofar as it means *division* (de Man's translation of *Zwiefalt*), while the same phrase projected by de Man onto the 1939 text on the *Feiertags*-hymn (in which it does not appear as such) is made to denote Heidegger's distortion of the poet's true insight.

We see then that de Man's reading of Heidegger is fundamentally determined by Heidegger's own reading practice, and in the conclusion to the central argument of 'Exegeses' the stakes in this encounter are sketched with what comes close to programmatic clarity. But before we turn to this conclusion, and to the reading it announces, we should perhaps allow for the continuous interruption of an overwhelming question: what is the good of this dialogue in these inward times?

A Resistance of History

> The schematic exposition of his conversion as it is ordinarily
> sketched, beginning with a diabolical phrase *[sic]* and progres-
> sively elevating itself to serenity, is far too simplistic.—Paul
> de Man, 'Biographies and History' (*Le Soir*, February 1942)

Our inward age' is an age of 'deep crisis,' not only for
poetry but also for 'the minds in general'—such is the
starting point of 'The Inward Generation.' We are
'trapped' in an era of 'oppression,' 'passivity,' and 'sterile silence' in
which the best the young can do is 'making up the inventory of the
failures they have inherited' ('IG' CW, 12). The echo of the inventory can hardly be ignored, but we must also register an amazing
change of sign: the imitation of the attitude which only two years
earlier was praised in Montaigne is now subjected to a severe critique, and this critique marks a moment of singular importance
in de Man's explication of the disastrous implications of the past.
The critique takes the shape of a narrative which is by no means
sufficient, but it is certainly necessary.

Nineteenth- and early twentieth-century thought and poetry
were also fundamentally preoccupied with the 'sterility' of their
present, but this preoccupation was always accompanied by 'in-
dignation, hope, rebellion, sheer desire for self-preservation,' by a
'will for change,' by the projection of 'a prophetic vision, a turning away from an erring present to a new beginning' (13). It is
this 'essentially revolutionary' quality (found in Hölderlin, Keats,
Baudelaire, Rimbaud, Yeats, and Rilke, and in Hegel, Nietzsche,
and Heidegger) which de Man now declares to be a thing of the
past. But this declaration can no longer content itself in the re-

treat of ironic observation; instead, it moves toward a rhetorical question that must be given a ring of urgency and cries out for an answer.

> We must ask ourselves what motives stand behind this retreat, not only because the resulting silence often seems unbearable, but also because one cannot take the risk of giving up such a long and vital effort for the wrong reasons. When are we being deceived: is it when we try to think within a context of death and rebirth, failure and its transcendence, nothingness and being— or is it when we abandon ourselves to a stream of passive permanence? Today, we seem inclined to prefer acceptance; but can we be certain that, in doing so, we are not about to abdicate because we are no longer able to stand the strain of the increasing difficulty of invention? Is not what is sometimes called modern conservatism just another form of nihilism? (13)

Yes, of course. But this is not a matter of course. It needs a narrative. Or rather, at least two narratives, neither of which can come to rest in an answer.

The first narrative seeks to ground 'modern conservatism' as a 'reaction against the weaknesses of the prewar era.' De Man selects four protagonists as representatives of the 'blend of revolutionary spirit and aesthetic refinement' (14) characteristic of that era. He does not specify the point, but it is significant that two of these, Jünger and Pound, were involved in totalitarian politics, while the other two, Malraux and Hemingway, combated such politics.[18] Characteristic of all four is that they were 'forcefully committed politically,' but ended up 'writing off this part of their lives completely, as a momentary aberration, a step towards finding themselves,' and that they were 'deeply committed to the defense of certain aesthetic values they had inherited from their symbolist ancestors,' although 'next to Proust, James and Rilke, their works seem to disappear in banality and imitation' (14). De Man then identifies the underlying principle of this double failure, which the war—'which here is as much cause as effect'—and 'a mounting mechanization and automaticism' served to expose:

> What happened is that the political as well as the aesthetic were being used, not for what they represent in themselves, but as a protection that shielded them from their real problems. Political systems of the left and of the right, and literary experimentations that had originated before them, provided an organized framework within which they could fit and act, without really returning to the questions out of which these systems and experiments had arisen. (14)

It is this insufficiency, then, which makes these representatives of the prewar era 'such vulnerable targets for today's conservatism—more vulnerable, in fact, than they deserve to be, because their predicament was not an easy one' (14).

The similarity between this 'conservative' reaction and the justificatory wartime narratives in which the parliamentary democracies functioned as favorite targets, and which de Man had himself repeatedly produced, is as striking as is his present refusal to take this narrative as read. Before the modern conservatives 'can claim any superiority, it should be proved that they are not just doing the same thing, in a more vicious and destructive way' (14). Which of course they are—a second relation is needed, and the logic of the first narrative requires that this second account return to the question the prewar 'political and aesthetic beliefs' had tried to cover up.

The name of this question is 'ontological crisis.' It is the product of an 'awareness of a deep separation between man's inner consciousness and the totality of what is not himself' which became prominent in Romanticism and is still crucially ours:

> Never have the truly great minds of romanticism, such as Rousseau, Hölderlin, or Hegel, been more familiar and more directly concerned with our own situation. The specific cluster of ideas that leads from the concept of separation to that of inwardness,

A Resistance of History | 121

and from inwardness to history, is the pattern of that period as it is of ours—with the difference that for us, it is more directly experienced, even to the point where it is often difficult to perceive the motion in which we are caught.' (15)

Or more important: even to the point where 'we' try to suppress this pattern in a 'studious avoidance, under a variety of pretexts, of the ontological question.' The principal reason why 'we' avoid this question is 'that we have no language to handle a problem that questions precisely the origin of the logic in which we have lived so long.' This, finally, is what relates modern conservatism to the failures it chooses for its enabling targets: whereas the prewar activist aesthetes sought refuge in systems that pretended to solve this problem, the modern conservatives go even further and embrace passive nihilism, but both are joined in their capitulation to the same 'temptation that exists in all of us: a desire for serenity that tries to forget and to repress the original anxiety'; both are seduced by the 'promise of serenity' which 'keeps us from facing the issues in which our being is at stake' (15).

The narrative is deceptively simple: its beginning is the ontological question, its middle is the answer to this question in a system, its end is the rejection of both answer and question in the spirit of nihilism. Only if it were that simple could this narrative straightforwardly answer de Man's initial rhetorical question. But matters are more complicated. The moment the ontological question arises it calls out for an answer and this answer must necessarily involve 'the conceptualization of history.' This conceptualization is itself already part of the system that will come to cover up the ontological question. And precisely because it tries to forget the question it is supposed to answer, this system is exposed to failure and is rejected in a rejection of what it was meant to conceive: history. 'When are we being deceived: is it when we try to think within a context of death and rebirth, failure and its transcendence, nothingness and being' (but when we try to think thus we are already engaged in a conceptualization of the question in a system that represses it), 'or is it when we abandon ourselves to a stream of passive permanence' (in which case we are engaged in a transcendence of the failure of the attempt to think in a context of failure and transcendence, and 'fall back on nothingness' [13])? It is this diabolical logic that robs the question of its rhetorical composure and makes it necessary to think a dialogue—with Heidegger, who is de Man's prime witness here.

The ontological question is not itself an answer: to think this question necessitates a thinking of its history, 'instead of submitting to some institution that accepts and perpetuates the separation between man and Being' ('HE' BI, 258).

> If we feel that our being is threatened, and we want to keep the hope that this threat may subside, then we must admit that even the all-encompassing concept of being is susceptible to change and that it has an existence in time; that, in other words, the ontological itself is historical. The meditation on being will then normally start as a meditation on historical time, the only way to reach a new metaphysical language; this evolution is characteristic of the work of a philosopher such as Heidegger, who begins to consider metaphysics only after having encountered, at the end of his first major work, the concept of time as the 'horizon' of all being. An attack on philosophy of history as such appears, therefore, as the best way to *forget* the ontological. ('IG' CW, 15–16) [19]

One such attack is Karl Löwith's critique of Heidegger in *Denker in dürftiger Zeit*, which de Man qualifies as 'mainly an extension of an article Löwith had published shortly after the war in Jean-Paul Sartre's review *Les Temps modernes*, as his contribution to a polemic on Heidegger's political attitude' (17). De Man's next comment is carefully—perhaps too carefully—balanced.

> Certainly, Heidegger's philosophy, which is full of traps and pitfalls and which has led many a mind to a kind of Lorelei-like perdition, requires a highly alert critical reading. But Löwith's main

argument consists in attacking Heidegger's historicism and the eschatological aspect of his thought. This constitutes precisely the most profound impulse that stands behind this philosophy, and it undoubtedly deserves a rigorous examination. Yet, as he starts from a preconceived and reactionary view of history as indifferent and meaningless repetition, Löwith's critique never reaches the level of a dialogue but always remains on that of a rather pointless polemic. (17)

De Man does not say enough: he does not explicitate Heidegger's political attitude, he does not explicitly condemn it, and he does not confess and condemn his own commitment to a similar politics (independent of any reading of Heidegger though it was). But this does not diminish the importance of what he does say: a critique of Heidegger's philosophy which starts out from a rejection of its eschatological aspect 'in the name of permanence (conservatism)' is pointless. Yet, was not the invocation of permanence itself asserted to be a favorite gesture of eschatological thought insofar as it is pitted against the noneschatological thinking of becoming? Is not Heidegger himself guilty of a capitulation to the temptation of permanence when he makes Hölderlin actually state the immediacy of Being, thus conferring on his poetry the power to found eternity in the anticipation of 'in Heidegger's terms, "that which *remains* in the process of becoming"' ('PP' CW, 64)? Precisely. That is why there should be a dialogue, not a polemic, 'a highly alert critical reading' and 'a rigorous examination' of Heidegger's answers to the ontological question, not an a priori rejection of the question itself on the basis of, in Löwith's terms, 'the untimely intuition [unzeitgemäße Anschauung] that man in the history that is known to us remains the same in the ground of his essence,' and that 'man is as he has always already [immer schon] been and will always be.'[20]

De Man does not say enough, but this does not diminish the importance of what he does not say. He does not say that a critique of Heidegger's political attitude is pointless. Neither does he suggest, unlike the editors of Les Temps modernes and unlike another participant in the polemic, Alphonse de Waelhens, that Heidegger's philosophy is essentially opposed to Nazism and fascism.[21] Nor does he make the essentially more radical claim, defended by Eric Weil, that Heidegger has 'falsified his philosophy' not so much in the sense that his particular political choice was incompatible with its principles but in the sense that this philosophy 'does not know politics' and hence cannot even ask political questions, let alone offer political answers.[22] In fact, as regards an abstract appreciation of the relation between Heidegger's political attitude and his philosophy, the narrative argument of 'The Inward Generation' brings de Man surprisingly close to Löwith's conclusion that 'the possibility of Heidegger's political philosophy does not arise from a "derailment" one could regret but from the very principle of his conception of existence which at the same time combats and assumes "the spirit of the times."'[23] But there is a decisive difference: de Man's double narrative can only be brought into agreement with Löwith's judgment if the two explanations for Heidegger's politics it presents as distinct alternatives only one of which is true, are both simultaneously admitted. Which, again, is why there must be a dialogue: a critical reading that acknowledges that it is 'Heidegger's *philosophy*' that 'has lead many a mind to a kind of Lorelei-like perdition,' while at the same time recognizing that this perdition is also incompatible with this philosophy; a rigorous examination that opposes the pointless polemic that implicitly rejects the very principle of combating 'the spirit of the times' by taking recourse to an acquiescence in the eternal essence of the human being, in 'the comfortable reassurance that whatever has been, will be.' Such a polemic is pointless to the precise extent that it repeats what it rejects ('in a more vicious and destructive way'): it rejects eschatology in the name of permanence without sufficiently realizing that any eschatology, as the logos of last things, is always in some way underway to permanence; it rejects the ontological question without thinking through the logic by which this question always prefigures, if not therefore performs, the answers that 'arise' (14) from it and reject it.

De Man could have gone further: he could have explicitly con-demned Heidegger's political attitude. But such a condemnation would have been caught in the imperative of a double *tu quo-que:* he would have had to apply it to his own wartime commit-ments, and he would have had to point up the specific proximity of Löwith to what this latter condemns in Heidegger. He could have brought together Löwith's implicit rejection of Heidegger's thesis that 'there is no such thing as an unchanging *[immer gleiche]* nature of man'; Löwith's concomitant invocation of 'our' connect-edness to unchanging nature;[24] his own admiration for 'the spirit of Jünger [which is] deeply rooted in the eternal bases of human nature' (LS, June 1942, 244); de Waelhens's characterization of fas-cist politics as incompatible with Heidegger's thought because 'a simple consequence of the existential attitude which fixes man in his determinations like a tree is fixed in its determinations';[25] and his own critique of Malraux's tree (his other example of an 'attack on the philosophy of history' ('IG' CW, 16) and its explicit con-nection to his critique of Heidegger's 'vegetative "doing/making *[faire]*"' ('TP' CW, 38; translation modified). He could have under-scored Löwith's inconsistency on the question of whether or not 'European nihilism' is an eminently German affair,[26] and he could have brought this problem to bear on Heidegger's persistent privi-leging of Germany, which in fact he characterizes in 'Exegeses' as a 'sentimental and national' 'secondary reason' for Heidegger's pref-erence for Hölderlin, in whose ' "national" poems' the philosopher 'finds an echo' for his 'anguished meditation upon the historical destiny of Germany' as 'thought out just before and during World War II' ('HE' BI, 254). He could have related this meditation to his own, supposedly nonsentimental, comments on the destiny of nations in his wartime journalism,[27] especially insofar as these com-ments lay claim to a privileged access to 'the historical necessities' which require 'the establishment of concrete methods permitting man to live a normal and healthy life' and thus reject the 'contem-plative evasion' in 'that much-vaunted anxiety *[inquiétude]*' which is nothing but 'an artificial invention of the idle' (LS, August 1942,

132)—a judgment that is precisely inverted in his present verdict that whenever 'concrete systems of organization . . . claim their ability to solve [the] problems that arise from [the] awareness of separation . . . they are in fact appealing to . . . a desire for serenity that tries to forget and to repress the original anxiety' ('IG' CW, 15). He could have further developed this account by considering the nationalist turn in Malraux[28] and the puzzling 1949 treatise in *Les Temps modernes* 'On the Character of the Belgians' (which de Man almost certainly had read at the time, even if only because it was coauthored by Alphonse de Waelhens) in which the Belgians are cast, by implication, in the role of Hölderlin's Greeks, with the crucial difference that, unlike these Greeks, they feel wholly contented in their privileged access to the sensible.[29]

But instead of all this, de Man turns to poetry—the important point being that, if thought through, this departure from what he calls 'a side issue' ('HE' BI, 254) decidedly moves to the heart of this same issue.

' "The world is the opening-up of wide paths created by the simple and fundamental decisions of a people from the interior of its historical destiny" ' ('TP' CW, 34).[30] De Man has no quarrel with this notion of national historical destiny and decision *(Entscheidung)*, provided it remains within the confines of what can be 'translated into Hegelian terms,' privileging 'a duality which is the structure of the dialectic' over 'a unity of being' (35).[31] It is only when this *Entscheidung* comes to be thought as that which would transcend the fundamental separation by gathering 'opposition in . . . unity . . . in a manner apparently permanent' that it has to be abandoned. For Heidegger, the *locus* of such gathering is the work of art, and Hölderlin's naming of Being its prime performance—witness the following lines from the *Erläuterungen* that de Man quotes elsewhere:

'The essence *(Wesen)* of what is named (Being) is revealed in the word,' writes Heidegger. 'By naming Being's essence, the word separates the essential from the non-essential. . . . And because it

separates *(scheidet)*, it decides *(entscheidet)* their struggle.' ('HE'
BI, 259)[32]

De Man does not agree:

> The play on the words *scheiden-entscheiden* is nonsense *[un con-
> tresens]*, because it is by virtue of the separation that it causes
> that the word prevents the struggle from reaching conclusion.
> It transfers the struggle within itself, which is why it is ever-
> renewed mediation. (256–60; translation modified)

Although de Man does not explicitly establish the connection between these two instances of the rhetoric of *Entscheidung* that he
selects from Heidegger's work, it is nevertheless in the necessity
of this connection that his dialogue with eschatologism must be
located if we are to appreciate his oblique but crucial resistance
to Heidegger's 'sentimental' appropriation of Hölderlin's poetry
in the name of national destiny. The moment Heidegger's reading
abandons mediation in favor of correspondence *(Entsprechen)* [33]
and moves to ultimate permanence, significantly on the back of a
pun so seductive that it carries one along,[34] de Man parts company.
It is necessary to underscore that the argument leading up to his
critique of a certain development suggested in Heidegger's essay
on the origin of the work of art follows an almost identical pattern. Having suggested how the *Entscheidungen* of a people, which
create the wide paths opened up as world, institute a struggle between world and earth which is that of 'becoming in the Hegelian
sense,' de Man continues with a further quotation from Heidegger
which, to him, conveys the same point:

> 'In this struggle, it is the unity of world and earth which is at
> stake. By this opening-up of the world are decided the victory
> and defeat, the happiness and the distress, the domination and
> the enslavement of a historical people. In revealing what remains
> undecided and unmeasured, the world just coming to birth re-
> veals the hidden necessity for decision and measure. But by the
> opening up of a world, the earth surges forth. Earth reveals itself

as the support of all things, as that which hides itself in its own law and refuses persistently to be unveiled. The world demands decision and measure, and it situates beings in the opening-up of their own paths. As foundation surging up, earth strives to remain hidden and to submit everything to its law.' ('TP' CW, 34; translation modified) [35]

Following de Man's suggestion, we could translate this into (his) Hegelian terms as follows: world is consciousness, earth is natural being, and what is at stake *(l'enjeu)* is their unity—a unity which, for de Man, is essentially forbidden. The intention of the struggle is to accomplish this unity by marshaling (earth) natural being to the measure of the decisions of (world) consciousness, but insofar as (earth) natural being (refuses persistently to be un-veiled) is intrinsically so superior that 'all attempts to master it are doomed at the outset' ('DA,' 13), this intention can never be ful-filled. This is why de Man 'understands less well the continuation of the passage from Heidegger' under consideration, in which, 'carried by verbal analogies' *(Riß, Grundriß, Auf-riß, Umriß)*, 'one leaps in a few moments over vertiginous distances, passing from the idea of struggle to that of contour' ('TP' CW, 35). And the mo-ment the struggle—the act of mediation which intends to bring natural being under the measure of conscious decision—is aban-doned, the path is cleared for Heidegger's potential capitulation to the temptation of permanence in a submission to earth:

Heidegger speaks more and more in the name of earth. Malraux could allow to subsist from human existence only the passive gestures in which the biological part of our nature reveals itself at moments of supreme crisis; these are the gestures that de-cide in the place of the historical decision. In thinking 'doing/making *[faire]*' in the sense of 'remaining, dwelling,' Heidegger ends up in a similar climate of thought. It is a question of a vege-tative 'doing/making' and one rediscovers more and more . . . examples and metaphors borrowed from the life of the earth. . . . ('TP' CW, 38; translation emended)

In 'The Inward Generation,' these 'gestures that decide in the place of the historical decision' are made even more explicit, and it is not surprising that this should occur by way of a gloss on the 'seductive image' of Malraux's tree:

> Conscious and self-willed history, by means of which man tries to give form to the tensions of his inner fate, is sacrificed to the unchanging. And the only stability that can be found in man is the animal, the vegetative; no wonder that Malraux's symbol is a tree and his subject, as it appears in the parts of the novel that deal with the two world wars, those semi-herdlike reactions of shapeless impulse, sometimes generous, always gregarious, which make up human behaviour in times of collective crisis. ('IG' CW, 16)

It will be clear that the decision de Man here wants to prevent from being replaced by the decisions of the crisis-reactions of shapeless impulse is not the decision *(Entscheidung)* which Heidegger's pun in the *Erläuterungen* names as the transcendence of separation *(Scheidung)*, but rather its exact opposite. The decision abandoned in Malraux and in the 'vegetative' Heidegger is abandoned precisely in favor of a decision of the struggle, which to de Man can never be decided and must therefore continue in the consciousness of decision, separation, mediation. The moment the struggle is declared to be decided in favor of permanence and gregarious, if generous, unconsciousness, introduced by way of puns, verbal analogies, or seductive images borrowed from the life of the earth, de Man measures his distances and demands a proper reading, or a dialogue.[36] Which is also to say—and this is of primary importance—that he must emphatically disagree with Löwith's comments on Heidegger's readings of Hölderlin.

For Löwith, Heidegger's *Erläuterungen* are 'as subtle as they are exaggerated,'[37] but the reasons for his reservations are diametrically opposed to those that motivate de Man's opposition:

> One can noncommitally accept *[unverbindlich hinnehmen]* Heidegger's elucidations of Hölderlin's poetry as an impressive

whole, or one can also examine them in detail from a literary-historical perspective. But as the elucidation of a poet by a thinker they must be questioned with consideration for the problem of history. For what is allowed for the poetic word is not therefore valid *[stichhaltig]* for a critical and discriminating thought *[ein kritisch-unterscheidendes Denken]*.

For de Man, to the contrary, Heidegger's readings are in error to the extent that they effectively allow the poetic word to have the prerogative that Löwith deems proper to it, but which, to de Man, is no more valid for poetry than it is for thought: 'A commentary on Hölderlin's poetry must essentially be critical, if it wishes to be faithful to its author's definition of poetry, just as this poetry is critical of its own certitudes, their illusory character unveiled' ('HE' BI, 263). Heidegger's first mistake is that he confers the power to found eternity on poetry—the fact that he then appropriates this power for his own discourse is only an effect of this initial mistake, a mistake that is Löwith's as much as it is Heidegger's. In this connection, it is not surprising that Löwith should also approvingly cite Nietzsche's canonization of art and religion as the supreme 'eternalizing powers,'[38] for it is this Nietzsche whom de Man chooses (or probably even borrows) as the 'direct ancestor' of the poetic eternalism to be attacked in the name of becoming ('PP' CW, 65–66). For Löwith, as for Heidegger as he functions here, poetry is the place where the limitations of thought are transcended, and in this they both perform the eminently metaphysical gesture which consists in the constitution of a realm of the aesthetic where what cannot be thought can be said in order to ensure its subsequent availability for the language of, precisely, thought. For de Man, such subterfuges—which, we must recall, he himself had explicitly praised in his wartime readings of Jünger—are no longer acceptable: one can never 'noncommitally' accept a certain poetic license as an alternative to a reading of the question of history in poetry, for no sooner has this license to found permanence and eternity been granted, than it is invoked as a truth with which to underpin 'an ideal of political supremacy' (74), or as a justification of the modern conservative nihilist acquiescence of an 'age of fatigue' for which 'history has become painful' ('TP' CW, 31–33).

De Man does not say enough. His opposition to the use of poetry as a refuge for conservatism and nationalism is explicit, but it does not suffice to confront the fundamental problem of the decision and the destiny of nations.[39] Moreover, his paradoxical but not therefore simply inconsistent emphasis on the development of 'inward meditation' as 'the quintessential historical act' (33) with which to combat the nihilism of 'our inward age' ('IG' CW, 17) is more poignantly pathetic than it is critically convincing. And yet, we cannot sufficiently emphasize his marked rejection of the serene retreat into the irony of the inventory. The argument is flawed, and the dialogue is promised rather than articulated,[40] but the intention to resist, by way of the decision to elaborate an adequate critical language, the resistance of history that informs the quarantining of poetry in the realm of eternity, is pertinent enough to be pursued on its own terms.

The Critical Choice

In the main conclusion to 'Heidegger's Exegeses of Hölderlin,' de Man sums up his differences with Heidegger in the general terms of what he diagnoses as the central problem for any exegetical method, namely, 'how to elaborate a language capable of dealing with the tension between the ineffable and the mediate.'

> The ineffable demands the direct adherence and the blind and violent passion with which Heidegger treats texts. Mediation implies a reflection that tends toward a critical language as systematic and rigorous as possible, but not overly eager to make claims of certitude that it can earn only in the long run. ('HE' BI, 263; translation modified)[41]

The passage is crucial for an understanding of the reading practice under construction in these texts. First, it offers a way to (partially) negotiate the difficulty of the fundamental dissymmetry of the choice de Man projected onto the supposedly diametrically opposed poets Mallarmé and Baudelaire by locating this choice on the level of reading (and writing insofar as this always involves [self-]reading). For if Heidegger can, mutatis mutandis, be said to read Hölderlin as if this latter were Baudelaire (as de Man pictured him), we may begin to question de Man's reading of Baudelaire as if he were precisely (de Man's) Baudelaire. If Heidegger's exegesis of Hölderlin can be said to be wrong because it violently and blindly refuses a critical dialogue and, to modify Heidegger's own (Hölderlinian) image, mutes the poem by covering it in a precipitate of preestablished (mis)understanding, a similar suspicion may well arise—and has, in fact, already arisen—with respect to de Man's initial exegesis of Baudelaire (even, perhaps, with respect to his exegesis of Heidegger's own 'hymns'). In addition, we are now able to suggest, with de Man, that the torn contradictions in his own account of a Hegelian dialectic in poetry which would and would not culminate in a named synthesis, which would still preserve hope even though it has abandoned all hope (and so on), can be successfully approached only through an investigation of a difficulty of choice on the part of the critic reflecting on poetry, rather than through an investigation of such a choice as it, allegedly, can be observed (as opposed to read) in that poetry. Such a suggestion may well seem to verge on banality (perhaps because it has become overly familiar to us), and it certainly cannot be made to figure as a satisfying conclusion to the quandaries we have had to face in the preceding, but it nonetheless does mark a certain potential the pursuit of which is the main permanent concern of de Man's entire enterprise.

What we have, then, is clearly still a choice, and it also remains a very lopsided choice, as 'Heidegger's' method of exegesis as presented by de Man can hardly count as a serious alternative to the rigorous reflection so programmatically announced.[42] Yet, what we have gained is a clear statement of the task incumbent on those who make the right choice: to develop a critical language which is as rigorous and systematic as possible, which mediates the immediate (the ineffable) without precipitating itself into its own negation (the ineffable), but which also refuses to lay claims to an authority of certainty it has not yet merited. The projection of truth in this 'not yet' is the lingering trace of the projection of an Absolute (Spirit). As such, it also partakes of the pathos of the authentic choice, but this choice is now fully recognized as the choice of the critic, Paul de Man—among others. Just how this choice should be thought of remains as yet undefined, but its very institution as a choice for reading should suffice to dispel the erroneous conceptions fostered by speaking of de Man's early work as 'the properly *critical* face of his activities.'[43] A 'metacritical' problematic has never been absent from his work—and, in fact, one should even go further and ask whether most of his early writings can be said to be primarily 'properly critical' (in the sense of what used to be known as 'primary' criticism of literature) at all. Indeed, as the preceding discussion should have made clear, there is precious little 'in-depth analysis' of actual works of literature to be found in most of these early essays, their overriding concern being, grossly put, 'philosophical' rather than strictly literary critical in the then received sense.[44] A turn to an even more outspokenly metacritical essay that de Man wrote during this period, 'Impasse de la critique formaliste,' will help us to put this point in perspective.

CHAPTER SEVEN

The Critical Aspect: At Least Three Roads for Criticism

'J'appelle un chat un chat.'—Freud,
'Bruchstück einer Hysterie-Analyse'

The Single Aspect of Poetry and Reconciliatory Criticism

First published in French in 1956, 'The Dead-End of For-malist Criticism' presents an introduction to the climate of (New) criticism in the United States and a warning to those critics in France who are in danger of committing the same mistakes that mar the 'formalist' enterprises on the other side of the Atlantic.[1] More important for our present investigation, however, the essay also contains more general statements on the problems of criticism as such, and it is to these that we shall predominantly turn.

A first notable development in this respect is de Man's critique of I. A. Richards. For Richards the critic's task is to retrace the road that led to the form of the literary work of art by identifying the initial experience the author communicates in this form, and having done so the critic will have grasped the meaning of the literary work. This seems commonsensical enough, de Man concedes, but it implies in fact 'some highly questionable ontological presupposions,' the most fundamental of which is the very belief 'that language, poetic or otherwise, can *say* any experience, of whatever kind, even only a simple perception' ('DF' BI, 232). He then expands his doubts as to the grounds of this ontological presupposition through the feline figure so frequently favored in philosophical investigations:

> Neither the statement 'I see a cat' nor, for that matter, Baudelaire's poem 'Le Chat' contains wholly the experience of this perception. It can be said that there is a perceptual consciousness of the object, and an experience of this consciousness, but the working out of a *logos* of this experience or, in the case of art, of a *form* of this experience, encounters considerable difficulties. (232)[2]

One of these difficulties follows from the fact that language *constitutes* what appeared to be given in the expression of an experience: the form is not merely a mediation between the subjectivity of the author and the reader/critic, as Richards would have it, but a mediation between 'a being and a non-being.' The critic's task would then be to reflect on the question how language (the form) can at all succeed in creating (rather than imitating) the experience and, moreover, how this creation can subsequently come to be experienced by the reader as constituting an 'initial' experience.

For Richards, this poses no real problems, as he postulates 'a perfect continuity between the sign and the thing signified.' On perceiving the sign 'cat,' Richards would argue, the reader engages in a consciousness of the absent cause of the sign, the real cat, to which de Man, arguably in a Kantian spirit, adds that this would also have to entail the retrieval of spatial and temporal determinations, thus effectively requiring the constitution of an entire 'world.' The very nature of this complicated effort casts serious doubts on Richards's apparently untroubled (and largely unargued) faith in its fundamental possibility. The fact that Richards insists that criticism is not concerned with a material object but with a consciousness of such an object through the form as a sign of its initial experience does not solve anything; nor does his insistence on the primacy of the affectivity of poetic language over and against its referential function pacify de Man. For after all, the form upon which Richards would have criticism reflect is seen as the imitation of a mental experience ('the experience, the *mental condition* relevant to the poem') in a substance, and thus forms, for the reader, a signifying object referring to the affectivity of the author or poet relative to the initial experience or perception—which reintroduces the problematic referential function through the formalist critic's backdoor.[3]

Compared to de Man's previous work, this sketchy critique of formalism and its ontological presuppositions is surprising in its composure. Far from mobilizing grand variations on the eternal cleft of Being, the present exposition suffices by pointing out, quite impassively, that there is a problematic distance between language and whatever it purports to be about. In the continuation of the argument, the pathos we have encountered before is forcibly reintroduced, but the salient point is that now this pathos is identified, more explicitly than before, as a reaction to a state of affairs that is first circumscribed by way of a fairly placid factual observation of a particular (but general) linguistic difficulty.

The said reintroduction of pathos is adumbrated in de Man's identification of the ethical implications of Richards's principles. Praising their salutary influence on the development of a refined technical vocabulary, de Man nonetheless swiftly exposes the inadequacy of dealing with poetry in the climate of morally reassuring communicability suggested by Richards's method. In order to argue this point, de Man takes recourse to William Empson—'a brilliant student of Richards'—in whose *Seven Types of Ambiguity* he finds evidence of a growing, albeit implicit, rejection of Richards's precepts in the idea that 'a fundamental ambiguity is constitutive of all poetry' (236), an insight that culminates in 'a thought Richards never wanted to consider: true poetic ambiguity proceeds from the deep division of Being itself, and poetry does no more than state and repeat this division' (237). Richards, in fact, had always held that such conflicts could be contained in the ability of poetry to effect a reconciliation of contraries—but Empson's 'more tormented spirit' cannot rest satisfied at this:

> In a note added to the text [après coup], he [Empson] writes: 'It may be said that the contradiction must somehow form a larger unity if the final effect is to be satisfying. But the onus of reconciliation can be laid very heavily on the receiving end,' that is, on the reader, for the reconciliation does not occur in the text. The text does not resolve the conflict, it *names* it. (237)

The heightening drift of this passage is unmistakable: the hesitant wording of Empson's note is overwhelmed by de Man's categorical interpretations,[4] and this gesture gathers even more momentum in the continuation of the passage, in which de Man, marshaling support from Empson's reading of George Herbert's 'The Sacrifice,' drives home his familiar point:

> And there is no doubt as to the nature of this conflict. . . . [It] can be resolved only by the supreme sacrifice: there is no stronger way of stating the impossibility of an incarnate and happy truth. The ambiguity poetry speaks of is the fundamental one that prevails between the world of the spirit and the world of sensible substance: to found itself, the spirit must turn itself into sensible substance, but the latter is knowable only in its dissolution into nonbeing. The spirit cannot coincide with its object and this separation is infinitely sorrowful. (237; translation modified)

Predictably now, this dialectic is immediately identified as the movement proper to the unhappy consciousness, but de Man also equates it to the governing idea of the 'pastoral convention' studied in Empson's *Some Versions of Pastoral*. This may seem surprising, but not for very long: it is especially the famous octave from Andrew Marvell's 'The Garden,' which Empson analyzes as an instance of pastoral poetry, that catches de Man's attention—and this for rather obvious reasons (which also prompt him to suppress the first two lines of the passage, wherein the Mind is said to 'Withdraw into its happiness'):

The Mind, that Ocean where each kind
Does straight its own resemblance find;
Yet it creates, transcending these,
Far other worlds, and other Seas,
Annihilating all that's made
To a green thought in a green shade.

For de Man, this (doctored) sestet forms a supreme expression of the 'dialectical armature' typical of the pastoral convention. Consciousness contemplates its reflection in nature, but, realizing that a reflection is not an identification, it is excited into the desire to comprehend the otherness escaping its reflecting act, which in effect entails the destruction of this otherness. 'Thus the essentially negative activity of all thought and of poetic thought in particular is conceived: "Annihilating all that's made." One would be hard pressed to state it any more strongly' (239).[5] The apparently appeasing greenness of this destructive thought is nothing but 'the freshness, the greenness of budding thought that can evoke itself only through the memory of what it destroys on its way.' And de Man concludes, characteristically jumping from rhetorical question to irrefutable verdict, that the pastoral convention is itself 'the eternal separation between the mind that distinguishes, negates, legislates, and the originary simplicity of the natural. . . . There is no doubt that the pastoral theme is, in fact, the only poetic theme, that it is poetry itself' (239). Pretending to write a genre study, Empson has in fact written 'his ontology of the poetic'—and this ontology is established as de Man's own: all poetry is engaged in naming the eternal separation, and the problem of reconciliation that this name cannot help but invite can be properly understood only by considering the choices made at 'the receiving end,' in the reader. We are back on the road:

A conception of poetic consciousness as an essentially divided, sorrowful, and tragic consciousness (or as representing, in stoical or ironical guises, attempts to transcend this pain without eliminating it) forces a choice between different roads upon critical reflection. The impression of crisis and uncertainty that one gathers from reading contemporary criticism derives from these hesitations. Without simplifying excessively, we may distinguish three possible roads for reflection: historical poetics, salvational poetics, and naive poetics. (241; translation modified)

At least three roads, then, and three roads for criticism, poetry being increasingly confined to the one road we cannot not already know.

ROAD 1:

REDEMPTIVE OR SALVATIONAL CRITICISM

The governing feature of this type of criticism is its attitude toward time, which it seeks to conquer in a quest for origins and primal sources. 'Originary beginnings take on the appearance of privileged moments beyond time, and their remembrance serves as the promise of a new fruitfulness,' writes de Man (242). His terminology allows us to identify this type of criticism as what he previously called an eternalist poetics: a conception of poetry deployed in an attempt to conquer history and to seek shelter in the intemporal realm of a permanent presence. Still, de Man is less simply dismissive here than before and also identifies in this type of thought the, to him, laudable intention to preserve the lucidity of conscious mediation. Thus, this criticism is marked by the ambivalence of a 'hesitancy at the prospect of surrendering to a redemptive faith . . . together with a presentation of poetry as a presage of redemption' (243). Which is to say that redemptive criticism is admittedly sensitive to the essentially divided nature of consciousness, and thus registers the essential negativity of poetry, but that it is incapable of reading this difficulty as a 'true ontological ambiguity' rather than as a simple contradiction. In other words, it is not sufficiently Hegelian, although it does exhibit some sensitivity to the demands of (Hegelian) consciousness, and de Man concludes that rather than to reject this poetics as a sacrific of consciousness to faith, 'it is better to say that it alternates moments of faith without conscious-ness with moments of consciousness without faith. This is possible only if one simultaneously maintains overly simple notions of affir-mation and negation' (244; translation modified). Poetry itself, it is always understood, develops essentially beyond such alternatives by virtue of its resistance to just such simplifications.

If redemptive criticism is primarily distinguished by its belief in poetry's salvational transcendence of time, naïve criticism can be understood as conferring upon poetry a supreme power over space by endowing it with the reconciliatory capacity to offer an immedi-ate contact with substance through its sensible form. This type of criticism resembles Richards's poetics insofar as it, too, postulates a continuity between sign and signified, but it goes even further and seems to believe in 'an adequation of the object itself with the language that names it' (244). In an erroneous declaration of indebtedness to Husserl (erroneous because it fails to grasp the thrust toward the nonsensible transcendental in this thought), the criticism of sensation, like the poetry of substance criticized be-fore, pledges allegiance to the notion of a unification of object and subject. Redemptive criticism and the criticism of sensation thus turn out to be two faces—one temporal, one spatial—of an inade-quate understanding of the notion of presence as a self-contained unit; both pertain to a poetics of being rather than becoming which projects in poetry its 'hope' of 'reconciliation,' of 'filling the gap that cleaves Being.' Yet, instead of simply dismissing this hope, de Man takes pains to emphasize its near 'naming of the center of the problem.' 'For it reveals,' he writes,

> in the impatience of which it is the symptom, the desire that haunts modern thought: 'to communicate substantially with what is substantial in things.' One is far from the truth when,

with Jean-Pierre Richard, one describes Baudelaire as a happy poet whose word is capable of 'filling the depth by substituting for the emptiness of the abyss the warm plenitude of substance.' But one is also very close to it, in the sense that for Baudelaire it is this possibility that constitutes the supreme wager; however, since it must remain wager, it is substance itself that is the abyss. As long as that remains the case, there is left but the sorrowful time of patience, that is to say, history. (245)[6]

The similarity between this judgment of Richard and the earlier assessment of Heidegger is unmistakable. In fact, it is the logical consequence of de Man's growing realization that if he wants to identify a law of separating mediation central to all poetry, he has to revise his earlier judgments of the poetry of substance supposedly produced by Baudelaire et al. and replace them by judgments of a critical poetics of substance that can be erroneously read into Baudelaire's language. Thus, Baudelaire's 'gageure suprême' is gradually moving in the direction of Hölderlin's 'gageure' ('HE' BI, 263) and Mallarmé's 'Jeu suprême' ('PN' CW, 23)—as indeed it had to, lest de Man would himself become subject to his criticism of the formalist postulate of a continuity between the poet's experience and the form 'resulting' from this experience.

It goes without saying that this by no means solves all difficulties, even if only because the notion of the wager itself continues to imply at least some knowledge of the consciousness of the poet, and de Man will indeed try to preserve a limited access to such knowledge in most of his earlier writings, as well as a margin within which differences between particular poets can still be argued for—in fact, in a crucially modified form, such access (and such margins) will always figure in his criticism. But before we continue to investigate this difficulty, we must turn to the third road, which will also allow us to take up the note of history into which the passage just quoted—and with it the entire essay—retreats.

ROAD 3: HISTORICAL POETICS

De Man immediately cautions that a true historical poetics does not exist as yet, and that it can consequently only be considered in a conditional or hypothetical mode. Not even Marxist criticism qualifies as true historical criticism, 'for it is bound to the necessity of a reconciliation scheduled to occur at the end of a linear temporal development, and its dialectical movement does not include time itself as one of its terms' ('DF' BI, 242): it is not in error because it is a dialectical criticism, but because it postulates a final term of reconciliation in a dialectic that does not contain temporality (i.e., becoming). De Man still seems to uphold a certain synthesis that would contain this temporality—such, after all, is the alleged nature of the synthesis that Hegel 'had the audacity to name'—but once again he abstains from naming it, and instead rejects Marxist criticism because it does name its term as an absolute that slights 'true' history. This judgment is consistent with his earlier expression of approval at the *bon mot* he gleans from Empson (slightly twisting it while doing so) following which Marxist thought, too, is a pastoral thought, but one that introduces the absolute prematurely. As de Man writes, 'the pastoral problematic, which turns out to be the problematic of Being itself, is lived in our day by Marxist thought, as by any genuine thought. In motivation, if not in its claims, Marxism is, ultimately, a poetic thought that lacks the patience to pursue its own conclusions to their end' (240).[7]

According to de Man, one of the chief merits of this (Empson's) conclusion is that, having truly recognized the fundamental necessity of 'the ontological question,' it simultaneously warns against certain 'Marxist illusions' which would have the unfortunate effect of obfuscating the pursuit of this fundamental necessity by substituting the insight that separation resides in Being itself with a focus on what are actually only side-effects of this ineluctable separation. It should be noted that this verdict is in keeping both with de Man's previous attacks on 'nihilist conservatism' ('IG' CW, 15), and with his consistent reduction of the separation between the poet's 'own being and whatever is not himself: the world of natural objects, of other human beings, society, or God' ('DA' 6) to what is, to him, the essence of this separation: the split between consciousness and its objects, which finds its 'purest' instantiation in the conflict between the mind and the world (or, more accurately, the earth) of natural being. The acknowledgment of this last point is a rigorous necessity, for only in thinking it through can one adequately enter into a dialogue with the common accusation that de Man's is a theory steeped in a sovereign indifference to matters political, social, and (even) historical. The point is that there is a difference between indifference and the insistence on a difference in priority between foundations and side-effects, irrespective of the considerable and at times quite maddening vacillation to which this latter attitude is subject.

The present point, in any event, is clear enough, and de Man illustrates it by quoting a thesis from Roland Barthes's *Writing Degree Zero* which he deems to be effectively demolished by Empson's 'irrefutable critique by anticipation.' 'It is because there is no reconciliation in society,' Barthes writes, 'that language, at once necessary and necessarily oriented, institutes a torn condition for the writer.' Moreover, for Barthes, this lack of reconciliation in society is an identifiable modern historical condition which can be set off against a truly universal classical period, and which can also be superseded by 'a "new Adamic world where language would no longer be alienated,"' a view which, to de Man, falls 'all at once into all the traps of impatient 'pastoral' thought: formalism, false historicism, and utopianism' (241).[8] Evidently, the future of criticism must be sought elsewhere.

Of what, then, can a true historical poetics consist? Once again,

it is essential to note that de Man's (possibly rather too facile) denunciation of Marxist criticism in general and Barthes's historical
narrative in particular by no means entails an antihistorical attitude.[9] Contrary to what is often averred, de Man's critical views on
what is called 'history' are themselves fundamentally prompted by
an explicit commitment to acquire a more adequate understanding
of history. It may well be objected that such an avowed commitment, especially as it styles itself in the mode of conclusive pathos,[10]
is in itself not sufficient as proof of an actual commitment, but
such an in-itself undoubtedly healthy suspicion is what remains to
be grounded precisely, and such grounding must always occur as
a reading. What, then, again, is Road 3?

> A profoundly historical poetics would attempt to think the sepa-
> ration in truly temporal dimensions instead of imposing on it
> cyclical or eternalist schemata of a spatial nature. Poetic con-
> sciousness, which emerges from this separation, *constitutes* a cer-
> tain time as the noematic correlative of its action. Such a poet-
> ics promises nothing except the fact that poetic thought can
> keep on becoming, beyond its failure to ground itself in space.
> Although it is true that a poetics of this kind has not found ex-
> pression in an established critical language, it nonetheless lies,
> at times in a conscious form, at the basis of great poetic works.
> (242; translation emended)

The passage is of deceptive brevity, for it in fact rehearses almost
every problem we have come across up to this point—as is only
right, since it implicitly styles itself in the optative mode of an
announcement of future investigations into these problems, a modality that our commentary must try to respect.

A first point is that de Man does not, strictly speaking, mention a profoundly historical *criticism* and collapses the 'poetics' that
he does refer to with poetic consciousness as such, a move that
evidently follows from his implicit (and sometimes explicit) claim
that only this, as yet undeveloped, type of criticism can pretend to
a true understanding of the essence of poetry. Yet, with respect to

this last thesis, there is evidence of a profound vacillation on de Man's part: the question is whether all language called poetry can be said to partake of the essence of poetry, or whether only that poetry that actually does so is truly entitled to the name of poetry and thus worthy of concentrated reading by the true critic. We will encounter this ambiguity throughout de Man's work (although later on he will prefer to speak of literature rather than poetry). Indeed, this is one of the constitutive features of his work that has rankled his critics most immediately, for the fairly obvious reason that in one of its components such ambiguity appears to give rise to theses on the privileged nature of the literary over and above anything else, theses which have the further hypostatizing effect of restricting 'the literary' to a more or less circumscribed 'kind' of literature usually deemed coterminous with what is generally called Romanticism.[11] But what must interest us more specifically for the moment is de Man's statement to the effect that the true poetics he celebrates lies at the roots of (some) great works of poetry and this 'at times in a conscious form.' We recall that the initial difference between Baudelaire and Mallarmé pivoted upon the difference in self-consciousness ascribed to both poets respectively, and we saw how this differentiation brought with it some exceptionally heady conundrums. Here, as the emphasis has shifted onto the act of criticism, the difficulty can be restated (albeit not resolved) in terms that no longer need foreclose critical dialogue by forcing particular poets into a conscious and categorical *parti pris* for or against consciousness which is then said to be consistent or inconsistent with their shared commitment to language. Indeed, the task incumbent on the critic can now be understood as a tracing of the way in which a certain poetic consciousness, 'accessible' only (and only relatively so) through the opacity of poetic language, has '*constituted* a certain time as the noematic correlative of its action.' And given the ultimate inaccessibility of the actual, empirical consciousness of the individual poet, the critic will have to undertake this task in a reflection on his or her own conscious reading of the language that constitutes this noematic correlative—whether it be 'Baudelaire's' or 'Mallarmé's.' Or 'Hölderlin's.'

But what exactly is a 'noematic correlative'? In what we by now recognize as a characteristic bracketing of expository explicitness (perhaps partially prompted also by his assumption of and in a certain discourse then dominant), de Man stops short of explaining this concept, but the telling references to Husserl (and Roman Ingarden) elsewhere in the essay, as well as the earlier passage on the modalities of existence of the (Baudelaire's) cat, allow us to gain some insight into its meaning and, more in particular, its function in de Man's critical project. All too briefly put, noemata can be conceived of as 'objective correlatives' (not, to be sure, in the Eliotian acceptance of the term) pertaining to and constituted by consciousness. They are the 'unreal' *(irreell)* entities or units *(Einheiten)* that form the 'gegenständliche Sinn,' (the 'content,' so to speak) of the 'real' subjective (noetic) *Erlebnisse*. When it is said that all consciousness is consciousness *of* something, the noema is that to which this 'of' properly refers, but on no account is it to be confused with the real object envisaged by consciousness. This latter, on the contrary, is ultimately always the unattainable substratum of the noema itself. Thus, the something that consciousness is consciousness of is itself properly that which is constituted by consciousness in an intentional act as the intentional object which figures as a predicate of, and consequently does not coincide with, the real (or intended) object. Which is also to say that the noema is wholly dependent on the constitutive act of consciousness, whereas the real intended object, by its very nature, remains radically 'outside' of consciousness.[12] To paraphrase Sartre's self-confessed simplification of an example given by Husserl: if I see a cat, the noematic correlative of my real (noetic) act of perception is 'cat-perceived,' not, it should be stressed, the 'real cat.'[13] The fact, however, that the noema is not 'real' does not mean that it does not exist—its existence, precisely, resides in its being the intentional object of the intentional act, and thus also in its non-

The Future of Criticism | 149

coincidence with the real (intended) object (the cat in the flesh—and the bones).

We have seen that de Man often glosses this noncoincidence as a destruction of the object, and in this respect his reference to the (Husserlian notion of the) noema is a timely reminder that we should not take this gloss at face value (which, after all, would be somewhat inconceivable, unless one adheres to occult (and most impractical) doctrines of the withering word): the destruction or annihilation in question is, rigorously speaking, only a destruction of the illusion of coincidence itself, precisely insofar as it, to put it tautologically, *is* the separation that bars consciousness from having immediate access to the object—from 'communicating substantially with what is substantial in things.' The negation of the real object in consciousness is, more properly put, a negation of the inalienable otherness of this real object: the object itself is never reached, and the noema in effect only negates the possibility of a non-negating comprehension of the real object, which is also to say that it negates the possibility of a real negation through comprehension of that object. Constituted by consciousness, the noema negates the real object as a real object in consciousness only, and it is in this 'invulnerability' of the real object that, as de Man sees it, the notion of its (ontological) priority or superiority over consciousness is rooted, as an acknowledgment of the ultimate ineffectualness of the negation of the object's otherness in consciousness, as a recognition of the fact that this negation is, in the final analysis, only ever a mute and blind affirmation of what must of necessity exceed all discursive practice.

But in the passage under scrutiny, de Man is no longer speaking of cats but of the separation itself as an object of consciousness. The reason for this shift is that the passage considers language and history rather than 'mere' perception. Language, we recall, *states* the essential separation because of its status as mediation; it introduces the separation in its most forbidding reality because, as mediation, it 'negates' immediacy. This is true of all language, but the language of poetry, insofar as it draws attention to itself, forces the reading consciousness to reflect upon this separation. And it is this reflection, itself also the reflection of the poetic consciousness as such, which constitutes 'a certain time'—that is, true temporality—as its noematic correlative. Exactly how the link between the reflection on separation and temporality is established is not explicitated. De Man submits that this reflection constitutes time as the 'content' of its intentional act, and this insofar as it discovers the impossibility for consciousness to found itself in space (that is to say, in an identification with real substance which would also enable the reflection to coincide with itself by homologizing its act with the object constitutive of that act), and insofar as such reflection necessarily develops, dialectically, in time; but he does not elaborate the point and indeed confesses that it has not yet been established in a critical language. Such a critical language would, presumably, have to go beyond merely *stating* that the noema of poetic consciousness (which could be circumscribed as 'separation-thought' (or 'separation-intended') is temporality in its true, nonspatial dimension and that this temporality is, finally, the 'sorrowful time of patience, that is to say, history' (245). It would have to argue the case.

In de Man's doctoral dissertation, defended some four years after the publication of 'Impasse de la critique formaliste,' this is not exactly what happens, but the 'same' statement is rendered there in a way that manages to pinpoint the crucial problems of the dialectic still under construction here. Speaking of Mallarmé, de Man writes,

> The poet chooses the road of consciousness, in full awareness of the danger this road involves. Indeed, it is by becoming fully aware of the danger of its predicament that the mind reaches the highest point of its development. . . . By making his decision in favor of thought and of the poetic work, man creates for himself an extremely tenuous entity: the unreal and fragile *time* of the poetic fiction. . . . thought, as Mallarmé conceives of it, *engenders* time as the mediating entity between consciousness and the chaos of immediate reality. The language of thought

contains time as a substance in which consciousness can remain suspended. Within this temporal substance can take place the 'legs à quelqu'un' which . . . characterize the historicity of a universal consciousness. ('PHD M,' 114–16)

Despite (because of) their authoritative tone, these theses remain very problematic. They are, in fact, the problems that the critical language de Man speculates on in 'Impasse de la critique formaliste' will have to come to terms with if it is ever to gain a true understanding of poetry—if ever it will. And terms, of course, remain themselves the problem—or, rather, *the* term remains the problem: the term named, for instance, by Hegel as the culmination of the dialectic (the 'universal consciousness' in the foregoing passage is, after all, quite as audacious as Hegel's *Geist*—or perhaps even Husserl's *Bewußtsein*). The project of a historical poetics is still, essentially, that of a promise, and the promise remains a choice for a direction indicated by a signpost on a map whose lines gradually grow less discernible. The term of the promise as it is stated in 'Impasse de la critique formaliste' is, moreover, initially negative only: this project promises nothing, de Man writes, except for the future of a poetic thought that will, discontinuously, continue to become, 'beyond its failure to found itself in space' ('DF' BI, 247; translation emended). And even though this promising voice is increasingly identified as that of the poetic consciousness essentially understood as a reading, 'interpreting' consciousness, this is evidently not to say that the rhetoric of volitional pathos has been left behind, and we will find it lingering on for a long time still in the work to come, at times even more prominent than we have yet encountered. The underlying structure that forces this pathos to declare itself is, again, the dialectic of desire in which the project is caught up: the poetic consciousness desires a solid foundation, is forced to reflect upon the essential separation that forbids such foundation, and is sent off into (the) becoming (of history) again.

The structure remains that of a repetition—not, however, as de Man takes pains to point out in a later essay, the repetition of an originary experience of lost unity, but the repetition of a desire for such repetition, which is always the repetition of the failure of the repetition of the originary experience of unity. Language, poetic language, does not repeat the experience of unity but only repeats itself, language. The reader (or the poet as reader) can be deluded into believing that (his or her) language actually repeats the unity, and this precisely, and understandably, because this language repeats the desire for this unity—but, ultimately, only the desire is repeated, not the unity of the originary, which remains radically silent. As de Man observes,

> It is . . . in the hope of breaking the silence that [the poet] invents words. But inasmuch as the words are only his own, they repeat *themselves;* they do not repeat *anything else.* If that were not so, Orpheus would not have had to address himself to creatures; he would only have had to listen to them. Art is not an imitation (or a repetition) but an endless longing for imitation, which by virtue of imitating itself, hopes finally to find a model. In other words, poetic language is not an originary language, but is derived from an originary it does not know; consequently, as a language, it is mediate and temporal. ('F' CW, 87; translation emended) [14]

Those who think otherwise, as we know now, are goaded by the 'impatience of a period whose predominant quality consists in the acuity of its self-consciousness'—and only in the painful time of patience (history) that such consciousness really demands and constitutes can criticism begin to read (87). [15]

De Man's poetics are still founded in a reactive attitude feeding off the ontological bad faith of others—but we also note that an increasing interest in actual problems of reading and interpretation, seen to be inseparable from questions of history, comes to supplement (and thus promises to recast) the aprioristic extralinguistic ideological dichotomies that served as an initial scaffolding for this poetics. But as de Man's next move shows, to read this note as a synopsis of a comprehended history of his thought is (un)fortunately impossible.

CHAPTER EIGHT

Reversal of
Priority

He for whom what is of the order of the thing *[das Dinghafte]*
is radically evil, and who wishes to dynamise everything that
is into pure actuality, is inclined to hostility against the other,
the alien, the name of which does not sound in alienation for
nothing.—Adorno, *Negative Dialektik*

A s its title already indicates, 'Structure intentionnelle de
l'Image romantique' (first published in 1960) proposes
to pursue yet again the inextricably coimplicit fundamental concerns of de Man's previous essays: the question of language
(as intentionality) and the question of history (here present as the
problem of Romanticism).[1] This, however, is not necessarily to say
that this pursuit also implies a felicitous methodological or critical
sophistication. On the contrary, rather, 'Structure intentionnelle'
in many ways marks a regression from some of the more promising insights de Man had been trying to articulate elsewhere—
although, as a regression from a rigor not yet attained, this development was also always already eminently possible.[2] It is the first
essay in which de Man devotes focused (albeit still rudimentary)
attention to the formidable English and French counterparts of
his initial favorite Hölderlin—Rousseau and Wordsworth—but it
is only in his later readings of these poets that the potential of
this enlarged scope is substantially worked through. It is therefore

somewhat unfortunate that this text has been frequently singled out as a major and representative instance of de Man's early work. Alternately, however, the essay does have the advantage of sketching in an accessible fashion the difficulties central to our purpose (by failing, in fact, to live up to the level of rigor they require), so that a brief consideration of its argument can profitably serve as a provisional conclusion to de Man's work of the 1950s.

But before we can move on to this conclusion there is another, more polemical issue to be dealt with, an issue that does not as such dominate the essay but which has been its burden ever since Frank Lentricchia marshaled it as a platform from which to launch his surprisingly influential attacks on de Man.[3] Enough has been said already about Lentricchia's crude conception of critical debate as a rap act for real men with attitude set to sounds sampled from Ennio Morricone scores (it is catching), so perhaps we had better move to his level at once and accept the challenge: Lentricchia shows us his early de Man as a don 'in the philosophical garb of the Sartrean existentialist,'[4] and the garments indeed tell a plain tale—but who owns them, and who makes the marionette move?

Unclaimed Garments

Lentricchia presumably had not read de Man's 1950s work when he wrote *After the New Criticism;* if he had, he would not have asserted that de Man 'almost never quotes (or even alludes) to *[sic]* the primary philosophical texts.'[5] Still, Lentricchia has read Sartre's 1940 study *L'Imaginaire* (to which de Man, incidentally, refers in 'Tentation de la permanence' [CW, 36]), so it is slightly surprising that he does not point out that the title of de Man's essay, 'Structure intentionnelle de l'Image romantique,' echoes and expands the title of Sartre's 1938 article 'Structure intentionnelle de l'image,' which became the first part of *L'Imaginaire.* The allusion, however, if any, does not stop there, and neither does de Man's use of the term 'noematic correlative' find its sufficient ground in Sartre's use of it in the same 1938 article 'Structure intentionnelle de l'image.'[6] Such a ground should rather be looked for in Husserl's phenomenology, on which Sartre avowedly relies, and while it is likely that de Man's interest in Husserl was stimulated by Sartre, this hardly stands up as evidence for his having been a Sartrean existentialist.[7]

But Lentricchia is above this kind of philological niggling: he has found 'solid conceptual clues in de Man's writing which point us directly to Sartre.' One of these clues is that the opposition between consciousness and object as deployed by de Man merely 'picks up and accommodates to romantic literary contexts *pour soi* and *en soi,* the key terms of Sartre's phenomenological ontology.' One feels foolishly pedantic in pointing this out, but the fact that *en soi* and *pour soi* indeed play prominent parts in Sartre's philosophy does not really make Hegel (or Husserl, or Kant) a follower of Sartre (the reverse, it will be agreed, is altogether more likely).[8] Apparently, the impact of Sartre on a certain kind of intellectual historiography is so overwhelming that it can transform bad logic into a solid conceptual clue at the turn of an unread page. Lentricchia's second clue consists of the link between 'Sartre's' analytic dichotomy and the dynamics of good and bad faith, authentic and inauthentic existence, and here he is almost convincing in arguing that de Man follows Sartre in the latter's attempt to evade Heidegger's tendency to equate *logos* and *physis* in his later work. Almost: for as I have tried to show, de Man's dialogue with Heidegger is more complicated than such a narrative of aversion can suggest, and the principal opposition to a possible inauthentic acquiescence in Heidegger's work in this dialogue derives from Hegel and Heidegger himself, not from Sartre.[9] Still, if it were merely a matter of establishing de Man's sources, our disagreements with Lentricchia would be fairly trivial in that they would only suggest that Sartre was less important as an influence than were Heidegger and Hegel. Thus to revise a genealogy can be entertaining but rarely adds up to an argument, and in this case it runs the further risk of being nothing more than yet another contribution to the gutting of Saint-Germain-des-Prés. This is why it is important to specify that the real interest of this debate lies elsewhere, in a difference between de Man and Sartre that has more to do with literature than with a philosophical fancy-dress party.

The title of de Man's 1960 essay, 'Structure intenionnelle de l'Image romantique,' already contains this difference by expanding Sartre's title in a reference to literature and its history: indeed de Man is primarily concerned with the *Romantic* image, and his reading of this image as literature substantially differs from Sartre's. What is arguably at stake here is a certain development in Sartre's thought on literature, leading from his remarkable close readings of the late 1930s and the first half of the 1940s (later collected in *Situations I*), which certainly caught de Man's admiring attention,[10] to a hardening of what was already problematic in these readings in the essays that came to make up Sartre's *Qu'est-ce que la littérature?* (1948). It is partly as a largely implicit resistance to what became prominent in this later work, rather than as an 'accommodation' of Sartrean terms to literature, that de Man's writing of the 1950s takes shape.

Already in his triumphalist 1939 celebration of Husserl, Sartre had hailed the notion of intentionality as a deliverance from the reign of Proust, whose 'vie intérieure' he regards as particularly noxious to any viable conception of the imagination.[11] Although this rejection of Proust is not yet a consistent feature of Sartre's thought at the time,[12] it does participate in the general movement (oddly neglected by Lentricchia) toward 'committed' realism *(littérature engagée)* in his aesthetics, which is also evident in his expressions of deep admiration for an author like John Dos Passos ('the greatest writer of our time,' as Sartre put it in 1938).[13] In his 1956 review of Nathalie Sarraute's *L'Ere du soupçon*, de Man leaves no doubt as to what he thinks of this privileging of Dos Passos over Proust, which he calls a 'historical concoction . . . whose chief culprits are the Sartre of *Situations I* and the Claude-Edmond Magny of *L'Age du roman américain*,' and which bases itself on arguments 'that have nothing to do with literature' ('SN' CW, 62). The point is, for de Man, that such authors as Proust and Joyce 'question the novel's *possibility of being;* their work implies the failure of the fictive, in the same way that Mallarmé's implies the failure of the poetic,' whereas such authors as Dos Passos, Hemingway, and Steinbeck write novels that run no such risk, 'and with reason: we do not expect to see a good producer declare the merchandise he manufactures to be useless or dangerous.'[14]

We have seen that Mallarmé's poetics of failure are conceived of by de Man as a predicament intimately related to Romanticism, and in this respect it is useful to relate de Man's rejection of Sartre here to the blind spot in Sartre's earlier history of the image in *L'Imagination* (1936), which occurs precisely at the moment where Romanticism should have been considered. The passage is curious and can be taken as symptomatic of Sartre's inability to come to terms with Romantic thought: in the course of one paragraph, he jumps from the suggestion that Romanticism 'might have spelled a complete renewal of the problem of the image' along lines very different from those of the classical metaphysical systems he opposes, to the observation that already in 1865, this Romantic conception was being ousted by determinism and mechanicism.[15] What Romantic conception? Romanticism itself is never properly engaged, and I would suggest that it is this neglect, and the gross myth of a deliverance from a literature of interiorization through committed realism that it entails (this is the *telos* of literature Sartre has the audacity to name), that de Man must have found unacceptable.

A further disagreement between de Man and Sartre, closely linked to their different views on the history of literature, concerns the definition of language and literature as such. Already in *L'Imaginaire* (1940), Sartre ventures a thesis on the role of the word in signification as a purely instrumental one,[16] but it is in *Qu'est-ce que la littérature?* (1948) that the implications of this view are categorically spelled out:

> Poets are men who refuse to *utilize* language. Now, since the quest for truth takes place in and by language conceived of as a certain kind of instrument, it is unnecessary to imagine that they aim to discern or expound the true. Nor do they dream of *naming* the world, and, this being the case, they name nothing at all, for naming implies a perpetual sacrifice of the name to the object named, or, as Hegel would say, the name is revealed as the inessential in the face of the thing which is essential.[17]

What must interest us here is not so much the exaggerated opposition between poetry and prose in which this passage functions,[18] but rather the characterization of poetry as a project singularly unconcerned with what is true and thus opposed to the sacrifice of naming. For while Sartre's echo of Hegel here is echoed in de Man's assertion against Heidegger that the separation effected by language leaves 'all the inessential on the side of the word' ('HE' BI, 259), the point of the echo is that for de Man this *is* precisely the process of poetry. Poetry is emphatically concerned with naming, in this naming it establishes the separation, and it is in its recognition of this separation that it performs its commitment to what is true. Where Sartre sees an essential difference between the service of the word in poetry and the sacrifice of the word in prose, de Man sees a sacrificial service of the word in a concern for what is true, which is itself the essence of true literature. From de Man's 1950s perspective, the reification of the word that Sartre ascribes to poetry is precisely what poetry always opposes, and it is only in its resistance to such a reification that reading can save poetry from being relegated to the realm radically beyond the reach of critical dialogue and thus of commitment in which *Qu'est-ce que la littérature?* would want to confine it.

This resistance is in fact analogous to that against Löwith and certain aspects of Heidegger: it emphatically does not consist of a dissociation of poetry from commitment but opposes precisely the poetics that would impose such a dissociation. One of de Man's most categorical statements in this respect occurs in his dissertation, in a discussion of 'whether political action should not take precedence over poetic speculation,' where he writes that the only way to seriously confront this issue is not by taking recourse to 'collective, historical aspects of reality' but by following Mallarmé's 'admirably uncompromising attitude.' The 'way to be present to one's own time begins in total inwardness, certainly not out of an indifference towards history, but because the urgency of one's concern demands lucid self-insight; action will follow from itself, when this insight has been gained' ('PHD M,' 102). Whether or not one cares to subscribe to this extraordinary faith in the efficacy of poetic reflection,[19] it certainly cannot be denounced as a refusal to engage the question of commitment: to the contrary, what de Man here proposes amounts to a critique of Sartre's concept of commitment as not nearly going far enough.[20]

Again, none of this is to say that Sartre was not also an influence on de Man. The point is that the influence that Sartre clearly did exert was neither idiosyncratic nor decisive; more important, if one wanted to usefully assess this influence it would be better not to exaggerate the nonspecific similarities when the differences are so much more fruitful. Fruitful, by the way, is an appropriate word here. First, because it calls to mind Sartre's metaphor for the poet's conception of words: 'They are natural things which sprout naturally upon the earth like grass and trees.'[21] And second, because it is precisely this conception that de Man's 'Intentional Structure'—Lentricchia's prime body of evidence—vehemently combats. I am not certain whether this conceptual conflict is an allusion, a solid conceptual clue, or some other intertextual effect, but I doubt whether it could be adduced as evidence for de Man's ever having been a Sartrean existentialist. In any event, the distance here measured between Sartre and de Man should suffice to unsettle Lentricchia's score and to open the 1960 essay up to a more responsible, and in fact more critical, reading.

Temptational Structure of the Romantic Image

D e Man begins 'Intentional Structure' with the observation that the status of the image as a unit of Western literature is subject to historical variations; he suggests that a history of literature could be conceived on the basis of an investigation into the modifications of this unit. For the time being, however, he narrows his scope down to the development of Romanticism since the end of the eighteenth century and observes the emergence of 'a dialectic that is more paradoxical than may appear at first sight' ('IS' RR, 2): the simultaneous increase in the poetic attention devoted to material substance (nature) and to metaphorical diction. The image—whether one calls it symbol, or metaphor, or even myth—becomes, as he states elsewhere, 'the most revealing stylistic unit of all romantic poetry' ('WBY' RR, 151), and what it reveals is a tension 'which never ceases to be problematic' ('IS' RR, 2) between the 'immediate presence of matter and of physical elements' in the object and the 'non-presence of the object' in the image.[22] De Man then briefly illustrates his point by considering the intentional structure of the Romantic image insofar as it is marked by a tension apparent in what he elsewhere calls 'anomalies of language' in the poet's production ('WBY' RR, 147). Such anomalies occur when language reaches out for a self-justification or foundation that belongs to a 'meta-logical' or 'anti-logical' realm and overreaches itself in doing so; when, in other words, a certain 'experience'—which may itself be 'coherent'—comes to be voiced in its supposed 'linguistic equivalence,' which, however, 'falls prey to the logical discontinuity that disrupts the natural image' (157–58).

A prototype of these anomalies of the logos is the concluding line of the fifth stanza of Hölderlin's 'Brod und Wein':

> . . . nun aber nennt er sein Liebstes,
> Nun, nun müssen dafür Worte, wie Blumen, entstehen.

> [. . . but now he names his most treasured possession,
> Now for it words like flowers leaping alive he must find.] [23]

De Man immediately points out that the choice of the verb 'ent-stehen' reveals that the 'Worte' in question cannot be read as 'those of ordinary speech,' for in everyday language words are instruments of communicative transaction, which, precisely, are not supposed to originate as something new. Everyday words are like fixed names and thus do not properly participate in the *act* of naming, which is known by the poets as 'a return to the source, to the pure motion of experience at its beginning' ('IS' RR, 3). Initially, this characterization of the act of naming is surprising, for has not de Man also taught us that 'poetic language is not an originary language' ('F' CW, 87) and that it establishes 'the eternal separation between the spirit that distinguishes, negates, legislates, and the originary simplicity of the natural' ('DF' BI, 239), thus developing 'an initial experience into an infinity of associated experiences that spring from it' (236)? But at closer consideration this contradiction reveals itself as part of the dialectic of contradictions that de Man is not only trying to expose but in which he also uneasily participates throughout the essays written in this period. In fact, the principle of (a specific poetic) intentionality was introduced precisely in response to this difficulty—even though, as we shall see, this gesture by no means resolves the problem.

The verb 'entstehen,' de Man continues, also functions as the specific *tertium comparationis* of the metaphor. 'The fundamental intent of the poetic word is to originate in the same manner as what Hölderlin here calls "flowers" ' ('IS' RR, 3). The poetic word intends to name 'Being as presence' and projects this intention into a desire to coincide with the origination of the 'flower'—enter the anomaly, as indicated by the reservation of the quotation marks, for that is exactly what language can never do. According to de

Man, the desire to name the *parousia* of Being is an absolutely impossible (and hence supremely possible) desire, since naming necessarily implies mediation and thus separation. The image of the flower owes its attractiveness precisely to its power to deceive consciousness into believing the opposite: that it can truly partake of Being in an act of naming which would not separate. For the flower, as in fact any (intended) real (as opposed to intentional and *irreell*) object, is marked (albeit imaginarily) by just that 'absolute identity with itself' (6) which would overcome this separation.

The conception of the 'entstehen' of the flower as a model for the production of language also contains an ontological paradox that further contributes to the seductive power of the image: flowers cannot properly be said to 'originate' in the first place, since their becoming and development is at all times identical to their source—theirs is the movement of growth already attacked in Malraux's trees. They are thus entirely literal (where literal may be read as a linguistic nonconcept for the nonlinguistic, as a metaphor for the real, as an index of the dream of language to move beyond its constitution as language).[24] And this forces the image into an irresolvable contradiction, which, however, is overruled by the desire to be seduced invested in it. De Man, needless to say, is determined not to be taken in:

> It would follow then, since the intent of the poetic word is to originate like a flower, that it strives to banish all metaphor, to become entirely literal.
>
> We can understand origin only in terms of difference: the source springs up because of the need to be somewhere or something else than what is now here. The word 'entstehen,' with its distancing prefix, equates origin with negation and difference. But the natural object, safe in its immediate being, seems to have no beginning and no end. Its permanence is carried by the stability of its being, whereas a beginning implies a negation of permanence, the discontinuity of a death in which an entity relinquishes its specificity and leaves it behind, like an empty shell.

Entities engendered by consciousness originate in this fashion, but for natural entities, like the flower, the process is entirely different. (4)

There are, then, two deceptions in the image of the flower: first, it seems to offer consciousness a foundation in the undivided realm of the natural object; and second, it introduces the positivity of growth and nonconscious movement as a permanent and continuous alternative for the discontinuities of the becoming proper characteristic of consciousness. The fact that flowers actually also fade, wither, and die, which would appear to disrupt the illusion of continuity, is of no consequence: apart from the fact that such vegetal death can always be recuperated in *si-le-grain-ne-meurt* narratives, the exteriority of the flower to consciousness, which the image in fact pretends to overcome, paradoxically also prevents consciousness from participating in the death of the flower as its own, that is, from experiencing the discontinuity in the death of the natural object *as* discontinuity.[25] There seem to be no limits to what images can get away with ('R' AR, 62).

The poetic word correctly understood, however, admittedly may intend to name the undivided 'origin' of the natural, but, as de Man puts it later on in the essay, it inevitably remains caught in the process of naming '*pure* origin' only, the origin of that which has no reality prior to (or otherwise outside of) the act of its origination, which has in fact no (Husserlian) reality at all. Such true origination, therefore, is always divided and discontinuous:

> For it is in the essence of language to be capable of origination, but of never achieving the absolute identity with itself that exists in the natural object. Poetic language can do nothing but originate anew over and over again; it is always constitutive, able to posit regardless of presence but, by the same token, unable to give a foundation to what it posits except as an intent of consciousness. The word is always a free presence to the mind, the means by which the permanence of natural entities can be put

into question and thus negated, time and again, in the endlessly widening spiral of the dialectic. (6)

This passage would appear to imply that insofar as Hölderlin's line seems to state the very opposite, he too would have to be denounced (alongside Malraux, Baudelaire, Heidegger . . .) for having fallen prey to the temptation of permanence. Such, however, is predictably—and consistently—not the case. Apart from the fact that this particular trope is, as de Man says 'en passant,' 'far from exhaust[ing] Hölderlin's own conception of the poetic image' (7), and in keeping with the assertion that if Hölderlin's rhetoric, like that of Yeats, 'is able to deceive the reader, it can never deceive the author' ('WBY' RR, 205), the fundamental point is that the burden of the problem indeed lies on the shoulders of the reader (be he the author) as the critic entrusted with the task to develop a critical language (i.e., to read) with which to read this possible deception as it is read by the poet. Needless to say, this tautology once more leaves in suspension the actual grounding of the particular judgment applied to particular poets, and the remainder of the essay makes it embarrassingly clear that de Man is still very far from being ready to offer a viable and articulate answer to this unavoidable question. Yet, the analysis of this disappointing revelation is itself singularly instructive.

In the third section of the essay, de Man proposes to explore how this type of image *has* in fact been read by the heirs of Romanticism. The conception underlying the Romantic natural image, he rehearses, is itself founded on the assurance of an 'intrinsic ontological primacy of the natural object,' and the language used in an intention governed by this assurance unfolds its becoming in accordance with the desire to attain this ontological status: but 'this movement is essentially paradoxical and condemned in advance to failure,' as is evident in the profound 'crisis of the poetic imagination' in nineteenth- and twentieth-century poetry.[26] We are already all too familiar with this deadlock to have to spell it out again; what is new (apart from the only relatively important fact that this is the first time that de Man actually speaks of the *ontological* primacy of the object in so many words), is that after having made some remarks illustrating his thesis (mainly on Mallarmé), de Man suddenly launches himself into a decisive rhetoric of redemption which not only relapses into the muddle of the dichotomous choice projected onto the poet, but which also opens up to a critical suggestion which, if pursued, would seriously impair the potential for rigorous reading we have found tentatively promised at various stages in this early work.

To escape from the deadlock inscribed in the contradictory intentional structure of the Romantic image, de Man suggests, poetic thought has to return to the founding premise of this image (the ontological primacy of the object), which means, in practical terms, that to find indices of what this could amount to, the critic would be well advised to turn to the precursors of Romanticism, in whose thought this founding premise was not yet consolidated but only 'one among several alternative roads.'[27] The final movement of the essay then answers this suggestion by looking at the 'other roads' that still lay open for Rousseau, Wordsworth, and Hölderlin. We are not here primarily concerned with the (poor) technical detail of de Man's analysis of a long extract from *Julie,* some forty lines from *The Prelude,* and about twenty lines from the first two stanzas of 'Heimkunft'—what matters is, again, the conclusion that de Man draws from this swift reading.

All three passages describe the ascent of consciousness from a position of being caught in a deeply divided and paradoxical nature, toward a consciousness that is no longer fettered in this contradiction but is appeased at last in the inner tranquillity it had lost. In each case the ascent develops in response to a transfer of the ontological priority 'previously' ascribed to the natural object onto something which, unlike the flower, is no longer an object: the word no longer originates 'like' a fruit of the earth (which, of course, it never really did), but is now asserted to have become the 'fruit of the sky.' This means that the 'ontological priority' now resides where it had never resided before, 'in an entity that could still . . . be called 'nature,' but could no longer be equated with matter, objects, earth, stones, or flowers' (15). Ultimately, the three poets are said to resemble Wordsworth's clouds—they become 'Cerulean ether's pure inhabitants' and theirs is the imagination lifting itself up as 'unfather'd vapour' in Wordsworth's famous apostrophe of this faculty after the Simplon-letdown. In the light of what we have read in his earlier essays, de Man's description of this imagination is deeply disturbing:

> It marks a possibility for imagining and thinking consciousness to suffice unto itself, independently of all relationship with an exterior object, and without being moved by an intention aimed at such an object. (16; translation modified)

It is clear that this type of imagination is radically incompatible with the notion of eternal separation established by language as a necessarily mediating and thus temporalizing instance.[28] It in fact marks the reverse image of the temptation of permanence sought in natural being by introducing the temptation of the permanence of a completely self-contained self-reflection—a temptation to which de Man is unfortunately close to succumbing in this particular passage, and to which he indeed does fall prey in a hypothetical mode. Circling back to the problem as we have sketched it before, we can say, with some overstatement, that it is at this point (more so even than at the *locus* of the 'universal consciousness' we referred to earlier on) that de Man imitates the imprudence of Hegel in giving a name to the *telos* of his dialectic (it is not merely by accident that the imagination invoked here *'lifts itself up'*), although one should perhaps add that this particular *telos* bears more similarity to a rather cheerful reading of Hegel's *das leblose Einsame* (or his stoic, or his Master) than to his *absoluter Geist;* or, similarly, we can submit that it is here that we find de Man, mutatis mutandis, imitating Heidegger's 'violent and blind exegetic passion' by imposing unity on the very instance that must, by its ineluctable law, forever foreclose such imposition. It is true that de Man does not go so far as to explicitly state that this imagination can lay claim to ontological priority, but the fact that the 'sky' for which it is said to nostalgically yearn and which does receive such priority as its distinctive feature is by implication thought of as internal to the imagination (which does not entertain any relations to the external and instead 'se suffit à elle-même') already indicates that the underlying movement engendering this new notion in the final analysis leads to just that: the ontological priority of consciousness. It is not insignificant that this problematic turn occurs at a moment when de Man explicitly considers, for the first time in his work, the canonical poets of interiority and self-reflection, Wordsworth and, above all, Rousseau. One is tempted to imagine a story in which this encounter figures as the event leading the critic to 'a kind of Lorelei-like perdition' ('IG' CW, 17), but there is every reason for handling such alluringly intelligible narratives with extreme caution.

However this may be, the fact that we are, after all, engaged in a dialectic entails that the damage wrought by the present thesis (which, moreover, is presented as a possibility rather than an actuality) may be limited only, and de Man enforces the hypothetical mode of his untenable name in the conclusion to the essay.

> We do not know, to be honest, whether the poetic language coming from such an imagination would still produce images similar to those we are familiar with. The works of early romanticism, with the sole possible exception of certain poems of Hölderlin written shortly before his madness, give us no actual examples, for they are, at most, *underway* toward such intuitions and come from the mixed and self-contradictory regions that we encountered in the three passages. We still misunderstand these poets, as criticism has traditionally called 'pantheistic' the writers who are perhaps the first, in the Western Hellenic and

Christian tradition, to have put into question, in the language of poetry, the ontological priority of the sensible object. In further reflecting on this oscillation in the ontological status of the image, perhaps we can better understand the true nature of the crisis that seems to leave contemporary poetic language under the steady sign of menace, even while it leaves it the depository of hopes of resurrection that no other activity of the spirit seems able to offer. ('IS' RR, 16–17; translation modified) [29]

The rhetoric of renunciation, of hope, of the road, the menace and the crisis, points us in the right direction. As we have repeatedly observed, these figures play prominent parts in the insecure dialectic that de Man tries to develop in his early essays, and the distressing *telos* of the self-sufficient imagination can be regarded as the all-too-obvious escape that any dialectic is bound to shadow forth as an answer to its own logic and the problems it generates.

The name of the unfathered imagination, and, more crucially still, the postulate of its hypothetical offspring, are a quasi-mechanical consequence of the very model of the choice we have seen to be operative throughout. We noted how this choice gradually revealed itself to be an imperative to renounce the temptation of reconciliation on a trajectory which would take the shape of a succession of failures, or 'deaths,' and how this imperative claimed to be completely subservient to a law of language wholly indifferent to the wishful thinking of the alienated mind. This notwithstanding, the trajectory commanded by this imperative would not be a mere mapping out of a static paralysis; far from being a succession of completely meaningless failures, it would consist of an incremental (or perhaps ceremental) repetition in which the mind would somehow 'grow' in consciousness. This growth would style itself against a capitulation to the ontological priority of natural being, but it would not therefore deny this priority—that is precisely the purpose of the introduction of the (Husserlian) notion of the intention as an activity that would honor the insurmountable separation without therefore rejecting the superior reality of the intended object. Yet, at the same time the principle of intentionality in de Man is still overdetermined by a powerful charge of intentionality considered as volition, and this volition in turn mar(k)s the dialectic with the rhetoric of existential pathos that echoes the seductive rhetoric of the deluded (Baudelaire, Malraux, Heidegger . . .) almost word for word.

This, then, is the double bind of de Man's project as it is outlined here: the imperative of renunciation[30] opposes the temptation of a reconciliation that would consist of a surrender to the ontological superiority of the natural object projected onto the seductive power of poetic language; but this imperative itself is voiced in a pathos-ridden discourse encumbered by an equally powerful suggestion of a different reconciliation, one that would preserve the precritical hierarchical dichotomy of the ontological difference in status by simply reversing the oppositional couple and claiming superiority for the subject rather than for the object.

Again, in terms of the rhetoric of sacrifice: de Man's earlier conception of the sacrifice of the object in the poetics of becoming ensured a persistent appreciation of the separation by virtue of the impossibility to actually accomplish this sacrifice, an impossibility that inflected the sacrificial act and directed it at the word itself, which in this inflection was revealed as the inessential. Now, with the concept of the autonomous imagination, the path is open for this rhetorically projected sacrifice to be completed along the *via negativa* of an exclusion of the object which is so absolute that, as against Sartre's conception of poetry, it also excludes the promotion of the word to the status of object. De Man's language, in short, is liable to lure him (and his reader) into the very trap whose danger he diagnosed in Heidegger's language. That is, having recognized the fallacy of a reconciliation of mind and nature, the rhetoric of the abyss in which de Man states this recognition invites the apotropaic refuge in another, but equally deluded, reconciliation; namely, the imagination as an entity wholly sufficient-unto-itself—a faculty which, if allowed to develop into a governing construct, would foreclose any ulterior reflection on reading and its supplementary relation to time and history, and would thus effectively end up in an ontological absolute beyond dialogue and commitment. But perhaps there is a dialogue, an 'unremitting *Auseinandersetzung*,' even if only in the order of sheer coincidence.[31]

The Question after Serenity

I n 1955, Martin Heidegger spoke his first public word *(Wort)* in Messkirch, his native town *(Heimatstad)*, on the occasion of a commemoration of his fellow native Conradin Kreutzer. The address is carried by an elegiac question:

> Is there still for man a quiet dwelling *[Wohnen]* between earth and sky? Does the meditating spirit *[der sinnende Geist]* still rule over the land? Is there still a home to take root in *[wurzel-kräftige Heimat]*, in whose soil *[Boden]* man can stand permanently *[ständig steht]*, that is to say, be native/rooted in the soil *[boden-ständig]*. . . . Or will everything be caught in the grip of planning and calculation, of organisation and automatic activity? [32]

In 1955, Paul de Man quotes a fragment from Rilke that expresses 'the disquiet of our age in the face of the menacing development of the technological world' by lamenting the substitution of our grandparents' intimate relation to 'a house, a well, a tower' by the empty and indifferent attitude to things he associates with America. De Man adds that it is not surprising that this text should also have been quoted by Heidegger, 'whose thought is so profoundly inspired by the horror he feels for any enslavement to technology' ('TP' CW, 30), but he immediately measures his distance, which is the distance of 'one [who] lives in this land of inhumane technology.' For 'under the immense skies of America stretches earth essentially unmarked as yet by technology, earth and sky that swallow the monstrous cities of industry.' In this emptiness, one has no support 'save that of thought,' in which one can think the

'virtue' of technology: that 'it is too rude to offer even a simulacrum of appeasement,' and can thus open up a critical reading of
the appeasement of the Old World:

> The security of Rilke's melancholy dreams, the security of our
> ancestors in their houses and vestments—was this real or is it
> merely a product of our imagination? And the appeasement we
> feel ourselves in thinking that they possessed this serenity—a
> thought that satisfies the spirit and lulls it to sleep at the same
> time—can we rely on this? Perhaps in the degree to which it
> is impoverishment and burns history without leaving material
> residue, technology forces us to rid ourselves of what is only a
> false serenity. (30–31) [33]

This European serenity is false in that it looks for 'shelter among
beautiful houses polished by history and among fields marked by
ancestral labour,' thus obscuring the 'essential' 'struggle' of man:
'the elaboration of his history with this physical entity that is given
to him and that, with Heidegger, one could name the Earth' (31).
This struggle takes the shape of the 'eternal conflict' between the
'resistant,' 'opaque,' and 'passive' earth and the 'transparency' of the
sky, in which man finds 'the model of the total liberty for which
he searches, and which is a perfect approximation of his action to
his being.' We know this movement to be that of the Hegelian dialectic of consciousness, a movement in which man often 'believes
in the triumph of one of these opposed forces': 'In the moments
of vigor and zest, it is to the sky that man believes himself equal,
and he escapes from all heaviness, rises towards pure transparency.
But in moments of fatigue, he hides himself in earth and believes
he finds repose there' (31). The rest of the essay is devoted to a
searching critique of this refuge in the earth as it is celebrated in
Malraux's trees and made possible in Heidegger's 'serene idea of
dwelling' (37), set off against the dialectic of true history which it
is the essential task for poetry as 'the quintessential historical act'
(33) to perform. But the rise toward the pure transparency of the
sky is left in suspension.

✱

In 1959, Heidegger published the text he had read in Messkirch in 1955. It is much more than a mere reaction of horror in the face of technology, and instead calls for another and finer relation with the technical world than that of simple opposition, a relation that both acknowledges technology's merits and keeps it in check—refusing to see it as 'the work of the devil' while simultaneously registering its potential preparation of 'an attack on life and on the essence of man.'[34] This threat can be read, perhaps more than for instance, in a 1955 statement of 'the American chemist Stanley,' quoted by Heidegger: 'The hour is near in which life will rest in the hand of the chemist, who can break down, build up, and change the living substance at will.' Heidegger proposes to name this 'attitude of a simultaneous Yes and No to the technical world with an old word: the *Gelassenheit* towards things.'[35] And when this *Gelassenheit* takes shape, he foresees a new future for the words of the poet he had quoted toward the beginning of his address:

> When the *Gelassenheit* towards things and the openness for the secret awaken in us, we could reach a new way, which leads to a new ground and soil *[Grund und Boden]*. In this soil the creating of lasting works *[bleibender Werke]* could strike new roots *[neue Wurzeln schlagen]*.
>
> Thus, in a changed manner and in a changing era, what Johann Peter Hebel says would anew become true: 'We are plants that—whether we like to admit it or no—must rise with their roots out of the earth, so as to be able to bloom and bear fruit in the ether.'[36]

✱

'Structure intentionnelle,' published in 1960, is de Man's first (and last) text in a Belgian journal since the war.[37] It speaks of a new way for poetry on which poets would become clouds and their words 'the fruit of the sky' ('IS' RR, 14–15). The goal of this way as it is projected in passages from Hölderlin, Rousseau, and Wordsworth, is peace:

The passages describe the ascent of consciousness, trapped within the contradictions of a half-earthly, half-heavenly nature which puts itself 'in opposition to itself,' towards another consciousness, in which this duality is appeased and in which is recovered 'that inner peace which (we had) lost for such a long time.' (It goes without saying that . . . this peace is far from having been definitively conquered. Yet it does not remain less true that . . . it is the existence of this moment of peace which definitively seals the destiny of the respective authors and marks it as being an essentially poetic destiny.) (15)[38]

Unlike Heidegger's practitioners of *Gelassenheit,* de Man's poets here emphatically do not occupy the in-between of earth and sky. Closer to Hebel's dictum, perhaps, they are radically uprooted, no longer connected to any native ground but raised to the total transparency of inner peace, released from 'the power of earthly things' (14). Like Heidegger's *Dasein* in *Sein und Zeit,* de Man's poetic consciousness now at last lays claim—albeit still only by implication—to the status of ontological superiority, and in this claim it envisages a term for the conflict of earth and sky in a 'nostalgia' for this latter, radically opposed to the pathos of the native soil pervading Heidegger's *Gelassenheit.* Here as much as in 1955, de Man's thought is of a nature to denounce this return to the native condition as an acquiescence in 'false serenity' ('TP' CW, 31), but such a denunciation is not pronounced (neither, for that matter, is Heidegger's name). Instead, de Man politely points out that Gaston Bachelard is mistaken in exclusively classifying 'images of repose with earth and not with air' ('IS' RR, 14) and warns that this 'nostalgia for the sky' should not be confused with a Christian nostalgia, as Christianity is a religion of incarnation: 'When a pure Christian like Alyosha Karamazov has his moment of truth, it is the earth which Dostoyevski makes him embrace.'[39] The echo of the criticism leveled at the passage in Malraux's *L'Espoir* in which a dead woman presses into and becomes part of the earth ('TP' CW, 31) is clear, but the more ringing echo is that of the illusory 'repose' sought in the earth by those who have abdicated the task of consciousness. Here, at least, it would appear that the opposition to the temptation of permanence can confidently expect its own, legitimate, repose in the sky, and perhaps it is this confidence which makes it no longer necessary to explicitly denounce those seeking refuge in the earth. Perhaps, in short, de Man's poet has finally recovered serenity.

'Sérénité' does occur (as does 'serein'), but only by way of the quotation from Rousseau from which the phrase 'paix intérieure' is lifted ('IS' RR, 10–11), which makes its absence in the passage on the ascension of the poets to the peace of the transparent sky (where serenity is etymologically at home) all the more conspicuous. For would not the ontologically superior sky of consciousness be the most appropriate realm for a recovery of, precisely, *true* serenity? For all that, de Man does not assume the word, and the peace that can be said to take its place '(is far from being definitively conquered)' (15). In fact, de Man takes pains, even against the grain of his argument (hence his parentheses), not to release poetic destiny from the labor of the negative and closes his essay in an exercise of commitment to the dialect of constant crisis and the hope of resurrection.

Perhaps 'serenity' (which can be translated as *Gelassenheit*) [40] is too loaded to be assumed, perhaps it is so strong that to assume it would too literally invite the end and the indifferent negation of the history that remains to be critically founded. Perhaps it would too overtly unmask the self-sufficient imagination as the faculty of complacency. [41] It is in a reflection on this excessive 'perhaps' that de Man's potentially disastrous capitulation to the celestial imagination must begin to be read. This reading lies ahead, and one of its principal moments is de Man's rereading of the poets here so enigmatically written into the sky—which is to say that our resistance to this apocalypse can provisionally take shape as a proleptic performance of the pathos of imperative return: from serenity to crisis. But this promise can never be more than a preface.

Notes

PREFACE

1. Eagleton 1983, 144.
2. Holdheim 1988, 4.
3. See 'AD' RR, 77.

PART ONE

1. For some reconstructions of this context the reader is referred to the volume of responses published as a companion to the facsimile edition of de Man's wartime journalism (Hamacher, Hertz, and Keenan 1989). A serious assessment of the more than 300 contributions to the debate on this journalism published to date cannot be given here.

CHAPTER ONE

1. In this, as in other respects, he followed in the footsteps of his uncle Hendrik de Man, who, some forty years earlier, had also turned from the natural sciences (in which, however, he was less successful than his nephew) and civil engineering to social sciences (cf. Hendrik de Man 1941, 44). For an instructive account of a possible relation between Hendrik de Man and Paul de Man, see Pels 1991. As I shall try to demonstrate, however, Pels is mistaken in casting Paul de Man as fundamentally a nationalist critic of 'cold' rationalism (39).
2. A full bibliography of de Man's wartime writings can be found in WJ, 388–99. I am indebted to E. Dedye, registrar at the Université Libre de Bruxelles, and to A. Despy-Meyer of the archives of that university, for their kind help in tracking the records of de Man's university years.
3. A particularly helpful sketch of the history of this demand is Lepenies 1988.
4. For further comment on this essay, see Bahti 1989, 2–3; and Hamacher 1989, 460–61.

5. De Man does not name sociology, but it is no coincidence that the authors he indicates as representatives of the model superseded by the psychological novel (especially Galsworthy, Wells, Bourget, and Mann) all wrote novels that were praised and/or condemned for their 'sociological' ambitions. On this score, see Lepenies 1988.

6. It is difficult not to suspect the influence of Hendrik de Man here, who, in his 1926 book on *The Psychology of Socialism,* came to castigate the Marxist analysis of society precisely on account of its putative inability to accommodate the psychological—as distinct from the socio-economical—motives of human behavior. Cf. Dodge 1966, 65–89.

7. LS, June 1941, 107. The analogy is de Man's, not Marañon's. The laboratory does appear in Marañon's methodological introduction, but only as 'the mystificatory laboratory of the pedagogues,' and he also registers some reservations as to the application of 'biological disciplines' to the study of history (1941, 3–4), a problem de Man must have been particularly sensitive to if, as is almost certainly the case, he took Raymond Jeener's course in the social sciences program of the Université Libre on 'Biology in its relations to the social sciences.' This is not the appropriate place for a discussion of Marañon's method—the important point is that we recognize de Man's presentation as a significant distortion.

8. In Marañon 1941, ix. De Monzie, apart from mentioning Marañon's intervention in the transition to the Republic that de Man refers to (see also Flesch 1989, 184), also rather gratuitously makes use of the occasion to underscore that the French people have never harbored any sentiments of Germanophobia.

9. Werner Hamacher accurately grasps this point when he writes that de Man's collaboration 'was *not* founded on pro-Nazi sympathies, but rather on a realism to which force appears as an authority that produces facts and justice' (1989), 454). Only a very few readings of de Man's actual writings under the occupation can compare with Hamacher's, and my only intent in response to it here is to specify the roots of de Man's realism in different detail.

10. Again, Hamacher, along with others, has admirably made this point: only when we ask not what 'motivated' de Man's collaboration but rather what '*did not prevent*' it, can we hope 'to isolate factors in the situation of intellectuals that would still, even today, not prevent a comparable commitment to a no less disastrous politics' (1989, 440).

It is not clear how carefully Hamacher has weighed the term 'isolate' here, but it is highly appropriate.

11. Here, too, de Man is close to his uncle, who associated abstraction, analysis, and mathematics (but also Marxism and metaphysics) with 'Jewish' as opposed to 'Germanic' thought, although he immediately added that that association was itself too abstract and general (Hendrik de Man 1941, 46; see also Pels 1991, 44–45).

12. Goethe, *Die Wahlverwandtschaften*, I, 4. The pun on *Scheidung* (separation, divorce) and *Scheidekünstler* (chemist) still works in Dutch *(scheiding, scheikunde)*. It is also explicitly signaled in the French translation de Man reviewed (Goethe, n.d., 60).

13. An almost exactly parallel but less developed argument appears in ls, April 1942, 218–19.

14. Carette, understandably, was not amused, as witness his oblique reply in an interview with de Man a week later, where he rejects the maxim that the author should be ruled by his characters as 'preposterous' and claims for the novelist 'the right to use his intelligence' (ls, March 1942, 210).

15. The point is repeated almost verbatim in bd, January 1943, 376. For a further analysis of Jünger's 'comprehension,' see de Graef 1990.

16. See also bd, January 1943, 376, where this same novel is praised for the scope it owes to the 'general data of a sociological nature' that it introduces.

17. The shift deserves to be stressed: most commentators on de Man's reviews of Jünger only indicate the early 'aesthetic,' 'apolitical,' or 'anti-epistemological' reading, not the later significant reversal that concerns us here (see e.g. Krueger 1989, 300; Stoekl 1989, 376–77).

18. Jünger's *Auf den Marmorklippen* was suspected of being an anti-Nazi allegory and was indeed banned in Germany at the time. See e.g. Krueger 1989, 302.

19. In fact, both nationalism and socialism are seen in *Der Arbeiter* as mere phenomena of transition toward the totalitarian state of the worker, a view which, at least as far as nationalism is concerned, is close to that expressed by Hendrik de Man at the time (see Dodge 1966, 177–78; 1979, 201). In any event, in 1932 Jünger was at least right about one thing: 'In a short while there will no longer be a political unity which does not try to operate through an appeal to socialism and to nationalism, and it has to be recognized that this phraseology is available

to anyone who has mastered the use of the twenty-four letters of the alphabet' (237).

20. At the end of November 1942 de Man ceases his publications in the daily press and in March 1943 he disappears from the pages of the *Bibliographie Dechenne*.

CHAPTER TWO

1. See the 'Editor's Notes' to Colinet 1989, 434 n. 6.
2. The 'Etymology' and the 'Extracts' are wholly cut, as are chapters 90, 95, 101 through 105, and 115, plus some of the author's notes and the odd paragraph. None of these cuts are acknowledged and it is impossible to ascertain whose responsibility they were. A partial explanation may perhaps be found in Helicon's being a publishing house aiming at a wide readership primarily interested in a good story.
3. Melville 1945, 12.
4. Ibid., 417. The passage appears as a footnote to the final paragraph of chapter 91. For another allegory of de Man and *Moby Dick*, see Felman 1989.
5. Montaigne 1988, 479.

CHAPTER THREE

1. The letter is quoted in full in Waters 1989, lxiv.
2. The reference to Sartre is unmistakable; it is extended in de Man's expression of mock surprise at the fact that Montaigne is 'honored by a (very judicious) study in one of our reviews whose very title seems to indicate a lack of interest in authors of such remote times,' an allusion to Merleau-Ponty's 'Lecture de Montaigne' in *Les Temps Modernes* (1947a), a text in which, incidentally, the author begins to demarcate his difference from Sartre, which was to lead to his leaving the journal in the same year de Man's essay was published (see Boschetti 1985, 268).
3. Apart from recalling Merleau-Ponty's philosophy of ambiguity, the phrase has also a distinctly Heideggerian ring, but an exploration of this resonance with *Being and Time* can be postponed for the time being.
4. Throughout this book, my translation of de Man's 'esprit' is 'spirit' rather than 'mind.'
5. The presence of Husserl could already be felt earlier in the text, specifi-

cally in its insistence on the principle of intentionality, but here too, this point can be suspended for the moment.

6. Hendrik de Man 1944, 35.
7. Ibid., 36; cf. Montaigne 1988, 31 (I, VII).
8. Hendrik de Man 1944, 169–70; cf. Montaigne 1988, 820 (III, III).
9. Hendrik de Man 1944, 21–22.
10. Claeys-Van Haegendoren 1972, 361.
11. Hendrik de Man 1944, 170.
12. Ibid., 53, 54.
13. *Nouveau Petit Larousse Illustré: Dictionnaire Encyclopédique* (Paris: Larousse, 1952), 1431.
14. From a letter to Frida Vandervelden, dated 3 January 1939. Monthouet was a small isolated inn in the Belgian Ardennes run by a Russian engineer, Alexandre (Sascha) Schor, and his Berlin wife. De Man stayed there in the course of 1938.
15. Hendrik de Man 1944, 240–41. It is unlikely that Jünger would have returned the sentiment, given the tone of his diary entry on their encounter at the Didiers in Paris in November 1943 (1963a, 192), which is probably the same encounter that de Man refers to. For Jünger's anesthetization of war, see also Chatwin 1989b and de Graef 1990.
16. Hendrik de Man 1944, 169; cf. Montaigne 1988, 617 (II, XV).

PART TWO

1. As indeed it did its subsequent readers (cf. Fletcher 1972, 14; see also Klein 1973, 33).
2. A notable exception here is de Man's 1960 dissertation—a genre which, after all, requires a certain amount of name-dropping.
3. 'Rompre ici avec les airs de famille, . . . éviter les tentations généalogiques . . . ,' Derrida 1987, 602.
4. Letter to Wlad Godzich, quoted in Waters 1989, lxxii, n. 92. The quotation comes from Hölderlin's project in prose for the 'Feiertags-Hymne' and occurs also in 'HE' BI, 262, and in 'PT,' 28.

CHAPTER FOUR

1. In his later work de Man will mount a consistent attack on this orthodox reading which, he argues, is only 'the canonical *idée reçue* of the poem' and has little to do with 'the poem read' ('MR' RT, 53; see also 'AT' RR, and 'HRJ' RT, 65–70). An excellent discussion of de Man's Baude-

laire readings is Newmark 1989; an excellent de Manian reading of Baudelaire is Chase 1986.

2. For Blake's 'minute particulars,' see also 'IS' RR, 5.

3. De Man's use of the category of not-being here is in fact closer to Hegel than it is to Heidegger, in the sense that not-being is still conceived of, albeit only for the sake of a negative argument, as something that may be accommodated to (and thus forgotten in) the development of metaphysical thought. For a particularly helpful commentary on this issue, see De Schutter 1990, 44–47. As for the focus on the figure of Parmenides, a plausible resonance here is the use made of Parmenides by Alexandre Kojève in his introductory lectures to Hegel's *Phenomenology* (quoted in Descombes 1979, 50)—the influence of Hegel (and Kojève) on de Man's thought will be discussed more extensively later.

4. For Heidegger's notion of ontological priority, see § 4 of *Sein und Zeit* (1977, 15–20; 1962, 34). The question of whether de Man's implicit ontology here in fact constitutes a deliberate and considered departure (or regression) from Heidegger (he had certainly read *Sein und Zeit* by this time [see 'IG' CW, 16]), or should rather be conceived of as a set of unreflected postulates, comes close to being irresolvable—in any event (and possibly also consequently), the answer to this question would appear to be of only a subordinate importance: what matters is the repercussion of this initial swerve on de Man's further commentary on Heidegger (and indeed on his entire thought), and we shall have ample occasion to develop this issue later on.

As for the 'deeper roots' of de Man's tendency to situate Being in sensuous substance, these can arguably be traced back to the kind of dualist ontology developed in Kojève's reading of Hegel and which was widely disseminated at the time (see Descombes 1979, 47–49). The point being, as Descombes convincingly argues, that while this type of ontology sets out to recognize an essential difference in being between the being of natural objects and the being of (conscious) man, it quasi-inevitably invites a reduction of Being to identity, this latter being the initial property of the being of natural beings. Further helpful backgrounds on Hegel in France are Poster 1975; Kelly 1981; Boschetti 1985, 87–89; Melville 1986; Taylor 1987; Roth 1988. See also Allan Stoekl's 1990 edition of texts by and on Bataille, another prominent figure in the discourse in which de Man participates.

5. My translation for de Man's 'sensible' throughout this study is 'sensible' rather than 'sensory' or 'sensuous.'

6. The reference is to the 'swan of past days' in the second of Mallarmé's 'Plusieurs sonnets.' A few years later, de Man, apparently incongruously, states that both swans (Baudelaire's and Mallarmé's) are really 'the same' ('WBY' RR, 199), but this shift can be explained in the light of a larger modification of the oppositional presentation of the two poets in his thought. The apparent contradiction in de Man's silent introduction of an animal—which would seem to belong on the side of natural being—as a proper analogue for poetic consciousness is implicitly dealt with in his later development of the notion of the emblem (as distinct from the natural image). An emblematic swan in Yeats is read in so many words in 'SL' RR, 140.

7. Throughout this study, I translate de Man's 'devenir' as 'becoming' rather than as 'process.' Although I accept, up to a point, the justification of this latter choice offered by the translators of this essay (CW, 75), I would still hold that 'becoming' has the double advantage of marking the opposition to 'being' central to de Man's thought here, and of following de Man's own use of the phrase in his English writing of the period (e.g. 'DA,' 14).

CHAPTER FIVE

1. De Man's naming of, in particular, Jünger and Pound and his reference to Löwith's critique of Heidegger's politics, to which we shall return, already establishes the link in question ('IG' CW, 14, 17), but even without these names the mere mention of 'nihilism' would already have achieved the same. In this respect, two specific moments in the extensive discourse on nihilism of the period deserve to be mentioned: the first is the famous *Festschrift* exchange between Jünger (1950) and Heidegger (1955) on the diagnosis and possible cure of nihilism (see Jünger 1963b and Heidegger 1978b); the second is the 1953–54 exchange between Hans Egon Holthusen and Heinrich Schneider on Jünger, Heidegger, and nihilism, which de Man in all probability translated for Henry Kissinger's Harvard journal *Confluence*. Holthusen had published an article titled 'The Literary and Cultural Situation of Postwar Germany,' to which Schneider had objected by accusing Holthusen, among other things, of dangerously misrepresenting what he calls nihilism (in, among others, Jünger's work) as 'a sign of returning health' (1953, 136). Holthusen replied in turn with a letter repeating the substance of his initial article and explicating his understanding of the various meanings of the term 'nihilism' and of Jünger as 'a diag-

nostician of the situation, including its nihilistic features,' rather than as 'a prophet of nihilism' (1954, 115–16). The insistent isotopy of diagnosis and therapy in these exchanges calls to mind de Man's critical reservations on 'mechanistically historical' explanations ('DA,' 6), but an adequate account of this viral rhetoric, which would also have to reflect on Hendrik de Man's simultaneous rejection and recuperation of its implications in his 1951 *Massification and the Decline of Culture* (1974, 51), cannot begin here.

2. Malraux 1948, 130.

3. This 'fact' masks the fact that trees, too, must die, and after having done so turn, precisely, into 'mere logs of wood,' but as we shall see, far from being an idiosyncratic view on vegetal life on the part of de Man, this masking betrays a core concept in the tradition of thought he participates in here.

4. A conservatism, he adds, 'which it can seem curious to see establishing itself most solidly in the Western country that has the least to conserve, the United States of America' (33). We should perhaps recall here that 'The Temptation of Permanence' was written in French for a French audience—in the originally American 'The Inward Generation,' de Man is more diplomatic and justifies his choice of the example from Malraux by saying that it may serve 'to indicate that the phenomenon is by no means confined to America' ('IG' CW, 17).

5. Payne 1973, 256. Malraux's eponymous trees are indeed walnut trees *(noyers)*, but in 'The Inward Generation' de Man refers to them as 'chestnut trees' ('IG' CW, 16). The slip may be trivial, but it is tempting to read it as prefiguring his rejection of the received reading of the apostrophe to the chestnut tree in Yeats's 'Among School Children' as 'a splendid statement glorifying organic, natural form, its sensuous experience and fundamental unity' ('WBY' RR, 197).

6. Nietzsche 1980, 1:330.

7. Hyppolite 1974, 18 (de Man refers to this commentary in 'PHD M,' 67; see also 'HE' BI, 264–65; and Warminski 1985, 273). This is also the thought that allows de Man to gloss over the death of Malraux's trees: nature has no history, and its movement is not a dialectic—or, as de Man also writes, 'Mallarmé would say with Hegel that mere "life" has no history, since it has neither future nor development' ('PN' CW, 25). Two more voices of death may have to be heard here. Around the time that de Man wrote these essays (1955), Bataille was thinking Hegel's 'doctrine of death' in the light of sacrifice, and it is not unlikely that

de Man borrowed some lines from this thought (cf. Bataille 1990a, 15). Bataille also noted that Kojève's Hegel drew some of his strength from Heidegger, and in this respect we may recall the statement by Alphonse de Waelhens—de Man's guide to Heidegger (cf. 'INT II' RT, 119; and Milic 1989)—that Heidegger 'was in no way interested in the biological phenomenon of death' (1971, 136) and tried to think it otherwise. We will come back to this.

8. De Waelhens 1971, 92–93.

9. This is not to suggest that de Man was not yet acquainted with Husserl's principle of intentionality at the time (we shall document this later on), but only that the difficulties in which he is here trapped arise from an insufficient winnowing away of intention as *volition* from intention as *noetic act*. (I bracket the question whether such a pure distinction can ultimately be maintained, on which see Levinas 1968, 490.) A parallel of this complication can be observed in de Man's wavering attitude on the question whether the 'essential separation' has come about 'by our own volition' ('PP' CW, 64; translation modified) or 'by the volition of Being itself' ('IS' [original 1960 version], 72—the English version of 1970 drops this phrase).

10. Consciousness as a requirement for the tragic here not only refers us to the moment of anagnorisis in the tradition of tragedy, but also to the identity in Hegel of what Hyppolite calls 'pantragedism' and 'panlogism' (1974, 31).

11. Hegel 1988, 550.

12. We are not primarily concerned with the accuracy of de Man's presentation of Hölderlin's theoretical attempt, and it suffices to summarily follow this presentation through on its own terms. A cautious disapproval of de Man's reading of this fragment is De Schutter 1989, 106–7.

13. Hölderlin 1969, 788.

14. As indeed we should be, when feeding the notion back into the distinction between the Flemish and the French as it figures in de Man's wartime journalism—we shall return to this.

15. Unless indicated otherwise, all quotations and translations from Hölderlin are taken from de Man's text. An exhaustive summary of the intensive debate on this quarrel cannot be given here. In what follows I must limit myself to a few cursory references, but I will say here that it takes a particularly vicious incompetence to be able to conclude from de Man's comments that he 'finds no . . . blindness in Heideg-

ger's readings of Hölderlin' (Hirsch 1988, 336), and to suggest that this is probably because, unlike Husserl, Heidegger was not 'a Jew': there seem to be no limits to what the House Un-American Reading Committee thinks it can get away with.

16. Derrida 1986, 7 and 79. See also Derrida 1987, 610; and 'ROB' BI, 136, for de Man's famous use of this defiant reasoning in his reading of Derrida.

17. Derrida 1986, 7.

18. Heidegger 1981a, 55.

19. In his last work, de Man would return to this unbridgeable distance between the teacher and the student in terms that are, even in their decisive difference, remarkably similar to those used here (see 'RT' RT, 4). To read these terms carefully is to understand that he was also aware of the danger that the very thought of this distance can itself become the doctrine that closes it and those who mouth the accusation that de Man engaged in a pedagogical practice which is 'politically ugly' in that it encouraged 'hero worship' (Lehman 1991, 212) might want to think this through. A good way to begin doing so is plotted in Christensen 1990.

20. Heidegger 1981a, 72.

21. The phrase is taken from the notes of Merleau-Ponty's 1952–53 course at the Collège de France (1968, 26)—de Man certainly followed Merleau-Ponty's lectures in 1955 (Waters 1989, lxv), but it is unlikely that he did so in 1952–53.

22. De Man establishes this connection in a footnote that is so exasperatingly rife with potential avowedly left undeveloped that I will quote it in full: 'It will suffice to indicate in passing how closely this transition resembles the dialectic of the unhappy consciousness, as well as its counterpart in the second part of Hegel's *Phenomenology,* which leads from the spiritual work of art to religion, with some notable differences (such as the absence, in Hölderlin, of the stage of comedy at this point) having to do with the essence of the distinction between poetical thought and philosophical thought. The problem of the relation between Hegel and Hölderlin is inexhaustible' ('HE' BI, 263 n. 6; translation emended). A necessarily equally inexhaustible problem is that of the relation between Hegel and Mallarmé, whose minds, as de Man puts it in a later text, in terms we need not comment upon further, 'are related by the similarity of their trajectory,' by 'a parallelism between the roads they have travelled' ('PHD M,' 73). The reference to

'the second part of Hegel's *Phenomenology*' in the footnote just quoted may betray once more de Man's indebtedness to the French Hegel dominant at the time: strictly speaking, the *Phenomenology* does not have a first and second part (on this issue, see the editorial matter in Hegel 1988, 547–48), but in the discourse on Hegel initiated by, in particular, Kojève and Hyppolite, such a division was commonly (and justifiably) assumed. Kojève's detailed organization of the *Phenomenology* appeared as an appendix to his 1933–39 lectures as they were published in 1947 (1947, 576–97); Hyppolite's division is established in the break between the two volumes of his 1939 translation of the work (a break accounted for in his preface, v–vi). It seems most likely that de Man's division was borrowed from the latter, even if only because in his dissertation he repeatedly uses the references 'PHEN. I' and 'PHEN. II,' while his actual quotations are taken from the 1952 Hoffmeister edition which contains no such division. For another reference to the 'bipartite structure' of the *Phenomenology*, see 'F' CW, 84.

23. See e.g. Hyppolite 1974, 74. Cf. also Bataille's implicit characterization of this passage as 'ambiguous' and 'extremely difficult' as well as 'comic' (1990a, 13).

24. Hegel 1977, 493. The concluding lines are adapted from Schiller's 'Die Freundschaft.' Hegel alters 'des ganzen *Seelen*reiches' and appropriates '*die* Unendlichkeit.'

25. The reference (through Golgotha) to a narrative ending in a named apotheosis in this grand finale also recalls two other stories with which the problem may be posed: the narrative of the *Phenomenology* as the *Odyssey* of the Spirit and the more complicated account of the act of philosophy, in Hegel, as symbolized in the figure of Oedipus. The combat that de Man sees as essential to Being is the experience *(Erfahrung)* of separation between consciousness and what is not consciousness from which Hegel sets out, and which corresponds, in turn, to Ulysses' experiences while away from Ithaca; but Ulysses, or so we are told, did come home (to his throne), as apparently does Hegel's Absolute Spirit. De Man's poet, on the contrary, who also starts out from the experience of separation, apparently is destined to roam forever. It should be clear by now that the problem resides precisely in this 'apparently,' and in de Man's reluctance to take a definite stance on this issue of modality. As for the figure of Oedipus in/as the performance of the final act of (Hegel's) philosophy, i.e., the figure 'erected' by Hegel as symbol of the 'heliological' trajectory of thought which ends in the solution to

the riddle in the name of the Spirit, see Lacoue-Labarthe 1986, 214–17. As de Man knows ('HE' BI, 247), this figure has one eye too many, but he cannot close, let alone gouge, it.

26. *Versöhnung*, incidentally, translates as 'reconciliation,' which de Man, as we saw, elsewhere rejects as *not* pertaining to either the Hölderlinian or the Hegelian dialectic ('HE' BI, 265). Another passage of this text rehearses the relation between poetry and philosophy in general as follows: 'True philosophers deal with the issues common to all men. The difference between their expression and that of poets (or artists, in general) is one of terminological exactness, and not of matter or intent' ('KH' CW, 48). A similar thought is expressed in de Man's dissertation when he counters the demand for explicit proof of a relation of influence between Hegel and Mallarmé with the bold statement that

> contacts between minds are more subterranean. When Hegel speaks of a *universal* consciousness, one should at least grant him that it is by virtue of its universality that such a consciousness can be transmitted, not as one imposes an opinion, but as a truth is revealed. The analogy between Mallarmé and Hegel does not indicate that the poet is dependent on the philosopher, his elder by more than twenty years [a slight understatement, seeing that Hegel had been dead for a good decade when Mallarmé was born]. It merely indicates that Hegel's 'experience' which he declares to be absolutely universal, is at least sufficiently so for two different minds, born in very different national traditions, to share some of its elements. The experience is not that of Hegel alone; it would be the most damaging of all criticism to define as a personal anomaly a system of thought that aims at transcending the singularity of individual convictions. The system certainly does not express absolute Truth, but it indicates one of the roads that is to lead towards it. Mallarmé chose this road with the freedom which constitutes the distinctive prerogative of a true dialectic.' ('PHD M,' 79–80)

Crucial as this fragment may be as evidence for de Man's own anxious awareness of the dilemma he has written himself into, its attempt to actually overcome this dilemma by rephrasing the Absolute Spirit as itself, indeed, a signpost to (one of) the road(s) to itself, cannot reasonably be said to succeed in pacifying the dialectical torment. As for the political implications of the claim to universality in this passage, they will require our attention at a later stage of this study.

1. 'Moira (Parmenides, Fragment VIII, 34–41)' was first read in 1952 and was published in 1954. De Man points out this latter date in a footnote, which, as we shall see, is not unimportant. For the original German of the passage just quoted, see Heidegger 1954a, 252. The present translation is Dan Latimer's ('TP' CW, 34); the French translation given by de Man is probably his own.

2. De Man translates *Zwiefalt* (which, admittedly, is a somewhat odd word) as if it were *Zwiespalt*. The use of this slight distortion will become clearer as we go along.

3. For suggestions toward a more detailed account, left in abeyance here, see Stoekl 1985, 39–40; and Milic 1989. One remark, however, is perhaps in order: it is strange to note that neither Stoekl nor Milic indicate that de Man quite blatantly misquotes Heidegger in the first passage he translates from the 'Ursprung.' When Heidegger writes, 'Welt und Erde sind wesenhaft voneinander verschieden und doch niemals getrennt. . . . Das Gegeneinander von Welt und Erde ist ein Streit' (1980a, 34), de Man translates, 'The world and the earth are essentially different from each other but without ever being separated. . . . The opposition of the sky *[ciel]* and the earth is a struggle' ('TP' CW, 34; translation emended). One can argue at length about the translatability of Heidegger's German, but it is not likely that a translation of 'Welt' as 'ciel' (semi-assonant though the words may be) can be condoned in the absence of any explanatory note from the translator. This 'slip' is particularly significant as it allows de Man to smuggle in the concept of the sky ('ciel,' 'Himmel') from which he set out and which he needs for his subsequent argument—a quite inexcusable gesture as the word 'Himmel' is not even mentioned in the immediate context of de Man's 'quotation.' The word 'Himmel' does occur, however, in two later texts de Man also refers to (both dating from 1951)—'". . . Dichterisch wohnet der Mensch"' (1954c) and 'Bauen Wohnen Denken' (1954b)—and especially with respect to his reading of a central passage in this latter essay, in which he uses and in fact expands his earlier distortion as if it were an actual argument, one can hardly help feeling somewhat led on. The passage in question is Heidegger's well-known reading of

the thing as a bridge gathering the *Geviert* (earth and sky, the divine and the mortal, 153). De Man comments, with some insolence, that, a bridge being a junction between two *separated* entities, such a gathering bridge is difficult to conceive of, as 'Heidegger has said to us that the division of the sky and the earth was of the order of difference and not of separation' ('TP' CW, 37–38). We shall return to this doctored dialectic of earth and sky, but we may already underscore that its pertinence is not diminished by this distortion. (The English translation of 'Tentation de la permanence' by Dan Latimer correctly quotes/translates Heidegger (and not de Man's 'translation' of Heidegger), which has the unfortunate effect that de Man's subsequent reference to his own abusive quotation becomes even more incomprehensible than it already was.)

4. De Man's central evidence here is Heidegger's reading of the line 'Voll verdienst, doch dichterisch, wohnet der Mensch auf dieser Erde' (Full of merit, but poetically, man dwells on this earth), which is taken from the so-called *Phaëton-Segmente* (also known as 'In lieblicher Bläue . . .'). Heidegger quotes from the first 'complete' Hölderlin edition by von Hellingrath. De Man follows Beißner, editor of the second complete edition, who classifies the *Segmente* as being of dubious origin (see Hölderlin 1951, 372–74 and 990–91), which leads de Man to annotate his reference to the line in question: 'We are dealing here with a poem probably apocryphal, at least in part, and which perhaps owes its strange power of suggestion to chance. We can use it when we clearly specify that Hölderlin is not at stake and that we are not talking about him' ('TP' CW, 40; translation emended). The remark is, again, slightly disingenuous, as in fact de Man subsequently aligns his own reading of the line in question to his larger appreciation of Hölderlin against Heidegger—an appreciation that emphasizes the oppositional 'but' over and against Heidegger's stress on dwelling as 'zufrieden sein,' 'zum Frieden gebracht sein,' 'eingefriedet bleiben,' etc. (1954b, 140). See also 'HE' BI, 254. In the most recent critical Hölderlin edition, Sattler convincingly argues in favor of the authenticity of the *Segmente* (Hölderlin 1983, 33).

5. Christopher Norris also quotes this passage but deletes the phrase I have underscored (1988, 167). The reasons for this not entirely innocent move presumably can be found in Norris's marked dislike of Heidegger (and of Hegel and Nietzsche), which goes hand in hand with his persistent attempts to 'salvage' de Man as an unsung ava-

tar of enlightened *Ideologiekritik*. The point I shall make later is that it is precisely in phrases such as the one Norris suppresses that de Man's most effective contribution to a critique of certain ideologies is adumbrated. For an incisive commentary on Norris's 'caricatures' of de Man's 'favorite' philosophers, see Redfield 1989, 38.

6. De Man's caution recalls a passage from a 1962 lecture by Adorno, in which, after having been treated to a caustic but entertaining reading of Heidegger's 'Warum bleiben wir in der Provinz?' we are told that 'we cannot get beyond these formulations of Heidegger when we simply polemicize against them; here too, we must first . . . determine the need or the truth they contain' (1973, 157).

7. All quotations taken from §§ 144–47 of the *Phenomenology* (1988, 101–3; 1977, 87–89). Limited space is the only excuse for this crude reduction. The case is argued more responsibly in, *inter alios*, Hyppolite 1974, 125–28; Marx 1971, 28–29; and Opiela 1983.

8. A very rash suggestion here would be that such a desire can be (mis)-read in Kant's development of the postulates of reason in the second *Critique*.

9. Hegel 1988, 62; 1977, 51. The translation here is modified to fit de Man's own reference to this passage ('DA,' 13). See also 'PHD M,' 67.

10. Hegel 1988, 66; 1977, 55.

11. As did a considerable number of Hegel commentators of his time. In 1946, Hyppolite observed that 'most contemporary thinkers deny the possibility of such a synthesis of the in-itself and the for-itself, and it is precisely on this ground that they criticize Hegel's system as a system. They generally prefer what Hegel calls "unhappy consciousness" to what he calls "spirit." They take up Hegel's description of self-consciousness which fails to be in-itself but which, nonetheless, exists only through its transcendence toward that in-itself; but they abandon Hegel when, according to him, specific self-consciousness—subjectivity—becomes universal self-consciousness—thingness—a movement through which being is posed as subject and subject is posed as being. They accept Hegel's phenomenology but reject his ontology' (Hyppolite 1974, 204–5).

12. The implicit identification suggested here between Heidegger's *Dasein* and Hegel's (unhappy) consciousness and/or Absolute Spirit as received by de Man can be partially grounded in the remarkable similarity between de Man's description of consciousness and the characterization of *Dasein* by Alphonse de Waelhens as marked 'by the permanent

relation of instability it entertains to itself,' as never 'a finished thing, an acquired result, an accomplished event,' and as 'always again put into play': 'A thing is what it is, and remains blocked in itself. Its inertia, its total determinability are entirely opposed to the unstable existence always to be won which *is* Dasein' (1971, 26–27). We have seen how for de Man's consciousness this instability is closely connected to interiorized death as distinct from exterior biological death ('TP' CW, 32). De Waelhens's paraphrase of Heidegger's attempt to distinguish the death of *Dasein* from 'the ripening that accomplishes the Being of fruit' and from the 'Being-at-an-end' as at 'a limit imposed from the outside' suggests that the problem of the *telos* of Hegel's interiorizations of death we are concerned with here is equally pertinent to this version of Heidegger's Being-towards-death: '*[Dasein] is-towards-the-end,* an end that is not exterior to *Dasein* but that inexorably ripens in it' (140). It is perhaps the proximity of this 'inexorable ripening' to Hegel's 'unhalting progress' that should be kept in mind when we take up de Man's suggestion, in a discussion with Hyppolite in 1966, that on the problem of death Heidegger has 'taken up again certain essential themes of the Hegelian tradition' ('C,' 185).

13. This, perhaps, is what is implied by de Man's suggestion that 'the promise of repose and peace contained in the word "dwell"' (as opposed to '"being in time," an expression that contains division') is what Heidegger wants to gain 'in thinking the tension of Being with beings in place of thinking, as does Hegel, the tension of the object and the idea' ('TP' CW, 37). The point being that thinking this tension along lines which are not those of mediation but of gathering threatens to end up in a complacent forgetting of what is to be thought, in a betrayal of 'the movement of being' 'in the name of the earth' (38). Again, we find a possible source for this understanding of the trajectory of Heidegger's thought in de Waelhens: 'It seems . . . that from *Hölderlin und das Wesen der Dichtung* onward, Heidegger moves more and more toward a philosophy more concerned with *Seiendes* than with *Sein.* It is that *[Seiendes]*—originally pure unknowable—which is at present the avowed center of speculation, engendering little by little a philosophy of the Earth and of the Dionysian whose Hölderlinian and Nietzschean origins are evident' (1971, 318; see also 365). And again we may note the rejection, on similar grounds, of a certain Heidegger, paired to a rejection of an eschatological Hegel, in Bataille (see Besnier 1990, 179).

14. We should add that de Man is well aware of Heidegger's own repeated contention that his readings of Hölderlin are, emphatically, conversations or dialogues (1981b, 1981c), as witness his reference to Heidegger's use of the image of the snow-covered bell in these contentions ('HE' BI, 253). The pattern is too interesting not to be deliberate.

15. Reading—though not therefore necessarily careful reading—breeds such mechanical moves. Thus, it can be said (and not without some justification) that de Man out-Heideggers Heidegger by turning his philosophy against his readings of Hölderlin (Gearhart 1983, 67; but see 'MP,' CW, 158 for de Man's implicit rejection of this possibility). One could also say that de Man, speaking for Hegel, accuses Heidegger in terms reminiscent of Heidegger's own accusations of Hegel, or indeed of Hegel's accusations of Kant. And the pattern is further complicated when we emphasize that Hegel speaks for the Absolute Spirit, a privileged position which de Man also ascribes to Heidegger ('HE' BI, 251), claims for himself and his readers ('PHD M,' 1–2), and later ironically projects onto the persona of Lukács's *Theory of the Novel* ('GL' BI, 53).

16. It is not difficult to find instances of this—some good examples are Heidegger's statements that 'the poet is still never able to immediately name the Holy through himself *[von sich aus],*' or that 'Insofar as the Holy becomes Word, its innermost essence begins to waver. The law is threatened. The Holy threatens to become unstable' (1981a, 68, 73).

17. The connective 'or' in the parenthetical phrase is less innocuous than it may seem. In his later work, de Man would focus precisely on what could be called the ineluctable disjunction between reading and understanding, and it is appropriate that this disjunction should be paired to a systematic connection between understanding and lyrical poetry as opposed to (noncomprehending) reading and prose (see esp. 'AT' RR, 262). Although this insight is certainly not yet developed in the essays under consideration here, it is already embryonically present in the characterization of a certain 'bad' Heidegger as being, in a way, more of a hymnic poet than a rigorous thinker. A footnote from de Man's dissertation echoes this prefiguration with admirable consistency: 'Heidegger's *Erläuterungen zu Hölderlin's Dichtung* . . . are founded on an ontology of the poetic that is essentially lyrical, as in Staiger or Croce's reconciled world' ('PHD Y,' 127).

18. This is also, to my knowledge, the last mention of Jünger in de Man's work.

19. Apart from perhaps overemphasizing a privilege of metaphysics, this statement on Heidegger transforms the final question of *Sein und Zeit* into an assertion (cf. Heidegger 1977, 437).

20. Löwith 1953, 72.

21. The editors of *Les Temps modernes* opened the debate in 1946 with a prefatory note to two documents on Heidegger (de Gandillac 1946 and de Towarnicki 1946) in which they drew a parallel between Heidegger's acceptance of Nazism and Hegel's acceptance of the Prussian monarchy and his later reactionary attitude. A careful analysis, they claim, has already 'cleared the essence of Hegelianism, dialectical thought, from all suspicion,' and they predict that the same will happen with 'the essence of [Heidegger's] philosophy, existential thought. What is more: [such an analysis] will perhaps show that an "existential" politics is at the opposite extreme of Nazism.' The two final paragraphs of the note demand to be quoted here:

> The two documents that follow are not even a rough draft of this work [of analysis]. Here one will only find a few facts, together with the interpretations given them by the philosopher, the impressions of a reserved visitor, and finally those of an enthusiastic visitor. We submit these latter with all reservations. Politics of presence and double games, we know all that. Initial adherence, followed by regrets and even acts of courage, we have seen that as well. Between these two hypotheses, these documents do not permit to choose.
>
> The reader should therefore primarily look in these documents for an opportunity to observe, in Germany and in the case of an illustrious philosopher, the equivocations we have witnessed in France among so many mediocrities.

The next contribution to the polemic was the article by Löwith that de Man refers to (1946; see also Löwith 1986), presented in a new section of the review ('Opinions') and accompanied by a note to the effect that the editors do not necessarily agree with the argument. The following installment consisted of de Waelhens's severely critical response to Löwith, in which he also registered approval of the initial editorial note (1947, 114, 118–19); the same issue contained another response by Eric Weil. In 1948, Löwith answered de Waelhens (and Weil) in turn, and de Waelhens 'closed' the discussion in the same issue with an answer to that answer (cf. also de Waelhens 1951, 306 n. 5).

22. Weil 1947, 135.

23. Löwith 1946, 358; see also the more radical version in Löwith 1948, 370.

24. Löwith 1953, 12, 44, 48, 60.

25. De Waelhens 1947, 122.

26. Compare Löwith 1946, 358 and 360. We might also refer here to Löwith's several statements on the essential differences between Italians and Germans in the original text from which the present essay is an extract (see Löwith 1986)—it is true that such comparisons 'are only too easily set up in an endeavour to balance accounts' (Habermas 1989, 433), but this is not to say that they cannot function otherwise.

27. Hamacher's account of these meditations (1989, 442–43) is exceptionally pertinent here.

28. 'IG' CW, 14. Cf. Gaillard 1970, 178–81; Chatwin 1989a, 117.

29. Micha and de Waelhens 1949.

30. The sentence is quoted from Heidegger's 1936 text on 'The Origin of the Work of Art' (1980a, 34).

31. This compatibility of Heidegger and Hegel is also indicated by Löwith, but for exactly the opposite reasons. For de Man, Heidegger resembles Hegel insofar as he remains this side of absolute presence in eternity; for Löwith, Heidegger comes to resemble Hegel precisely insofar as his history of Being begins to be thought in function of such presence (cf. Löwith 1953, 44, 53–54). The point would be, on de Man's terms, that Löwith does not enter into a dialogue with either Hegel or Heidegger but instead reads them both as if they were Spengler (cf. also 'TP' CW, 32 and 'IG' CW, 16), as indeed Löwith explicitly does with Heidegger (1953, 56).

32. Cf. Heidegger 1981a, 58.

33. Cf. 'HE' BI, 257. Again, we must refer to Löwith, who underscores that in Heidegger 'a dialectic of "correspondence" *[eine Dialektik des "Entsprechens"]*' replaces Hegel's 'dialectic of mediation *[Vermittlung]*' (1953, 27)—but while for Löwith this replacement takes place in the realm of similarity, for de Man it is a matter of fundamental difference.

34. Here, too, de Man agrees with Löwith, who also warns against the 'persuasive *[überredend]*' (as distinct from 'convincing *[überzeugend]*' force of Heidegger's language (1953, 14).

35. Heidegger 1980a, 49.

36. The linguistic mechanism of these seductive moves is attractively repeated in a pun buried in de Man's comments on Malraux's walnut

trees: 'In becoming trees, we have lost the precarious situation of being *on* the earth to become creatures *of* the earth. This is to yield to the temptation of permanence, for art so considered is in reality only a sediment without life, which integrates itself with the soil instead of opposing it. Pretending to think being, Malraux thinks in reality earth, which he desires' ('TP' CW, 32). The pun only works in the original French of the final sentence: 'Prétendant penser l'être, Malraux pense en réalité la terre, qu'il désire.' The anagrammatic (or anaphonetic) shift from *être* to *terre* recapitulates the dangers of some versions of ontology in a nutshell, but as we shall see, an opposition to this desire for the earth—and the soil *(sol)*—is not necessarily an opposition to ontology as such.

37. Löwith 1953, 11.

38. Ibid., 66, 88.

39. An index of this insufficiency is that de Man's rejection of the ideological recuperation of Hölderlin's *vaterländische Umkehr* falls back in the logic it opposes by characterizing those who have defended it as 'hardly occidental' ('PP' CW, 74). Another significant instance here is the unfinished manuscript (probably written in about 1958) in which de Man wholly subscribes to Benedetto Croce's 'indictment of a messianic nationalism that makes use of Hölderlin's poetry' even while he insists, in a promise he does not fulfill, that this poetry cannot itself be held accountable for this abuse: 'I will have to come back later to what 'national' means in Hölderlin's poetry and it should then be clear that it has nothing in common with the extreme forms of twentieth century nationalism' ('HRT,' 3). The only thing he does add, in a syntactically ambiguous passage he later crossed out, is that Hölderlin's poetry is situated in 'a realm where there is no room for problems of personal or political expediency aside from those of pure poetic expression,' thus frustratingly opening up the challenging implication that there are 'problems of personal or political expediency' that *are* those of 'pure poetic expression.' We shall come back to this.

40. This is not only the case for the dialogue with Heidegger's eschatologism but also—and more strikingly—for the dialogue with Löwith and Malraux: both *Denker in dürftiger Zeit* and *Les Noyers de l'Altenburg* are summarily dismissed, and de Man suggests that 'both might well soon be forgotten' ('IG' CW, 17). It is difficult not to suspect a subtext for this dismissal, and, especially in the case of Malraux, the possible data for such a text are as fascinating as their narrative combination

is unreliable. Here, nevertheless, are some of the entries: *Les Noyers de l'Altenburg* is narrated in 1940 by a French prisoner of war of Alsatian origin; its hero is the narrator's father, Vincent Berger, who fought on the side of the Germans in the First World War (Alsace was under German rule from 1871 to 1919 and again from 1940 to 1944). The name Berger, later adopted by Malraux as his pseudonym in the resistance (Payne 1973, 265), can either be pronounced as French or as German (de Man's name, too, was and is pronounced as French or Germanic). If German, it invokes, among other things, mountains, and Montaigne, pronounced by one of Malraux's characters as 'Montagne' (1948, 122), is invoked as an exemplar of wisdom whose aim it was never to be surprised by man (117). The model for the narrator's grandfather was Malraux's own grandfather, who was Flemish, as was his father (Payne 1973, 12). The novel was first published in Switzerland, in 1943, under the title *La Lutte contre l'ange;* it was republished in 1945, and, under its new title, in 1946, with a notice by the author warning that 'This work will not be republished.' It was first reviewed in October 1943, in the clandestine *Les Lettres françaises,* where it was praised as an 'exemplary' response to the catastrophe of the times ('which dramatically confront man with his destiny'), in that, after having 'called into question, desperately,' 'everything about ourselves,' it allows to 'shine forth,' 'at the bottom *[fond]* of a tragical negation,' 'the secret that can found our living *[qui peut nous fonder à vivre]*' and allows 'us to suddenly recognize the great voice which, throughout the centuries, ensures our action and our duration': 'Malraux finds himself carried to search this duration almost instinctively, and, one could say, biologically.' The reviewer was Jean Lescure, the editor of the journal *Messages,* which de Man helped publish in December 1942 after it had been refused authorization by the German censor in Paris, an act which led to his dismissal from the German-controlled Agence Dechenne in March 1943 (Keenan 1989, 469–72). Further material for this unfounded narrative can be found in Payne 1973, 251–63; Caillois 1970; Tison-Braun 1975; Gaillard 1970, 121–32.

41. De Man adds a remark on the function of philology, which echoes his introductory remarks on that subject in the same essay (where he points out Heidegger's royal but not therefore inconsistent disdain for the niceties of text-critical science [see also Heidegger 1981c, 10]). In de Man's view, philology is extremely important as a discipline of resistance to the 'arbitrariness' of 'excessive mysticism' and to the pseudo-

rigor of 'excessive scientism' alike, and in this resistance, 'it gains in increased self-awareness and provokes the development of methodological movements within the discipline itself, which ultimately reinforce it' ('HE' BI, 264). The return to philology has never been absent from his thought.

42. Here too, as regards the question of exegetical method, de Man gives and takes away. Compare '[Heidegger] ignores altogether all matters of poetic technique that had certainly been of great import to Hölderlin; a number of anomalies and obscurities in these poems cannot be explained without reference to them. And one could go on listing Heidegger's heresies against the most elementary rules of text analysis' ('HE' BI, 250) with 'The passage of Heidegger is remarkable by its profound justification of poetic metrics—one thinks of perspectives that he opens on the quasi-obsessional metrics of a poet like Hölderlin, whose work the classical metrical analyses seem powerless to evaluate' ('TP' CW, 36).

43. Godzich 1986, x.

44. Of course, substantial sections of such criticism do figure in these texts, but they are always already subordinate to a larger, 'philosophical' and (at least implicitly) metacritical argument. This is especially obvious in 'Le néant poétique: Commentaire d'un sonnet hermétique de Mallarmé'—as indeed the title of the essay suggests.

CHAPTER SEVEN

1. As usual, we are not primarily concerned here with the accuracy of de Man's account of New Criticism and of the work of I. A. Richards, William Empson, and Philip Wheelwright. Some assessments of this matter are Culler 1971, 269–70; Martin 1983; Norris 1985, 1988, x–xii, 173–76; Eagleton 1986; Barzilai and Bloomfield 1986; Shusterman 1988, 393–95; Hartman 1989, 5–7; Waters 1989, xl–il; and Hertz 1990.

2. In 1982, this cat was to put in a late appearance in de Man's 'The Resistance to Theory' (RT, 5) and in its companion piece 'The Return to Philology' (RT, 26). Its present use not only echoes the French maxim of communicational integrity and reliability, but can also allude to the quarrel on the subject of the cat that developed between Sartre and Blanchot in the late 1940s. In an essay, published in 1947, that was later to conclude 'Qu'est-ce que la littérature?' Sartre wrote (I translate literally so as to preserve the idiom): 'The function of a writer is to call a cat a cat *[appeler un chat un chat]*. If words are sick, it is up to us to

cure them. Instead of that, many writers live off this sickness. . . . It is perfectly all right to write 'horse of butter' but in a sense it amounts to doing the same thing as those who speak of a fascist United States or a Stalinist national socialism' (1948, 341; 1988, 228). Without explicitly naming Sartre, Blanchot promptly replied in an essay, published in 1947, which later became the first part of 'La littérature et le droit à la mort,' published in 1949 in *La part du feu*. In this reply, Blanchot turned the tables on Sartre's inversion of Boileau's *bon mot* by resuscitating its original political-polemical conclusion: 'Often these days there is talk of the sickness of words. . . . Naturally, an author can see it as his ideal to call a cat a cat. But what he cannot claim is that he would therefore be on the road to recovery and sincerity. He is on the contrary more than ever a mystifier, for the cat is not a cat, and he who affirms it envisages nothing other than this hypocritical violence: Rolet is a rascal' (1949, 314–15). And one year later, in 1948, in what was to become the second part of that same essay, he added, in a typical rhetorical turn: 'Everyday language calls a cat a cat, as if the living cat and its name were identical, as if the (f)act of naming it did not consist of retaining of it only its absence, what it is not' (329). Blanchot is another of those whose presence in de Man's work could be the subject of an extensive study. De Man's explicit references to his work in these early essays are relatively scarce, and they are marked by the same duplicity we noticed in his attitude toward Heidegger: in one essay he is denounced as an 'eternalist' ('PP' CW, 65), whereas in the present text he is explicitly exempted from the criticism leveled at 'contemporary French criticism' ('DF' BI, 245). It is clear, however, that in the polemic between Sartre and Blanchot, de Man largely took sides with the latter (see also 'INT II' RT, 119).

3. The quotation is from Richards 1930, 11.

4. This becomes even more evident when we contrast de Man's partial quotation with the continuation of Empson's note: 'One could, of course, also introduce much philosophical puzzling about the reconciliation of contradictions. The German tradition in the matter seems eventually based on Indian ideas, best worked out in Buddhism. But I daresay there is more than enough theorising in the text here already' (1966, 193 n. 1). Not nearly enough for de Man, needless to say. Still, it should be added that de Man also confesses to having taken some liberties in his reading and admits that Empson might very well not agree ('DF' BI, 241 n. 21).

5. The act of naming as an act of annihilation: this, too, Hegel named and Blanchot quoted (Blanchot 1949, 325; see also Hyppolite 1974, 237).
6. The phrase 'to communicate . . . things' is taken from Jean Wahl. De Man also uses it in his dissertation on Yeats ('WBY' RR, 200). The notion of the wager, which, incidentally, is used by de Waelhens to characterize Heidegger's thinking of the truth in the work of art as an original leap (*Ur-Sprung;* 1971, 292), demonstrates yet again de Man's ambivalent attitude with regard to the status of the natural object: on the one hand, the wager is understood as a desire powered by the attraction of the 'chaude plénitude de la substance'—and de Man does not refute this diagnosis, which presupposes the intrinsic superiority of natural being—but on the other hand, the impossibility for the wager ever to be won transforms substance itself into the abyss of Being, which, however, in turn, does not mean that consciousness would therefore become superior.
7. De Man puts this judgment in the larger perspective of 'the apparent contradiction of the attraction exerted upon our generation by the problematic of poetry and the solution of Marxism' ('DF' BI, 240), and subsequently annotates this observation with a reference to the 'Brief über den "Humanismus,"' in which Heidegger praises Marx as the (one) disciple of Hegel who has thought the destiny of the world in a conception of history as 'Geschichte' which leaves far beneath it 'der übrigen Historie' (1978a, 336). The interest of this reference is that it names the triumvirate of thinkers (or, in Aimé Patri's contemptuous phrase, 'the intellectual and moral *ménage à trois*' [cf. Bloom 1980, vii]) that can be argued to have dominated a sizable portion of French intellectual life in the period in which these essays were conceived. De Man, through Kojève and Hyppolite, among others, was very much aware of this trinity, but it is equally beyond doubt that Marx captivated him far less than Hegel and Heidegger—see on this issue his 1955 letter from Paris to Harry Levin (quoted in Waters 1989, lvvi).
8. A more developed version of some of these charges is de Man's criticism of Barthes at the now legendary 1966 Johns Hopkins conference ('C'). De Man's most encompassing reading of Barthes's limits is 'RB.'
9. Even as (at least self-confessedly) sympathetic a critic as Christopher Norris refuses to acknowledge this and argues that 'the upshot of [de Man's] reading is to force Empson's text towards another kind of 'absolute,' one that negates historical understanding in the name of a more authentic "ontological" concern' (1985, 211). Norris misses the mark

to the extent that he does not recognize that this 'more authentic "onto-logical" concern' *is*, for de Man, precisely history itself. For Norris such a conception probably smacks too much of Hegel and, especially, of Heidegger, but by failing to even consider its explicit pretence to be an historical conception, he closes his reading to what is at stake in its object.

10. An excellent appreciation of this pathos in de Man is Redfield 1990.

11. Some of the very numerous instances of versions of this objection are Graff 1979, 174–75; Riccomini 1979, 2–3; Lentricchia 1980, 309; and Sychrava 1989, 102–3. See also Gearhart 1983, and 1984, 25–26; and Melville 1986, 119 and 126. It is only fair to point out that de Man at times quite explicitly claims the privilege in question here for the literary consciousness.

12. This all too concise account in no way pretends to do justice to Husserl's thought and is proposed solely as a tentative understanding of de Man's understanding of this notion (mentioned only twice in his work—see 'IR' RR, 41). An exemplary institution of the concept is Husserl 1962, 238. Further formulations are Jansen 1976, esp. 76–86; Jansen's entry in Ritter and Gründer 1984, 869–70; Breton 1956, esp. 125–50; Lauer 1955, esp. 199–211; and, importantly, Sartre 1936, 139–59; 1940; and 1947a.

13. Sartre 1936, 153.

14. This curiously ambiguous statement on poetry as a repetition in the face of separation which is at the same time not a repetition but a cre-ation (a statement which, incidentally, oddly prefigures de Man's later definition of allegory [see 'ROT' BI, 207]), points up one more impli-cation of de Man's thought in the discursive formations of his time: the reading of repetition in Lacan's 1950s repetition of its reading in Freud. Especially some passages from the 1953 *discours de Rome,* which stage the complex intertwining of language, interpretation, death, the destruction of the object, and history (1966, 203–4), almost read like a different version of de Man's reading of Mallarmé (e.g., 'PN' CW, 21–22). To the extent that they are versions, Lacan's and de Man's accounts are differently turned, but they turn around a common concern, as in-deed they have both explicitly stated (see 'JL' and Lacan 1976, 47–48). This is not the place to commence a reading of de Man's silent rela-tion to psychoanalysis (some steps in this direction have been taken in Klein 1973, Felman 1978 and 1985, Kamuf 1989, and Melville 1986), but I will say that, if strained, de Man's relation to psychoanalysis is no

more so than Lacan's own. As for Orpheus, it seems not improbable that, beyond the obvious archetype, de Man also had in mind the 'core' of Maurice Blanchot's *L'espace littéraire* (1955), 'Le regard d'Orphée' (227–34) and possibly also Geoffrey Hartman's 1955 essay 'The Fulness and Nothingness of Literature,' whose gloss on these pages of Blanchot's may help put the strange and strained attitude of de Man toward Blanchot into some perspective. 'The poet [Orpheus] is the one who by his recourse to language, breaks the immediacy of experience, destroys it by that "vibrating almost-disappearance" of which Mallarmé spoke, but who, also, because of such word-inherent power of negation, is able to force nature to reverse or even undo time ("Ecrire, c'est se livrer à la fascination de l'absence du temps"), and so to recover a far greater immediacy than that originally yielded' (1955, 71). If we accept this as an accurate portrayal of Blanchot's thought in the passage in question—and it is a very possible rendering of this thought—we may understand de Man's ambivalence: the destruction of the object in the poetic word is a concept he would willingly subscribe to (witness his own readings of the phrase from Mallarmé in 'PN' CW, 21), but the fascinating absence of temporality that this destruction would appear to entail for Blanchot would almost certainly (albeit not therefore necessarily legitimately) invite the charge of eternalism (cf. e.g. 'PP' CW, 65).

15. Cf. also 'RH' CW, 212.

CHAPTER EIGHT

1. The 1960 essay 'Structural intentionnelle de l'Image romantique' was translated and revised by de Man in 1970. As a rule, I shall use this translation ('Intentional Structure of the Romantic Image') and only indicate de Man's revisions when pertinent.

2. This conceptual regression in the 1960 essay is especially striking when one compares that essay to de Man's dissertation of the same year, which does succeed in maintaining the high level of (albeit problematic) reasoning of de Man's earlier work. In 1983, de Man justified the publication of about one third of this dissertation ('WBY' RR) (the remainder is still not available in print) by pointing to the 'unmistakable methodological trend' toward 'a rhetorical analysis of figural language' it already betrayed (RR, vii); certainly in technical detail de Man's readings in this dissertation are far more advanced than anything else he wrote in the period. Yet, this is not a simple watershed: even the mere

fact that the dissertation's original introduction equally legitimately justified its method not as a rhetorical reading but as a 'metaphysics of style,' and 'an interpretation of its intentional structure' ('PHD I,' II–III) should make us aware of the participation of these early rhetorical analyses in the equivocal metaphysics of his previous work. A further point that these two distinct justifications of the same work should underscore is that de Man's later enterprise (like every serious deconstructive practice) must remain fundamentally unread as long as one hypostatizes it in some exotopic realm identifiably outside of metaphysics. This also means that critics of de Man who think they have discovered something devastating when they recognize a metaphysical strand in his work, early and/or late, will always miss their polemical mark. For such an invention of hot water ('de Man used to be thoroughly metaphysical'), see Lentricchia 1980, 287.

3. See esp. Lentricchia 1980, 284–89. Uncritical approval of Lentricchia's arguments here is registered in, *inter alios,* Raval 1981, 277; Corngold 1982, 491; O'Hara 1985, 208; Melville 1986, 166–67; Berman 1988, 244. Some counterarguments are sketched in Parker 1981, 62, 68–69; Stoekl 1985; Milic 1989. An entertaining staging of the Lentricchia–de Man conflict is performed in Bretzius 1987. Further remarks on 'Structure intentionnelle' can be found in Baker 1986; Chase 1986, 134 and 1987, 76 n. 7; Sychrava 1989, 69–70, 102–3; De Schutter 1989.

4. Lentricchia 1980, 284. For Lentricchia's exhibitionist imperative— 'I've shown you mine, now you show me yours'—see Salusinszky 1987, 205.

5. Lentricchia 1980, 285.

6. Sartre 1940, 11.

7. De Man's interest in Husserl was certainly also stimulated by Merleau-Ponty, whose course at the Collège de France insistently entered into a dialogue with Husserl. De Man followed the course in 1955 (Waters 1989, lxv n. 5).

8. Cf. Descombes 1979, 64–70. Lentricchia admittedly acknowledges the presence of Hegel in Sartre and de Man but fails to develop it (1980, 285).

9. We may add that, by his own retrospective admission, de Man chose to side with Heidegger in the latter's 1946 conflict with Sartre over the question of existential philosophy and existentialism (see de Man's answer to Lentricchia's claim in 'INT II' RT, 118–19).

10. As indeed de Man affirms in 'INT II' RT, 118. Here one should also

reread Sartre's 1941 review of *Moby Dick,* which convincingly turns Melville into Hegel (reprinted in Contat and Rybalka 1970, 634–37).

11. Sartre 1947a, 32.

12. See e.g. Sartre 1940, 281, and 1947b, 69–75.

13. Sartre 1947c, 24.

14. There is an echo here of de Man's January 1940 privileging of Proust and Joyce over Bourget and Galsworthy (c, 16–18), but it is important to note that in 1940 this privilege had nothing to do with literature.

15. Sartre 1936, 21; 1962, 19–20 (translation modified).

16. 'The word is but a milestone [*jalon*]: it presents itself, awakens a meaning, and this meaning never returns to the word, it goes out to the thing and drops the word' (Sartre 1940, 50; 1972b, 23 [translation modified]).

17. Sartre 1948, 16; 1988, 29.

18. As de Man's comments on Proust and Joyce make clear, this is not a distinction that he deems decisive. For him, the question of *littérature engagée* 'should . . . be considered in relation to dramatic media rather than, as in Sartre's *What Is Literature?,* in relation to the novel, itself a confusingly ambiguous genre' ('PHD M,' 102).

19. This is a conception borrowed from Hegel and, especially, from Hölderlin's *Empedokles* ('PP' CW, 66). De Man will return more pointedly to these grounds of political action in his 1960s readings of Romanticism, which I will consider in detail in a later book.

20. It must be added that Sartre himself soon recognized the shortcomings of his notion of commitment, appropriately in the course of the unfinished reading of Mallarmé he set out on in the late 1940s (cf. Contat and Rybalka 1970, 262). The only part of this project that de Man could have read at the time is a brief 1952 essay (1972a) which also contains some oblique concessions to Blanchot's objections to *Qu'est-ce que la littérature?* But it is only in a 1960 interview that Sartre straightforwardly voices a new conception of commitment and even goes so far as to say of Mallarmé, to his interlocutor's significant surprise, that 'his commitment appears to me to be as total as possible: social as well as poetical' (1972b, 14). When Lentricchia, in a later text, obliquely abandoned his casting of de Man as a Sartrean existentialist on the basis of de Man's 1960 thesis on Mallarmé's commitment, which Lentricchia rightly recognizes as being in opposition to 'Sartre's Marxism of *littérature engagée*' (1983, 41), he should perhaps have realized that, by that time, Sartre was moving to a comparable position. Again, the

point is that this similarity between de Man and Sartre, apart from remaining inscribed in a considerable difference, is not an effect of a specific influence, but rather participates in an intense debate in which Sartre is only one name among many. Arguably, Sartre is a less important voice than Merleau-Ponty, whose 1947b qualifications of Sartre's commitment de Man had almost certainly read, given the fact that he refers to the issue of *Les Temps modernes* in which they appeared ('MT' CW, 3; see also Boschetti 1985, 246–49; and Pingaud 1971), or Bataille (1990b, Bataille's 1950 letter to René Char which tried to displace and rethink the 'misapprehended' 'incompatibility' of literature and commitment against Sartre), whom de Man in 1983 remembered as one of those 'whose relationship to the political (because they were very political) was more complex, more mediated than in the case of Sartre' and thus offered 'a way to resist the obvious attraction of Sartre's flamboyant presence on the scene' ('INT II' RT, 119).

21. Sartre 1948, 18; 1988, 29.

22. The summary statement of fundamental tension in the last two phrases is quoted from the original 1960 version (69). It was deleted from the 1970 version.

23. Translated by Michael Hamburger (Hölderlin 1990, 183). De Man deletes the last comma from the original, probably because its removal might seem to facilitate his subsequent reading of 'Blumen' as second subject of the verb 'entstehen.' In a footnote, he admits that another reading is possible ('Worte, die wie Blumen sind, müssen entstehen' rather than 'Worte müssen entstehen, wie Blumen entstehen') and archly adds that 'syntax and punctuation allow for both readings' ('IS' RR, 291). The English version restores the lost comma.

24. This reading requires some strain; it demands that we read de Man's suggestion that flowers 'are literally what they are, definable without the assistance of metaphor' as a thesis of impossibility: inasmuch as they are definable without the assistance of metaphor, flowers are not definable. We must remember that the project of the literal is that of the 'authentic word that fulfils its highest function in naming Being as presence' ('IS' RR, 3), and that as such its modality is quite as optative as that of Hölderlin's 'das Heilige *sei* mein Wort' ('HE' BI, 258). Thus, to object to de Man, as does Dirk De Schutter, that flowers can only be defined without the assistance of metaphor if 'their absolute identity has been mediated by language' (1989, 100), which is to say that they can not be defined (without the assistance of metaphor), is

entirely correct but it is not an objection. De Schutter takes de Man to task for having smuggled in 'metaphysical-ontological distinctions and concepts (such as the concept "metaphor")' prior to having fulfilled Heidegger's requirement for the introduction of such categories—'the naming of Being as such' (108). But apart from the fact that Heidegger himself, in *Sein und Zeit,* establishes such distinctions (in the definition of the triple priority of *Dasein,* for instance), the point would be that for de Man this a priori condition is literally impossible to fulfill, and that the nonconcept of the literal is the mark of that impossibility. Admittedly, Heidegger registers reservations as to his distinctions at the end of *Sein und Zeit,* and one could read these as prefiguring his move away from the analytics of *Dasein* as a prolegomenon to the fundamental ontology and toward the naming of Being as such, but the problem would remain the same in that de Man makes strategical distinctions prior to having been given license to do so, whereas Heidegger implicitly grants such license in a way that de Man cannot accept (by appointing Hölderlin as he who has named Being as such).

25. De Man does not explicitate this, but it will be clear that the underlying assumption is once more Hegel's notion of vegetal death. The reason why consciousness does not experience natural death as discontinuity is ultimately that such death is of the order of continuous succession, not in fact of the order of discontinuity at all. The fact, however, that de Man takes recourse to the alternative but equally natural image of the shell as an image that somehow would, be it only negatively, apply to language (despite its resonances with Baudelaire's 'rocs'), already points up what the continuation of the essay makes abundantly clear: the natural world of immediacy (which is '"merely" the world of Being' ('PHD Y,' 141) is not so easily contained. In the original 1960 version, de Man even implicitly speaks of the entity of consciousness's relinquishing its '*natural* specificity,' an inconsistency he understandably erased from the revised 1970 text.

26. The 1970 version has 'predicament' instead of 'crisis' ('IS' RR, 10).

27. De Man strengthens the same point in an unpublished essay, probably written in about 1958, where he suggests that it is the consolidation of this premise in nineteenth- and twentieth-century Romanticism that blinds us to the fact that 'Hölderlin as well as Rousseau differ from this pattern' ('HRT,' 13).

28. In this respect, it is interesting to observe that de Man explicitly distinguishes this conception of poetry from Mallarmé's, where the sky

and the constellation 'are always seen from the point of view of the earth' ('IS' RR, 15). The shift is so explicit that one risks not reading it, as is indeed the case in Allan Stoekl's comments on this passage, which render de Man's '*Unlike* Mallarmé's 'azur' . . .' as '*Writing now of* Mallarmé . . . de Man states . . .' (1985, 38).

29. This conclusion, which closely resembles the less optimistic conclusion to the published part of de Man's dissertation on Yeats ('WBY' RR, 238), is slightly less prophetic in the revised version, but Frank Lentricchia is still justified in singling it out as evidence for his thesis that de Man's 'apparent caution in speaking of this *telos* is undercut by his optative projection of the autonomous imagination as the virtual fulfilment of all of his critical desires' (1980, 280). Amusingly, Lentricchia's failure to register that the teleology he here denounces is radically opposed to the destruction of interiority that Sartre strove for in his reading of Husserl and in his initial promotion of *littérature engagée* prevents him from accusing de Man of having opposed what to Lentricchia ought to be commendable in Sartre (see also Stoekl 1985, 39; Milic 1989, 76).

30. Here, as elsewhere, the reader is referred to Minae Mizumura's seminal 'Renunciation' (1985), the first essay to have explicitly and seriously dealt with the rhetoric of sacrifice, temptation, and renunciation in de Man's work.

31. Weber 1989, 977.

32. Heidegger 1959, 9, 15–16.

33. At least as far as the first sentence of this passage is concerned, de Man is not as distant from Heidegger as he seems to suggest, witness Heidegger's remark that what Rilke projects onto America was already there in the time of our ancestors (1980b, 287). This is as good a place as any to reiterate that it is not our intention to comment on Heidegger but only on the possible perception of his thought by de Man.

34. Heidegger 1959, 22.

35. Ibid., 1959, 20, 23.

36. Ibid., 26. See also 'Hebel—der Hausfreund,' where the same lines are quoted in a variation on the theme of man's poetic dwelling on earth (1957, 28–29).

37. The *Revue internationale de philosophie* is a journal of the Université Libre de Bruxelles.

38. I translate from the original 1960 text; de Man's own 1970 translation deletes the word 'apaisé' and replaces one of the three occurrences of 'paix' with 'tranquillity.'

39. This remark on Christianity was deleted from the 1970 version.

40. Such, at least, is André Préau's decision in his 1966 translation of Heidegger's address. For an English translation Richardson suggests 'release' (1963, 504) and Anderson and Freund (who also point out that the word can mean 'composure,' 'calmness,' or—importantly—'unconcern') 'releasement' (Heidegger 1966, 54). The term also occurs in 'Vom Wesen der Wahrheit' (1976, 199), often seen as the pivotal point of Heidegger's *Kehre,* where it is variously translated as 'souplesse' (de Waelhens and Biemel 1948, 63) or as 'docility' (Richardson 1963, 253).

41. Malraux's trees offer an affirmation of earth as repose in which 'l'esprit se complaît' ('TP' CW, 32); the celestial imagination 'se suffit à elle-même': a literal Dutch translation would invite the word 'zelfge-noegzaam,' which is primarily used pejoratively ('complacent').

Bibliography

Primary Sources

The following list only comprises those items of de Man's bibliography cited in the text, with the exception of the individual items of his wartime journalism. The most complete bibliography of de Man's post-1950 writings is Thomas Keenan's 'Bibliography of Texts by Paul de Man' (RT, 122–27).

BOOKS BY PAUL DE MAN

Blindness and Insight: Essays in the Rhetoric of Contemporary Criticism. New York: Oxford University Press, 1971. 2d ed., with five additional essays and an introduction by Wlad Godzich. Minneapolis: University of Minnesota Press, 1983.

Allegories of Reading: Figural Language in Rousseau, Nietzsche, Rilke and Proust. New Haven: Yale University Press, 1979.

The Rhetoric of Romanticism. New York: Columbia University Press, 1984.

The Resistance to Theory. Foreword by Wlad Godzich. Minneapolis: University of Minnesota Press, 1986.

Wartime Journalism, 1939–1943. Ed. Werner Hamacher, Neil Hertz, and Thomas Keenan. Lincoln: University of Nebraska Press, 1988.

Critical Writings, 1953–1978. Ed. and introduction Lindsay Waters. Minneapolis: University of Minnesota Press, 1989.

Aesthetic Ideology. Ed. and introduction Andrzej Warminski. Minneapolis: University of Minnesota Press, forthcoming.

ESSAYS AND REVIEWS BY PAUL DE MAN
1953

'Montaigne et la transcendance.' *Critique* 79 (December 1953), 1011–22. Trans. Richard Howard as 'Montaigne and Transcendence,' CW, 3–11.

1955

'The Double Aspect of Symbolism.' *Yale French Studies* 74 (1988), 3–16. Transcription of manuscript probably written between 1954 and 1956.

'The Inward Generation.' *i.e., The Cambridge Review* 1:2 (Winter 1955), 41–47. Rpr. in cw, 12–17.

'Le néant poétique (commentaire d'un sonnet hermétique de Mallarmé).' *Monde Nouveau* 88 (April 1955), 63–75. Trans. Richard Howard as 'Poetic Nothingness,' cw, 18–29.

'Tentation de la permanence.' *Monde Nouveau* 93 (October 1955), 49–61. Trans. Dan Latimer as 'The Temptation of Permanence,' cw, 30–40.

'Les exégèses de Hölderlin par Martin Heidegger.' *Critique* 100–101 (September–October 1955): 800–19. Trans. Wlad Godzich as 'Heidegger's Exegeses of Hölderlin,' BI, 246–66.

1956

'Keats and Hölderlin.' *Comparative Literature* 8:1 (Winter 1956), 28–45. Repr. in cw, 41–60.

'Impasse de la critique formaliste.' *Critique* 109 (June 1956), 483–500. Trans. Wlad Godzich as 'The Dead-End of Formalist Criticism,' BI, 229–45.

'Situation du roman.' *Monde Nouveau* 101 (June 1956), 57–60. Trans. Richard Howard as 'Situation of the Novel,' cw, 61–63.

'Le devenir, la poésie.' *Monde Nouveau* 105 (November 1956), 110–24. Trans. Kevin Newmark and Andrzej Warminski as 'Process and Poetry,' cw, 64–75.

1957

'La critique thématique devant le thème de Faust.' *Critique* 120 (May 1957), 387–404. Trans. Dan Latimer as 'Thematic Criticism and the Theme of Faust,' cw, 76–89.

1958

'Hölderlin and the Romantic Tradition.' Unpublished manuscript.

1960

'Image and Emblem in Yeats.' RR, 145–238. Part of 'Mallarmé, Yeats and the Post-Romantic Predicament.' Diss. Harvard 1960.

'Structure intentionnelle de l'Image romantique.' *Revue internationale de philosophie* 51 (1960), 68–84. Trans. and rev. Paul de Man in 1970 as 'Intentional Structure of the Romantic Image,' rpr. in RR, 1–17.

1962

'Symbolic Landscape in Wordsworth and Yeats.' In *In Defense of Reading*, ed. Richard Poirier and Reuben Brower, 22–37. New York: Dutton, 1962. Rpr. in RR, 125–43.

1964

'Heidegger Reconsidered.' Review of *What Is Existentialism?* by William Barrett. *New York Review of Books*, 2 April 1964, 14–16. Rpr. in CW, 102–6.

1965

'L'Image de Rousseau dans la poésie de Hölderlin.' *Deutsche Beiträge zur Geistigen Überlieferung* 5 (1965), 157–83. Trans. Andrzej Warminski as 'The Image of Rousseau in the Poetry of Hölderlin,' RR, 19–45.

Entry under 'Modern Poetics: French and German.' In *Princeton Encyclopedia of Poetry and Poetics*, ed. Alex Preminger, 518–23. Princeton: Princeton University Press, 1965. Rpr. as 'Modern Poetics in France and Germany,' CW, 153–60.

1966

Comments. *The Languages of Criticism and the Sciences of Man (The Structuralist Controversy)*, ed. Richard Macksey and Eugenio Donato, 150, 184–85. Baltimore: Johns Hopkins University Press, 1970. Comments at the 1966 Johns Hopkins symposium.

'Georg Lukács's *Theory of the Novel*.' M L N *(Modern Language Notes)* 81:5 (December 1966), 527–34. Rpr. in BI, 51–59.

1967

'The Crisis of Contemporary Criticism.' *Arion* 6:1 (Spring 1967), 38–57. Rpr., rev. as 'Criticism and Crisis,' BI, 3–19.

'Patterns of Temporality in Hölderlin's "Wie wenn am Feiertage." . . .' Unpublished manuscript of third Gauss lecture delivered at Princeton University in 1967.

1969

'The Rhetoric of Temporality.' In *Interpretation: Theory and Practice*, ed. Charles S. Singleton, 173–209. Baltimore: Johns Hopkins University Press, 1969. Rpr. in BI, 187–228.

1970

'The Riddle of Hölderlin.' Review of *Poems and Fragments* by Friedrich Hölderlin. *New York Review of Books*, 19 November 1970, 47–52. Rpr. in CW, 198–213.

1971
'The Rhetoric of Blindness: Jacques Derrida's Reading of Rousseau.' In BI, 102–42.

1972
'Proust et l'allégorie de la lecture.' In *Mouvements premiers: Études critiques offertes à Georges Poulet,* 231–50. Paris: José Corti, 1972. Trans. and rev. Paul de Man as 'Reading (Proust),' AR, 57–78.

'Roland Barthes and the Limits of Structuralism.' *Yale French Studies* 77 (1990), 177–90. Transcription of manuscript probably written in 1972.

1974
Review of Harold Bloom's *The Anxiety of Influence. Comparative Literature* 26:3 (Summer 1974), 269–75. Rpr. in BI, 267–76.

'Nietzsche's Theory of Rhetoric.' *Symposium* 28:1 (Spring 1974), 33–51 (including question and answer session). Rpr. (without question and answer session) as 'Rhetoric of Tropes (Nietzsche)' in AR, 103–18.

1975
Introduction for Jacques Lacan, Yale University, 1975. *Yale French Studies* 69 (1985), 50–51. In French; Engl. trans. Shoshana Felman.

1979
'Autobiography as De-Facement.' *MLN (Modern Language Notes)* 94:5 (December 1979), 919–30. Rpr. in RR, 67–81.

1981
'Hypogram and Inscription: Michael Riffaterre's Poetics of Reading.' *Diacritics* 11:4 (Winter 1981), 17–35. Rpr. in RT, 27–53.

1982
'The Resistance to Theory.' *Yale French Studies* 63 (1982), 3–20. Rpr. in RT, 3–20.

Introduction. In *Toward an Aesthetics of Reception,* by Hans Robert Jauß, trans. Timothy Bahti, vii–xxv. Minneapolis: University of Minnesota Press, 1982. Rpr. as 'Reading and History,' RT, 54–72.

'The Return to Philology.' *Times Literary Supplement,* 10 December 1982, 1355–56. Rpr. in RT, 21–26.

1983
'Anthropomorphism and Trope in the Lyric.' In RR, 239–62.

' "Conclusions": Walter Benjamin's *Task of the Translator*.' *Yale French Studies* 69 (1985), 25–46. Edited transcript of the last of six Messenger Lectures, Cornell University, 4 March 1983. Rpr. with question and answer session, in RT, 73–105.

'An Interview with Paul de Man.' *Nuova Corrente* 93 (1984), 303–13. Conducted by Stefano Rosso, 4 March 1983. Rpr. in RT, 115–21.

Secondary Sources

Adorno, Theodor W. 1973. *Philosophische Terminologie*. Frankfurt: Suhrkamp.

———. 1981. *Negative Dialektik*. Frankfurt: Suhrkamp.

Bahti, Timothy. 1989. 'Telephonic Crossroads: The Reversal and the Double Cross.' In *Responses: On Paul de Man's Wartime Journalism*, ed. Werner Hamacher, Neil Hertz, and Thomas Keenan, 1–5. Lincoln: University of Nebraska Press.

Baker, John Jay. 1986. 'The Problem of Poetic Naming in Hölderlin's Elegy "Brot und Wein." ' *MLN (Modern Language Notes)* 101 : 3 (April), 465–92.

Barzilai, Shuli, and Morton W. Bloomfield. 1986. 'New Criticism and Deconstructive Criticism, Or What's New?' *New Literary History* 18 : 1 (Autumn), 151–69.

Bataille, Georges. [1955] 1990a. 'Hegel, Death and Sacrifice,' trans. Jonathan Strauss. *Yale French Studies* 78, 9–28.

———. [1950] 1990b. 'Letter to René Char on the Incompatibilities of the Writer,' trans. Christopher Carsten. *Yale French Studies* 78, 31–43.

Berman, Art. 1988. *From the New Criticism to Deconstruction: The Reception of Structuralism and Post-Structuralism*. Urbana: University of Illinois Press.

Besnier, Jean-Michel. 1990. 'Georges Bataille in the 1930s: A Politics of the Impossible,' trans. by Amy Reid. *Yale French Studies* 78, 169–80.

Blanchot, Maurice. 1949. 'La littérature et le droit à la mort.' In *La part du feu*, 305–45. Paris: Gallimard.

———. 1955. *L'espace littéraire*. Paris: Gallimard.

Bloom, Allan. [1969] 1980. Editor's Introduction. In Alexandre Kojève, *Introduction to the Reading of Hegel: Lectures on 'The Phenomenology of Spirit,'* assembled by Raymond Queneau, ed. Allan Bloom, and trans. James H. Nichols, Jr., vii–xii. Rpr. Ithaca: Cornell University Press.

Boschetti, Anna. 1985. *Sartre et 'les Temps modernes': Une entreprise intellectuelle*. Paris: Minuit.

Bretzius, Stephen. 1987. 'By Heaven, Thou Echoest Me: Lentricchia, *Othello,* de Man.' *Diacritics* 17:2 (Spring), 21–32.

Breton, Stanislas. 1956. *Conscience et intentionnalité.* Paris: Vitte.

Caillois, Roger. [1944] 1970. 'La vie est inépuisable.' *Les critiques de notre temps et Malraux,* ed. Pol Gaillard, 91–95. Paris: Garnier.

Chase, Cynthia. 1986. 'Getting Versed: Reading Hegel with Baudelaire.' In: *Decomposing Figures: Rhetorical Readings in the Romantic Tradition,* 113–38. Baltimore: Johns Hopkins University Press.

———. 1987. 'Monument and Inscription: Wordsworth's "Lines."' *Diacritics* 17:2 (Winter), 66–77.

Chatwin, Bruce. [1974] 1989a. 'André Malraux.' In *What Am I Doing Here,* 114–35. London: Picador.

———. [1981] 1989b. 'Ernst Jünger: An Aesthete at War.' In *What Am I Doing Here,* 297–315. London: Picador.

Christensen, Jerome. 1990. 'From Rhetoric to Corporate Populism.' *Critical Inquiry* 16:2 (Winter), 438–65.

Claeys-Van Haegendoren, Mieke. 1972. *Hendrik de Man: Biografie.* Antwerp: De Nederlandsche Boekhandel.

Colinet, Edouard. 1989. 'Paul de Man and the Cercle du Libre Examen.' In *Responses: On Paul de Man's Wartime Journalism,* ed. Werner Hamacher, Neil Hertz, and Thomas Keenan, 426–37. Lincoln: University of Nebraska Press.

Contat, Michel, and Michael Rybalka. 1970. *Les Écrits de Sartre: chronologie, bibliographie commentée.* Paris: Gallimard.

Corngold, Stanley. 1982. 'Error in Paul de Man.' *Critical Inquiry* 8:3 (Spring), 489–508.

Culler, Jonathan. 1971. 'Frontiers of Criticism.' *The Yale Review* 61:2 (December 1971), 259–71.

De Gandillac, Maurice. 1946. 'Entretien avec Martin Heidegger.' *Les Temps modernes* 1:4 (January), 713–16.

De Graef, Ortwin. 1989a. 'Aspects of the Context of Paul de Man's Earliest Publications followed by Notes on Paul de Man's Flemish Writings.' In *Responses: On Paul de Man's Wartime Journalism,* ed. Werner Hamacher, Neil Hertz, and Thomas Keenan, 96–126. Lincoln: University of Nebraska Press.

———. 1989b. 'Silence to Be Observed: A Trial for Paul de Man's Inexcusable Confessions.' In *(Dis)continuities): Essays on Paul de Man,* ed. Luc Herman, Kris Humbeeck, and Geert Lernout, 51–73. Amsterdam: Rodopi. Rpr. in *The Yale Journal of Criticism* 3:2 (Spring 1990), 205–23.

——. 1990. 'A Stereotype of Aesthetic Ideology: Paul de Man, Ernst Jünger.' *Colloquium Helveticum* 11/12, 39–70.

De Man, Hendrik. 1941. *Après coup (Mémoires)*. Brussels: Toison d'Or.

——. 1944. *Cahiers de ma montagne*. Brussels: Toison d'Or.

——. 1974. *Persoon en Ideeën, VI: Massificatie en Cultuurverval* [1951], ed. W. De Brock. Antwerp: Standaard.

Derrida, Jacques. 1986. *Mémoires: For Paul de Man*. Trans. by Cecile Lindsay, Jonathan Culler, and Eduardo Cadava. New York: Columbia University Press.

——. 1987. 'Désistance.' In *Psyché: Inventions de l'autre*, 597–638. Paris: Gallimard.

De Schutter, Dirk. 1986. *De voornaam van het zijn: Een lectuur van Heideggers filosofie van de tijd*. Diss. Louvain.

——. 1989. 'Words Like Stones.' In *(Dis)continuities: Essays on Paul de Man,* ed. Luc Herman, Kris Humbeeck, and Geert Lernout, 99–110. Amsterdam: Rodopi.

——. 1990. 'De smart van de schijn: Over Heidegger's filosofie van de kunst.' *Bijdragen, tijdschrift voor filosofie en theologie* 51, 38–67.

Descombes, Vincent. 1979. *Le Même et l'Autre: Quarante-cinq ans de philosophie française 1933–1978*. Paris: Minuit.

De Towarnicki, Alfred. 1946. 'Visite à Martin Heidegger.' *Les Temps modernes* 1:4 (January), 716–24.

De Waelhens, Alphonse. 1947. 'La philosophie de Martin Heidegger et le nazisme.' *Les Temps modernes* 2:22 (July), 115–27.

——. 1948. 'Réponse à cette réponse.' *Les Temps modernes* 3:35 (August), 374–77.

——. 1951. *Une philosophie de l'ambiguïté: L'existentialisme de Maurice Merleau-Ponty*. Louvain: Publications Universitaires de Louvain.

——. [1942] 1971. *La philosophie de Martin Heidegger*. Louvain: Nauwelaerts.

De Waelhens, Alphonse, and Walter Biemel. 1948. Introduction. In *Martin Heidegger, De l'essence de la vérité*, trans. into French by Alphonse de Waelhens and Walter Biemel, 7–64. Louvain: Nauwelaerts.

Dodge, Peter. 1966. *Beyond Marxism: The Faith and Works of Hendrik de Man*. The Hague: Martinus Nijhoff.

——. 1979. *A Documentary Study of Hendrik de Man, Socialist Critic of*

Marxism, comp., ed., and trans. by Peter Dodge. Princeton: Princeton University Press.

Eagleton, Terry. 1983. *Literary Theory: An Introduction.* Oxford: Blackwell.

———. 1986. 'The Critic as Clown.' In *Against the Grain: Selected Essays,* 149–65. London: New Left Books.

Empson, William. [1930, 1947] 1966. *Seven Types of Ambiguity.* New York: New Directions.

Felman, Shoshana. 1978. *La folie et la chose littéraire.* Paris: Seuil.

———. 1985. 'Postal Survival, or The Question of the Navel.' *Yale French Studies* 69, 49–72.

———. 1989. 'Paul de Man's Silence.' *Critical Inquiry* 15:4 (Summer), 704–44.

Flesch, William. 1989. 'Ancestral Voices: De Man and his Defenders.' In *Responses: On Paul de Man's Wartime Journalism,* ed. Werner Hamacher, Neil Hertz, and Thomas Keenan, 173–84. Lincoln: University of Nebraska Press.

Fletcher, Angus. 1972. 'The Perpetual Error.' *Diacritics* 2:4, 14–20.

Freud, Sigmund. 1982. *Hysterie und Angst,* Studienausgabe Band VI. Frankfurt am Main: Fischer.

Gaillard, Pol. 1970. *Malraux.* Paris: Bordas.

Gasché, Rodolphe. 1986. *The Tain of the Mirror: Derrida and the Philosophy of Reflection.* Cambridge: Harvard University Press.

Gearhart, Suzanne. 1983. 'Philosophy *Before* Literature: Deconstruction, Historicity, and the Work of Paul de Man.' *Diacritics* 13:4 (Winter), 63–81.

———. 1984. *The Open Boundary of History and Fiction: A Critical Approach to the French Enlightenment.* Princeton: Princeton University Press.

Goethe. n.d. *Les Affinités électives.* Trans. into French J. F. Angelloz. Paris: Aubier.

Godzich, Wlad. 1986. 'Foreword: The Tiger on the Paper Mat.' In Paul de Man, *The Resistance to Theory,* ix–xviii. Minneapolis: University of Minnesota Press.

Graff, Gerald. 1979. *Literature Against Itself: Literary Ideas in Modern Society.* Chicago: University of Chicago Press.

Habermas, Jürgen. 1989. 'Work and Weltanschauung: The Heidegger Controversy from a German Perspective,' trans. John McCumber. *Critical Inquiry* 15:2 (Winter), 431–56.

Hamacher, Werner. 1989. 'Journals, Politics: Notes on Paul de Man's

Wartime Journalism,' trans. Susan Bernstein, Peter Burgard, Jonathan Hess, Eva Geulen, and Timothy Walters. In *Responses: On Paul de Man's Wartime Journalism*, ed. Werner Hamacher, Neil Hertz, and Thomas Keenan, 438–67. Lincoln: University of Nebraska Press.

Hamacher, Werner, Neil Hertz, and Thomas Keenan, eds. 1989. *Responses: On Paul de Man's Wartime Journalism*. Lincoln: University of Nebraska Press.

Hartman, Geoffrey H. 1955. 'The Fulness and Nothingness of Literature.' *Yale French Studies* 16, 63–78.

————. 1989. 'Looking Back on Paul de Man.' In *Reading de Man Reading*, ed. Lindsay Waters and Wlad Godzich, 3–24. Minneapolis: University of Minnesota Press.

Hegel, G. W. F. 1977. *Phenomenology of Spirit*, trans. A. V. Miller, analysis of text and foreword by J. N. Findlay. Oxford: Clarendon Press.

————. 1988. *Phänomenologie des Geistes*, ed. Hans-Friedrich Wessels and Heinrich Clairmont, introduction by Wolfgang Beusiepen. Hamburg: Meiner.

Heidegger, Martin. [1952] 1954a. 'Moira (Parmenides, Fragment VIII, 34–41).' In *Vorträge und Aufsätze*, 231–56. Pfullingen: Neske.

————. [1951] 1954b. 'Bauen Wohnen Denken.' In *Vorträge und Aufsätze*, 145–62. Pfullingen: Neske.

————. [1951] 1954c. '. . . Dichterisch wohnet der Mensch.' *Vorträge und Aufsätze*, 187–204. Pfullingen: Neske.

————. 1957. *Hebel—der Hausfreund*. Pfullingen: Neske.

————. 1959. *Gelassenheit*. Pfullingen: Neske.

————. 1962. *Being and Time*, trans. John Macquarrie and Edward Robinson. Oxford: Blackwell.

————. 1966. *Discourse on Thinking: A Translation of 'Gelassenheit,'* trans. John M. Anderson and E. Hans Freund. New York: Harper & Row.

————. 1966. 'Sérénité,' trans. André Préau. In *Questions III*, trans. André Préau, Julien Hervier, and Roger Munier, 159–227. Paris: Gallimard.

————. [1930, 1943] 1976. 'Vom Wesen der Wahrheit.' In *Gesamtausgabe, 1. Abteilung, Band 9: Wegmarken*, 177–202. Frankfurt am Main: Klostermann.

————. [1926] 1977. *Gesamtausgabe, 1. Abteilung, Band 2: Sein und Zeit*. Frankfurt am Main: Klostermann.

————. [1946] 1978a. 'Brief über den "Humanismus."' In *Wegmarken*, 311–60. Frankfurt am Main: Klostermann.

———. [1955] 1978b. 'Zur Seinsfrage. In *Wegmarken*, 379–491. Frankfurt am Main: Klostermann.

———. [1935–36] 1980a. 'Der Ursprung des Kunstwerkes.' In *Holzwege*, 1–77. Frankfurt am Main: Klostermann.

———. [1946] 1980b. 'Wozu Dichter?' In *Holzwege*, 265–316. Frankfurt am Main: Klostermann.

———. [1939] 1981a. '"Wie wenn am Feiertage. . . ."' In *Gesamtausgabe*, 1. *Abteilung, Band 4: Erläuterungen zu Hölderlins Dichtung*, 49–77. Frankfurt am Main: Klostermann.

———. [1944] 1981b. 'Vorbemerkung zur Wiederholung der Rede.' In *Gesamtausgabe, 1. Abteilung, Band 4: Erläuterungen zu Hölderlins Dichtung*, 193–94. Frankfurt am Main: Klostermann.

———. [1950] 1981c. 'Vorwort zur Zweiten Auflage.' In *Gesamtausgabe, 1. Abteilung, Band 4: Erläuterungen zu Hölderlins Dichtung*, 8–9. Frankfurt am Main: Klostermann.

Hertz, Neil. 1990. 'More Lurid Figures.' *Colloquium Helveticum* 11/12, 205–40.

Hirsch, David H. 1988. 'Paul de Man and the Politics of Deconstruction.' *Sewanee Review* 96:2 (Spring), 330–38.

Hölderlin, Friedrich. 1951. *Sämtliche Werke (Grosse Stuttgarter Ausgabe). Zweiter Band. Gedichte nach 1800,* ed. Friedrich Beißner. Stuttgart: Kohlhammer.

———. 1969. *Werke und Briefe. Band 2: Der Tod des Empedokles—Aufsätze—Übersetzungen—Briefe,* ed. Friedrich Beißner and Jochen Schmidt. Frankfurt am Main: Insel.

———. 1983. *Sämtliche Werke: Frankfurter Ausgabe. Band 9. Dichtungen nach 1806. Mündliches,* ed. D. E. Sattler. Frankfurt am Main: Roter Stern.

———. 1990. *'Hyperion' and Selected Poems,* ed. Erich Santner. New York: Continuum.

Holdheim, Wolfgang. 1988. 'Fateful Swerve.' Letter to the Editor. *London Review of Books,* 17 March, 4.

Holthusen, Hans Egon. 1954. 'Letter to the Editor,' probably trans. Paul de Man. *Confluence: An International Forum* 3:1 (March 1954), 115–18.

Husserl, Edmund. [1913] 1962. *Ideas: General Introduction to Pure Phenomenology,* trans. W. R. Boyce Gibson. London: Collier-Macmillan.

Hyppolite, Jean. 1939. 'Avertissement du traducteur.' In G. W. F. Hegel, *La Phénoménologie de l'Esprit,* 2 vol., trans. into French by Jean Hyppolite, v–vii. Paris: Aubier.

———. 1946. *Genèse et structure de la 'Phénoménologie de l'Esprit' de Hegel*. Paris: Aubier.

———. 1974. *Genesis and Structure of Hegel's 'Phenomenology of Spirit*,' trans. Samuel Cherniak and John Heckman. Evanston: Northwestern University Press.

Jansen, Paul. 1976. *Edmund Husserl: Einführung in seine Phänomenologie*. Freiburg: Alber.

Jünger, Ernst. 1932. *Der Arbeiter: Herrschaft und Gestalt*. Hamburg: Hanseatische Verlagsanstalt.

———. [1949] 1963a. *Werke, Band 3. Tagebücher III, Strahlungen: Zweiter Teil*. Stuttgart: Klett.

———. [1950] 1963b. 'Über die Linie.' in *Werke. Band 5. Essays I, Betrachtungen zur Zeit*, 248–89. Stuttgart: Klett.

Kamuf, Peggy. 1989. 'Pieces of Resistance.' In *Reading de Man Reading*, ed. Lindsay Waters and Wlad Godzich, 136–54. Minneapolis: University of Minnesota Press.

Keenan, Thomas. 1989. 'Documents: Public Criticisms.' In *Responses: On Paul de Man's Wartime Journalism*, ed. Werner Hamacher, Neil Hertz, and Thomas Keenan, 468–77. Lincoln: University of Nebraska Press.

Kelly, Michael. 1981. 'Hegel in France to 1940: A Bibliographical Essay.' *Journal of European Studies* 11:1 (March), 29–52.

Klein, Richard. 1973. 'The Blindness of Hyperboles: The Ellipses of Insight.' In *Diacritics* 3:2 (Summer), 33–44.

Kojève, Alexandre. 1947. *Introduction à la lecture de Hegel: Leçons sur la 'Phénoménologie de l'Esprit.'* Taught from 1933 to 1939 at the École des Hautes Études, assembled by Raymond Queneau. Paris: Gallimard.

Krueger, S. Heidi. 1989. 'Opting to Know: On the Wartime Journalism of Paul de Man.' In *Responses: On Paul de Man's Wartime Journalism*, ed. Werner Hamacher, Neil Hertz, and Thomas Keenan, 298–313. Lincoln: University of Nebraska Press.

Lacan, Jacques. 1966. *Ecrits I*. Paris: Seuil.

———. 1976. 'Conférences et entretiens dans des universités nordaméricaines.' *Scilicet* 6/7, 3–63.

Lacoue-Labarthe, Philippe. 1986. 'Oedipe comme figure.' In *L'Imitation des modernes: Typographies 2*, 203–25. Paris: Galilée.

Lauer, Quentin. 1955. *Phénoménologie de Husserl: Essai sur la genèse de l'intentionnalité*. Paris: P.U.F.

Lehman, David. 1991. *Signs of the Times: Deconstruction and the Fall of Paul de Man*. New York: Poseidon Press.

Lentricchia, Frank. 1980. *After the New Criticism.* London: Athlone Press.
———. 1983. *Criticism and Social Change.* Chicago: University of Chicago Press.
Lepenies, Wolf. 1988. *Between Literature and Science: The Rise of Sociology.* Trans. R. J. Hollingdale. Cambridge: Cambridge University Press.
Lescure, Jean. [1943] 1970. 'La Lutte avec l'Ange.' In *Les critiques de notre temps et Malraux,* ed. Pol Gaillard, 90–91. Paris: Garnier.
Levinas, Emmanuel. 1968. 'La substitution.' *Revue philosophique de Louvain* 66:91 (August), 487–508.
Löwith, Karl. 1946. 'Les implications politiques de la philosophie de l'existence chez Heidegger,' trans. into French by Joseph Rovan. *Les Temps modernes* 2:14 (November), 342–60.
———. 1948. 'Réponse à M. de Waelhens.' *Les Temps modernes* 3:35 (August), 370–73.
———. 1953. *Heidegger: Denker in dürftiger Zeit.* Frankfurt am Main: Fischer, 1953.
———. 1986. *Mein Leben in Deutschland vor und nach 1933: Ein Bericht.* Stuttgart: Metzler.
Malraux, André. 1948. *Les Noyers de l'Altenburg.* Paris: Gallimard.
Marañon, Gregorio. 1941. *Tibère.* Trans. into French by Louis Parrot, pref. by Anatole de Monzie. Paris: Gallimard.
Martin, Wallace. 1983. Introduction. In *The Yale Critics: Deconstruction in America,* ed. Jonathan Arac et al., xv–xxxvii. Minneapolis: University of Minnesota Press.
Marx, Werner. 1971. *Hegels Phänomenologie des Geistes: Die Bestimmung ihrer Idee in 'Vorrede' und 'Einleitung.'* Frankfurt am Main: Klostermann.
Melville, Herman. 1945. *Moby Dick.* Trans. into Dutch by Paul de Man. Antwerp: Helicon.
Melville, Stephen W. 1986. *Philosophy Beside Itself: On Deconstruction and Modernism.* Foreword by Donald Marshall. Manchester: Manchester University Press.
Merleau-Ponty, Maurice. 1947a. 'Lecture de Montaigne.' *Les Temps modernes* 3:27 (December), 1044–60.
———. 1947b. Review of *Les Cahiers de la Pléiade. Les Temps modernes* 3:27 (December), 1151–52.
———. 1955. *Les Aventures de la dialectique.* Paris: Gallimard.
———. [1952] 1960a. 'Le Langage indirect et les voix du silence.' In *Signes,* 49–104. Paris: Gallimard.

———. [1954] 1960b. 'Sur les faits divers.' In *Signes*, 388–91. Paris: Gallimard.

———. 1968. *Résumés de cours (Collège de France 1952–1960)*. Paris: Gallimard.

Micha, René, and Alphonse de Waelhens. 1949. 'Du caractère des Belges.' *Les Temps modernes* 4:41 (March) 413–42.

Milic, Novica. 1989. 'Paul de Man and Alphonse de Waelhens: Reading and the Question of Self-Knowledge.' In *(Dis)continuities: Essays on Paul de Man*, ed. Luc Herman, Kris Humbeeck, and Geert Lernout, 75–83. Amsterdam: Rodopi.

Montaigne. 1988. *Les Essais*, 3 vols., ed. Pierre Villey. Paris: Quadrige/ P.U.F.

Mizumura, Minae. 1985. 'Renunciation.' *Yale French Studies* 69, 81–97.

Newmark, Kevin. 1989. 'Paul de Man's History.' In *Reading de Man Reading*, ed. Lindsay Waters and Wlad Godzich, 121–35. Minneapolis: University of Minnesota Press.

Nietzsche, Friedrich. 1980. *Sämtliche Werke. Kritische Studienausgabe*, 15 vols., ed. Georgio Colli und Mazzino Montinari. Munich: DTV.

Norris, Christopher. 1985. 'Some Versions of Rhetoric: Empson and de Man.' In *Rhetoric and Form: Deconstruction at Yale*, ed. Robert Con Davis and Ronald Schleifer, 191–214. Norman: University of Oklahoma Press.

———. 1988. *Paul de Man: Deconstruction and the Critique of Aesthetic Ideology*. New York: Routledge.

O'Hara, Daniel T. 1985. *The Romance of Interpretation: Visionary Criticism from Pater to de Man*. New York: Columbia University Press.

Opiela, Stanislas. 1983. 'Le problème de la chose-en-soi (Ding-an-sich) dans la philosophie de Hegel.' In *Kant oder Hegel? Über Formen der Begründung in der Philosophie*, ed. Dieter Henrich, 267–73. Stuttgart: Klett-Cotta.

Parker, Andrew. 1981. ' "Taking Sides" (On History): Derrida Re-Marx.' *Diacritics* 11 (Fall), 57–73.

Payne, Robert. 1973. *André Malraux (A Portrait of André Malraux)*, trans. into French by Pierre Rocheron. Paris: Buchet/Castel.

Pels, Dick. 1991. 'Treason of the Intellectuals: Paul de Man and Hendrik de Man.' *Theory, Culture & Society* 8, 21–56.

Pingaud, Bernard. 1971. 'Merleau-Ponty, Sartre et la littérature.' *L'Arc* 46, 80–87.

Poster, Mark. 1975. *Existential Marxism in Post-War France: From Sartre to Althusser*. Princeton: Princeton University Press.

Raval, Suresh. 1981. *Metacriticism*. Athens: University of Georgia Press.

Ray, William. 1984. *Literary Meaning: From Phenomenology to Deconstruction*. Oxford: Blackwell.

Redfield, Marc W. 1989. 'Humanizing de Man.' *Diacritics* 19:2 (Summer), 35–53.

————. 1990. 'De Man, Schiller, and the Politics of Reception.' *Colloquium Helveticum* 11/12, 139–67.

Riccomini, Donald Roy. 1979. *Literary Indeterminacy and Revolution in the Yale Criticism*. Ann Arbor: Xerox University Microfilms/University Microfilms International.

Richards, I. A. 1930. *Practical Criticism: A Study of Literary Judgement*. London: Kegan Paul, Trench, Trubner & Co.

Richardson, William J. 1963. *Heidegger: Through Phenomenology to Thought*. The Hague: Nijhoff.

Ritter, Joachim, and Karlfried Gründer. 1984. *Historisches Wörterbuch der Philosophie. Band 6*. Basel: Schwabe.

Roth, Michael S. 1988. *Knowing and History: Appropriations of Hegel in Twentieth-Century France*. Ithaca: Cornell University Press.

Salusinszky, Imre. 1987. *Criticism in Society: Interviews with Jacques Derrida, Northrop Frye, Harold Bloom, Geoffrey Hartman, Frank Kermode, Edward Said, Barbara Johnson, Frank Lentricchia, and J. Hillis Miller*. New York: Methuen. 1987.

Sartre, Jean-Paul. 1936. *L'Imagination*. Paris: P.U.F.

————. 1940. *L'Imaginaire*. Paris: Gallimard.

————. [1939] 1947a. 'Une idée fondamentale de la phénoménologie de Husserl: l'intentionnalité.' In *Situations I: Essais critiques*, 29–32. Paris: Gallimard.

————. [1939] 1947b. 'A propos de 'Le Bruit et la Fureur': La temporalité chez Faulkner.' In *Situations I: Essais critiques*, 65–75. Paris: Gallimard.

————. [1938] 1947c. 'A propos de John dos Passos et de "1919."' In *Situations I: Essais critiques*, 14–24. Paris: Gallimard.

————. 1948. *Qu'est-ce que la littérature?* Paris: Gallimard.

————. [1952] 1972a. 'Mallarmé (1842–1889).' In *Situations IX: Mélanges*, 191–201. Paris: Gallimard.

————. [1960] 1972b. 'Les Écrivains en personne.' Interview. In *Situations IX: Mélanges*, 9–39. Paris: Gallimard.

Sartre, Jean-Paul. 1962. *L'imagination: A psychological critique*, trans. Forest Williams. Ann Arbor: University of Michigan Press.

Sartre, Jean-Paul. 1988. *'What Is Literature?' and Other Essays*. Cambridge: Harvard University Press.

Schneider, Heinrich. 1953. 'Letter to the Editor,' probably trans. Paul de Man. *Confluence: An International Forum* 2:4 (December), 134–46.

Shusterman, Ronald. 1988. *Critique et poésie selon I.A. Richards: De la confiance positiviste au relativisme naissant*. Lille: Atelier National de Reproduction des Thèses.

Stoekl, Allan. 1985. 'De Man and the Dialectic of Being.' *Diacritics* 15:3 (Fall), 36–45.

———. 1989. 'De Man and Guilt.' In *Responses: On Paul de Man's Wartime Journalism*, ed. Werner Hamcher, Neil Hertz, and Thomas Keenan, 375–85. Lincoln: University of Nebraska Press.

———. 1990. 'On Bataille.' *Yale French Studies* 78.

Sychrava, Juliet. 1989. *Schiller to Derrida: Idealism in Aesthetics*. Cambridge: Cambridge University Press.

Taylor, Mark C. 1987. *Altarity*. Chicago: University of Chicago Press.

Temps modernes, Les. 1946. 'Deux Documents sur Heidegger.' Editors' Note. *Les Temps modernes* 1:4 (January), 713.

Tison-Braun, Micheline. 1975. 'Le Colloque de l'Altenburg ou les démons de la contingence.' *La revue des lettres modernes* 425/431, 161–73.

Warminski, Andrzej. 1985. 'Dreadful Reading: Blanchot on Hegel.' *Yale French Studies* 69, 267–75.

Waters, Lindsay. 1989. 'Introduction. Paul de Man: Life and Works.' In Paul de Man, *Critical Writings, 1953–1978*, ix–lxxiv. Minneapolis: University of Minnesota Press.

Weber, Samuel. 1989. 'Upsetting the Set-Up: Remarks on Heidegger's Questing after Technics.' *MLN (Modern Language Notes)* 104:5 (December), 977–91.

Weil, Eric. 1947. 'Le cas Heidegger.' *Les Temps modernes* 2:22 (July), 128–38.

Index

Absolute Spirit, 84–85, 92, 103, 104–5, 134, 152, 189n.25, 190n.26, 195n.15

Adorno, Theodor W.: *Negative Dialektik,* 155; *Philosophische Terminologie,* 193n.6

Aesthetics: and the ontological question, 121; as privileged realm, 131

Agence Dechenne, 199n.40

Allegory, 203n.14

Allemann, Beda, 103

America, specificity of, 29, 174–75, 186n.4

Anderson, John M., 210n.40

Bachelard, Gaston, 177

Bacon, Francis, 37

Bahti, Timothy, 179n.4

Baker, John Jay, 205n.3

Barthes, Roland, 202n.8; *Writing Degree Zero,* 146–47

Barzilai, Shuli, 200n.1

Bataille, Georges, 29, 184n.4; and committed literature, 207n.20; and Hegel, 186–87n.7, 189n.23; and Heidegger, 194n.13

Baudelaire, Charles, 64, 133; anti-historicism of, 76; authentic poetic commitment of, 87, 99–100, 106; and death, 54, 55, 56, 59; and Heidegger, 167, 172; and Hölderlin, 101, 144, 149; and Mallarmé, 62, 78, 89, 90–91, 101, 106, 133, 144, 148–49; and Malraux, 76, 167, 172; and Montaigne, 34, 35; and Nietzsche, 81, 91; and recovery of undivided Being, 51–53, 54, 55, 57–58, 62, 84, 167; revolutionary intent of, 119; and Richard, 144; and sacrifice of conscious-ness, 56, 59, 64, 65, 78, 81; 'Le Chat,' 138; 'Correspondances,' 51, 52, 60, 183n.1; 'Le Cygne,' 51, 52, 60, 62, 208n.25; *Spleen de Paris,* 81

Becoming. *See* Being: and be-coming

Being: and becoming, 56, 58, 69, 73, 75–76, 115; and nam-ing, 50, 93, 94, 97–100, 164, 208n.24; and not-being, 53, 54, 184n.3; preservation of, 77–78, 96. *See also* Ontico-

Being (*continued*)
ontological distinction; Onto-
logical superiority; Ontologism
Beissner, Friedrich, 192n.4
Berman, Art, 205n.3
Besnier, Jean-Michel, 194n.13
Bibliographie Dechenne, 182n.20
Biemel, Walter, 210n.40
Blake, William, 184n.2
Blanchot, Maurice: *L'espace
littéraire,* 204n.14; 'La lit-
térature et le droit à la mort,'
200–201n.2, 202n.5, 206n.20
Bloomfield, Morton W., 200n.1
Boileau, Nicolas, 201n.2
Boschetti, Anna, 182n.2, 184n.4,
207n.20
Bourget, Paul, 180n.5, 206n.14;
Le Démon du Midi, 7
Breton, Stanislas, 203n.12
Bretzius, Stephen, 205n.3
Brinckmann, A. E.: *Geist der
Nationen,* 17, 19, 21
Byron, Lord George Gordon, 90

Caillois, Roger, 199n.40
Carette, Louis (Félicien Marceau),
22–23, 181n.14
Char, René, 202n.20
Chase, Cynthia, 184n.1, 205n.3
Chateaubriand, François-René de:
Mémoires d'Outre-Tombe, 37
Chatwin, Bruce, 183n.15, 197n.28
Christensen, Jerome, 188n.19
Christianity, 177
Claeys-Van Haegendoren, Mieke,
183n.10
Colinet, Edouard, 182n.1

Collaboration and scientific truth,
12–13, 19–20, 180n.9
Commitment and literature, 120,
159, 160, 161, 173, 198n.39,
206n.18, 206–7n.20, 209n.29
Confluence, 185n.1
Consciousness: death of, 76, 103,
165, 194n.12, 208n.25; and
dialectic, 76–79, 83–86; intentional structure of, 31, 141,
149–50; and language, 50;
and object, 31, 49; ontological superiority of, 77–78, 114,
168–70, 172, 177, 202n.6; sacrifice of, 31, 59–60, 62, 64, 81,
103; temporality of, 56, 76–79.
See also Separation (between
consciousness and object)
Conservatism: in America,
186n.4; as anti-historicism, 71,
74; as nationalism, 74; as nihilism, 33–34, 70–72, 74, 120,
121, 122, 132, 146; as ritual, 33
Continuity, hope of, 32, 33, 34, 35
Corngold, Stanley, 205n.3
Crisis: as historical condition, 41,
119, 130; and literature, 25–
26, 42, 45, 86, 162, 167, 171,
178; and ontological question,
121, 178
Criticism: and ethics, 139; and history, 145–47; Marxist, 145–46,
147; and mediation, 133–34;
and objective truth, 21–22;
salvational, 142–43; and sensation, 143–44
Critique, 29
Croce, Benedetto, 195n.17,
198n.39

Culler, Jonathan, 200n.1

Dasein, 58, 78, 114, 177, 193–94n.12, 208n.24
Death: as biological phenomenon, 73, 76, 166, 186n.3, 186–87n.7, 194n.12, 208n.25; of consciousness, 76, 103, 165, 194n.12, 208n.25; as figure, 56, 60; as theme, 54–55, 56, 59–60; and unity, 54–55. *See also* Sacrifice
Deconstruction and metaphysics, 204–5n.2
Deduction, 12, 20
De Gandillac, Maurice, 196n.21
De Man, Hendrik, 3, 36–38, 179n.1, 181nn.11, 19; *Cahiers de ma montagne,* 36–38, 42; *Massification and the Decline of Culture,* 186n.1; *The Psychology of Socialism,* 180n.6
De Man, Paul: *Allegories of Reading,* xi; 'Anthropomorphism and Trope in the Lyric,' 183n.1, 195n.17; 'Autobiography as De-Facement,' 179n.3; Comments (Johns Hopkins Symposium), 194n.12, 202n.8; ' "Conclusions": Walter Benjamin's *Task of the Translator,*' 107; 'The Crisis of Contemporary Criticism,' 45; 'The Dead-End of Formalist Criticism,' 135, 137–52, 164, 201nn.2, 4, 202n.7; 'The Double Aspect of Symbolism,' 49–65, 67–68, 71, 90, 92, 101, 102, 106, 129, 146,

185n.7, 186n.1; 'Georg Lukác's Theory of the Novel,' 50, 195n.15; 'Heidegger's Exegeses of Hölderlin,' 85–86, 94–100, 101, 102–4, 107, 115, 118, 127–28, 131, 133, 144, 160, 183n.4, 186n.7, 188n.22, 190n.25, 192n.4, 185n.15, 197n.33, 199–200n.41, 200n.42, 207n.24; 'Hölderlin and the Romantic Tradition,' 198n.39, 208n.27; 'Hypogram and Inscription,' 183n.1; 'Image and Emblem in Yeats' (*see* 'Mallarmé, Yeats, and the Post-Romantic Predicament'); 'The Image of Rousseau,' 203n.12; 'Intentional Structure of the Romantic Image,' 155–56, 157, 158, 162, 163–73, 177–78, 184n.2; Interview with Stefano Rosso, 187n.7, 201n.2, 205nn.8, 9, 207n.20; Introduction for Jacques Lacan, 203n.14; Introduction to *Toward an Aesthetics of Reception,* 183n.1; 'The Inward Generation,' 67–72, 102, 119–24, 126, 127, 130, 146, 170, 186nn.4, 5, 197n.31, 198n.40; 'Keats and Hölderlin,' 105, 190n.26; Letter to Frida Vandervelden, 40; Letter to Georges Bataille, 29; Letter to Harry Levin, 202n.7; Letter to Wlad Godzich, 47; 'Mallarmé, Yeats, and the Post-Romantic Predicament,' 151–52, 161, 163, 167, 183n.2, 186nn.5, 7, 188–89n.22, 190n.26, 165nn.15, 17,

De Man, Paul (*continued*)
202n.6, 204–5n.2, 206n.18,
208n.25, 209n.29; 'Modern
Poetics,' 195n.15; 'Montaigne
and Transcendence,' 29, 30–
35, 39–40; 'Nietzsche's Theory
of Rhetoric,' 49; 'Patterns of
Temporality,' 183n.4; 'Poetic
Nothingness,' 102, 104, 144,
186n.7, 200n.44, 203n.14,
204n.14; 'Process and Poetry,'
59, 64, 68, 77, 78–79, 81, 87–
93, 101–2, 112, 131, 198n.39,
201n.2, 204n.14, 206n.19;
'Reading (Proust),' 166; 'The
Resistance to Theory,' 188n.19,
200n.2; 'The Return to Philology,' 200n.2; Review of
Harold Bloom's *Anxiety of Influence,* 67; 'The Rhetoric of
Blindness,' 188n.16; *The Rhetoric of Romanticism,* 204n.2;
'The Rhetoric of Tempo-
rality,' xi, 83, 203n.14; 'The
Riddle of Hölderlin,' 204n.15;
'Roland Barthes and the Limits
of Structuralism,' 202n.8;
'Situation of the Novel,' 159;
'Symbolic Landscape in Wordsworth and Yeats,' 185n.6; 'The
Temptation of Permanence,'
59, 71, 76–77, 83, 109–12,
115, 116, 117, 118, 126, 127,
128–29, 132, 157, 174–75, 177,
191–92n.3, 192n.4, 197n.31,
198n.36, 200n.42, 210n.41;
'Thematic Criticism and the
Theme of Faust,' 153, 164,
189n.22; *Wartime Journal-*

ism, xi, 3–26, 32, 72, 119, 121,
126–27, 131, 206n.14
De Monzie, Anatole, 12, 181n.8
Derrida, Jacques, 57, 183n.3;
Mémoires: for Paul de Man,
94, 95
De Schutter, Dirk, 184n.3,
187n.12, 205n.3, 207–8n.24
Descombes, Vincent, 184nn.3, 4,
205n.8
Destiny, 73, 89–90, 109, 127–28
De Towarnicki, Alfred, 196n.21
De Waelhens, Alphonse, 210n.40;
'On the Character of the Belgians,' 29, 127; *Une philosophie
de l'ambiguïté,* 196n.21; *La
philosophie de Martin Heidegger,* 78, 187n.7, 193–94n.12,
194n.13, 202n.6; 'La philosophie de Martin Heidegger et
le nazisme,' 125, 126, 196n.21;
'Réponse à cette réponse,'
196n.21
Dialectic: of consciousness, 76–
79, 83–86; final term of, 84–86,
87, 92, 96–98, 101–6, 112–
14, 134, 145, 151–53, 169–70,
171, 176–77, 189–90n.25,
190n.26, 193–94n.12, 197n.31,
209n.29; and history, 76–79,
109–10, 127, 145, 175, 186n.7;
and Marxism, 145; as mediation, 112, 129, 140, 197n.33; of
poetic image, 163
Dialogue, 111, 115–16, 118, 122–
24, 132, 133, 173
Dictatorship, 11–12
Didier, Edouard, 183n.15
Dodge, Peter, 180n.6, 181n.19

Dos Passos, John, 159
Dostoyevski, Fyodor, 177
Doubt, aesthetic recuperation of, 39–40

Eagleton, Terry, xi, 200n.1
Earth. *See* Object
Eliot, T. S., 184
Empson, William, 145, 146, 200n.1, 202n.9; *Seven Types of Ambiguity,* 139–40, 201n.4; *Some Versions of Pastoral,* 140–41
En soi, 157
Entscheidung, 127–28, 129–30
Erfahrung, 113–14, 189n.25
Eschatology, 92, 101–2, 103–4, 124, 125. *See also* Dialectic: final term of
Eternalism, 59, 74–75, 77, 111, 124, 125, 126, 131, 197n.31, 201n.2, 204n.14
Ethics, 30, 33, 39, 139
Existential categories. *See* Ontological question: and existential categories; Rhetoric: and existential categories
Existentialism, 156, 157, 162, 205n.9

Fact versus value, 19–20
Fascism, 124, 126
Felman, Shoshana, 182n.4, 203n.14
Flesch, William, 180n.8
Fletcher, Angus, 123n.1
Formalism, ontological presuppositions of, 137–38

Free University of Brussels, 5, 180n.7, 209n.37
Freud, Sigmund, 203n.14; 'Bruchstück einer Hysterie-Analyse,' 137
Freund, E. Hans, 210n.40
Friedrich, Hugo, *Montaigne,* 30, 33, 40

Gaillard, Pol, 197n.28, 199n.40
Galsworthy, John, 180n.5, 206n.14; *The Forsyte Saga,* 7
Gasché, Rodolphe: *The Tain of the Mirror,* 67
Gearhart, Suzanne, 195n.15, 203n.11
Godzich, Wlad, 134, 183n.4
Goethe, J. W. von, 31; as representative of complementary nationalism, 17, 25; *The Elective Affinities,* 17
Graff, Gerald, 203n.11

Habermas, Jürgen, 197n.26
Hamacher, Werner, 179n.4, 180n.9, 180–81n.10, 197n.27
Hamburger, Michael, 207n.23
Hartman, Geoffrey, 200n.1; 'The Fulness and Nothingness of Literature,' 204n.14
Hebel, Johann Peter, 176, 177
Hegel, G. W. F., 54, 67, 142, 145, 175, 187n.10, 192n.5, 193n.11, 193–94n.12, 195n.15, 202n.7, 203n.9; on experience *(see Erfahrung);* and Heidegger, 110, 111–15, 127, 128, 129, 184n.3, 186–89n.7, 193–94n.12, 194n.13, 195n.15,

Hegel, G. W. F. (*continued*)
197n.31, 202n.7; historical
symbolism in, 89; and Hölderlin, 96, 103–4, 105–6, 188n.22,
190n.26, 206n.19; and Kant,
111–15; and Mallarmé, 63, 86,
186n.7, 188n.22, 190n.26; and
negating power of naming,
202n.5; and Nietzsche, 102;
on organic life versus life of
consciousness, 76, 186–87n.7,
208n.25; and politics, 196n.21,
206n.19; revolutionary intent
of, 119; as Romantic, 121; and
Sartre, 160, 205n.8; and separation between consciousness
and object, 68, 157, 184n.4;
synthesis in, 64, 84, 85, 96,
102, 103–6, 112–14, 134, 152,
169, 189–90n.25, 190n.26 (*see
also* Absolute Spirit); unhappy
consciousness of, 71 (*see also*
Unhappy consciousness); *Phenomenology of Spirit*, 45, 76, 85,
96, 104–5, 112, 188–89n.22,
188–89n.25
Heidegger, Martin, 54, 107, 144,
160, 177, 192n.5, 201n.2,
202n.6, 203n.9; on authentic
interpretation of Being, 78,
158; and Baudelaire, 167, 172;
death of, 38; and death, 187n.7,
194n.12; on earth, world, and
sky, 191–92n.3; *Entscheidung*
in, 127–28; exegetical method
of, 133–34, 170, 195n.17, 199–
200n.41, 200n.42; *Gelassenheit*, 174, 176–78, 210n.40;
and Hegel, 110, 111–15, 127,

128, 129, 184n.3, 186–89n.7,
193–94n.12, 194n.13, 195n.15,
197n.31, 202n.7; and his-
tory, 109–10, 123, 124, 128,
129, 202n.7; and Hölderlin,
94–97, 110, 115–16, 118, 126,
128, 130–31, 133, 187–88n.15,
192n.4, 195n.14, 200n.42;
and Kant, 111–12, 114–15,
195n.15; and Malraux, 129–
30, 167, 172, 175; and Marx,
202n.7; naming of Being in,
94–95, 96–97, 102, 131, 207–
8n.24; and Nietzsche, 102,
139, 194n.13; 88n.15, 192n.4,
194n.14, 200n.42; on ontological priority, 57–58, 78, 114,
177, 184n.4, 208n.24; and
politics, 123, 124–26, 127, 128,
185n.1, 196n.21; and privileging of poetry, 131, 161; revolutionary intent of, 119; and
Rilke, 94, 174, 209n.33; and
Sartre, 158, 205n.9; seductive
language of, 115, 117, 125, 128,
172, 195n.17; and technology,
174, 176; and temptation of
permanence, 110–11, 114–
15, 129, 167; 'Bauen Wohnen
Denken,' 110, 118, 191–92n.3,
192n.4; 'Brief über den Humanismus,' 202n.7; 'Dichterisch
wohnet der Mensch,' 110,
191n.3; *Erläuterungen zu
Hölderlins Dichtung*, 93–97,
127–29, 130–31, 195nn.14,
16, 17, 199n.41; 'Hebel—
der Hausfreund,' 209n.36;
'Hölderlin und das Wesen der

Dichtung,' 194n.13; 'Moira,'
110, 111, 118; 'The Origin of
the Work of Art,' 110, 127,
191n.3, 202n.6; *Sein und Zeit,*
49, 57, 109, 114, 177, 182n.3,
184n.4, 196n.19, 208n.25;
'Vom Wesen der Wahrheit,'
210n.40; 'Warum bleiben
wir in die Provinz?' 193n.6;
'Wozu Dichter?' 209n.33; 'Zur
Seinsfrage,' 185n.1
Helicon (publishing house), 27,
182n.2
Hellingrath, Norbert von, 192n.4
Hemingway, Ernest, 120, 159
Herbert, George: 'The Sacrifice,' 140
Hertz, Neil, 200n.1
Hirsch, David H., 187–88n.15
History: and consciousness, 75–
79; and criticism, 145–47; and
dialectic, 76–79, 109–10, 127,
145, 178; and eternalism, 111,
112–13; and Marxism, 145–47,
202n.7; versus nature, 72–
75, 76, 186n.7; as noematic
correlative, 147, 149, 151; and
ontological question, 123,
202n.7, 202–3n.9; and poetry,
74–75, 77, 132, 147, 175; and
rhetoric, xi; and science, 11–12,
17–18, 75, 77; and separation
between consciousness and
object, 67–68, 89–91, 144,
150–52. *See also* Resistance as
repression: of history
Hitler, Adolf, 14
Hölderlin, Friedrich, 87, 155, 168,
176, 207n.24; and Baudelaire,

101, 144, 149; on conception
of poetic image, 163–67, 170;
and Hegel, 96, 103–4, 105–6,
188n.22, 190n.26, 206n.19;
and Heidegger, 94–97, 110,
115–16, 118, 126, 128, 130–
31, 133, 187–88n.15, 192n.4,
195n.14, 200n.42; and history, 102; and Mallarmé, 100,
101, 104, 144; and naming of
Being, 94–98, 99–100, 116;
on poetry of substance versus
poetry of becoming, 88–90;
and politics, 126, 128, 198n.39,
206n.19; revolutionary intent
of, 119; as Romantic, 107, 121–
22, 208n.27; and *vaterländisches
Umkehr,* 90, 91, 92, 198n.39;
'Andenken,' 94; 'Anmerkungen
zur Antigonä,' 89–90; 'Brod
und Wein,' 163–66; *Empedokles,*
105, 206n.19; 'Heimkunft,'
168; 'In lieblicher Bläue,' 118,
192n.4; 'Wie wenn am Feiertage . . . ,' 47, 95–97, 103, 118,
207n.24
Holdheim, Wolfgang, xi
Holthusen, Hans Egon, 185–
86n.1
Husserl, Edmund, 82; and humility of phenomenology, 33;
and principle of intentionality, 149–50, 159, 166, 171,
182–83n.5, 187n.9, 188n.15,
203n.12; and Merleau-Ponty,
205n.7; and Montaigne, 33;
and Sartre, 157, 159; transcendental consciousness in, 143,
152; *Ideas,* 203n.12

Huxley, Aldous, 7
Hyppolite, Jean, 189n.22, 202n.7;
    *Genesis and Structure of Hegel's
    'Phenomenology of Spirit,'* 76,
    187n.10, 189n.23, 193nn.7, 11,
    202n.5

Image, intentional structure of,
    163–69
Imagination, self-sufficiency of,
    169, 172–73, 178, 209n.29,
    210n.41. *See also* Consciousness
Induction, 18, 20
Ingarden, Roman, 149
Intentional structure: of con-
    sciousness, 31, 141, 150; of
    image, 163–69. *See also* Lan-
    guage, intentional structure
    of; Poetry of becoming, inten-
    tional structure of; Poetry of
    being, intentional structure of
Intention and volition, 172,
    187n.9
Intuition and truth, 24, 25–26
Irony, 32, 34, 35, 39–40, 42, 86,
    120, 132

James, Henry, 120
Jansen, Paul, 203n.12
Jeener, Raymond, 180n.7
Jews, 14–15, 181n.11, 188n.15
Joyce, James, 9, 159, 206nn.14, 18;
    Ulysses, 7
Jünger, Ernst, 131, 195n.18; and
    Hendrik de Man, 42; and poli-
    tics, 120, 181–82n.19; as rep-
    resentative of complementary
    nationalism, 25; and sociology,
    24–25, 181n.18; *Der Arbeiter,*
    5, 24, 25, 181–82n.19; *Auf den
    Marmorklippen,* 25, 181n.18;
    'Über die Linie,' 185–86n.1

Kafka, Franz: *Das Schloss,* 7
Kamuf, Peggy, 203n.14
Kant, Immanuel, 111–14, 138, 157,
    193n.8, 195n.15
Keats, John, 87, 105, 119
Keenan, Thomas, 199n.40
Kelly, Michael, 184n.4
Kinsey, Alfred: *Sexual Behavior in
    the Human Male,* 29
Kissinger, Henry, 185n.1
Klein, Richard, 183n.1, 203n.14
Kojève, Alexandre, 184nn.3, 4,
    187n.7, 189n.22, 202n.7
Kreutzer, Conradin, 174
Krueger, S. Heidi, 181nn.17, 18

Lacan, Jacques, 203–4n.14
Lacoue-Labarthe, Philippe,
    190n.25
Language: as agent, 99–101; and
    consciousness, 50; constitutive
    function of, 138, 148–49, 166;
    and ethics, 139; as identifica-
    tion, 50, 110–11; intentional
    structure of, 100–101; as me-
    diation, 50, 62–63, 87–88,
    97–99, 100, 111, 133, 138, 139–
    40, 150–51, 165; as negation,
    141, 142, 149, 166–67, 200–
    201n.2, 202n.5; as presence
    of being, 94; referential func-
    tion of, 138–39; as repetition
    of language, 152–53, 203–

4n.14; seductive power of,
115, 117, 128, 129–30, 195n.17,
197n.34, 197–98n.36. *See also*
Separation: linguistic origin of;
Symbol; Naming
Latimer, Dan, 191n.1, 192n.3
Lauer, Quentin, 203n.12
Law versus choice, 99–100, 117
Lehman, David, 188n.19
Le Libre Examen (student organi-
zation), 6
Lentricchia, Frank, 205n.4,
206n.20; *After the New Criti-
cism*, 156, 157–58, 159, 162,
205nn.2, 8, 9, 209n.29
Lepenies, Wolf, 179n.3, 180n.5
Lescure, Jean, 199n.40
Les Lettres françaises, 199n.40
Le Soir, 6
Les Temps Modernes, 123, 124, 127,
196n.21
Levin, Harry, 202n.7
Levinas, Emmanuel, 187n.9
Literal versus metaphorical, 165,
207–8n.24
Literature: and commitment, 120,
159, 160, 161, 173, 198n.39,
206n.18, 206–7n.20, 209n.29;
and crisis, 26, 42, 45, 86,
142; and intuition, 25; privilege of, 148, 203n.11; and
science, 6, 8–10, 18, 21–26,
199–200n.41; and sociology,
23–26, 180n.5. *See also* Poetry
Löwith, Karl, 161, 185n.1; *Denker
in dürftiger Zeit*, 123, 125,
126, 130–31, 197nn.31, 33,
34, 198n.40; 'Les implications
politiques de la philosophie

d'existence chez Heidegger,'
123, 196n.21; *Mein Leben in
Deutschland vor und nach 1933*,
196n.21, 197n.26; 'Réponse à
M. de Waelhens,' 196nn.21, 23
Lukács, Georg, 50, 195n.15

Magny, Claude-Edmond: *L'Âge du
roman américain*, 159
Mallarmé, Stéphane, 87, 168,
203n.14, 208–9n.28; and
Baudelaire, 62, 78, 89, 90–91,
101, 106, 133, 144, 148–49; and
Blanchot, 204n.14; and commitment to language, 100; and
Hegel, 63, 86, 186n.7, 188n.22,
190n.26; and history, 151–52;
and Hölderlin, 100, 101, 104,
144, 149; and Montaigne, 31,
34, 35, 86; and politics, 161,
190n.26; and Romanticism,
159; and sacrifice of object,
62–65; and Sartre, 206n.20;
and tragic progression of consciousness, 83–85, 101–2; *Un
Coup de dés*, 64, 84; 'Plusieurs
sonnets,' 62
Malraux, André: anti-historicism
of, 72–75, 126, 129–30; auto-
biographical elements in *Les
Noyers de l'Altenbourg*, 199n.4;
and Baudelaire, 76, 167, 172;
conception of art, 73–74; and
Heidegger, 129–30, 167, 172,
175; and Montaigne, 199n.40;
and nationalism, 74, 126;
and nihilist conservatism, 74,
186n.4; and organic life versus
life of consciousness, 72–74,

Malraux, André (*continued*)
83–84, 129–30, 165, 167, 175,
177, 197–98n.36, 199n.40,
210n.41; resistance to totalitarianism of, 120, 199n.40;
seductive language of, 130;
L'Espoir, 177; *La Lutte contre
l'ange*, 199n.40; *The Walnut
Trees of Altenbourg*, 72–74,
186n.5, 198–99n.40
Mann, Thomas, 180n.5; *Buddenbrooks*, 7
Marañon, Gregorio: opposition to
anti-Republican forces of, 12,
180n.8; *Tiberius*, 11, 180n.7
Martin, Wallace, 200n.1
Marvell, Andrew: 'The Garden,'
140–41
Marx, Karl, 202n.7
Marx, Werner, 193n.7
Marxism, 145–47, 180n.6,
181n.11, 202n.7, 206n.20
Mediation. *See* Language: as
mediation; Symbol: as media-
tion; Sacrifice: and mediation;
Dialectic: as mediation
Melville, Herman: *Moby Dick*,
27–28, 206n.10
Melville, Stephen, 184n.4,
203nn.11, 14, 205n.3
Merleau-Ponty, Maurice, 182n.3,
205n.7; on committed litera-
ture, 207n.20; *The Adventures
of the Dialectic*, 3; 'Indirect
Language and the Voices of
Silence,' 109; 'Lecture de Mon-
taigne,' 182n.2; 'On News
Items,' 27; *Résumés de cours*, 99
Messages, 199n.40

Messkirch, 174, 176
Metaphor versus literal language,
165, 207–8n.24
Metatemporality. *See* Eternalism
Micha, René: 'On the Character of
the Belgians,' 29, 127
Milic, Novica, 187n.7, 191n.3,
205n.3, 209n.29
Mizumura, Minae, 209n.30
Montaigne, Michel de, 28, 29;
and aesthetics, 30, 34–35, 39;
and Baudelaire, 34, 35; and
conservatism, 33–34, 119; and
epistemology, 30–32, 33, 39;
and ethics, 30, 33, 39; and existentialism, 30; and Hendrik
de Man, 36, 37; and Husserl,
33; ironic stance of, 31, 32,
34–35, 39–40, 41–42, 86,
119; and Mallarmé, 31, 34, 35,
86; and Malraux, 199n.40;
and Merleau-Ponty, 182n.2;
resistance in, 33–34; and transcendence, 30–35
Morricone, Ennio, 156
Mussolini, Bennito, 3
Myth, 25

Naming: and being, 50, 93, 94,
97–100, 164, 208n.24; as negation, 200–201n.2, 202n.5; of
pure origin, 166; of separation,
116, 140, 141, 160; true meaning of, 103, 164; and unity,
52–56, 60, 110–11
Narrative, necessity of, 3, 119,
120–22
Nationalism: as centre of factitious loyalties, 34, 39; comple-

mentary, 16–17, 18–19, 25; and
national temperaments, 16–
17, 23, 25, 181n.11, 187n.14,
197n.26; and poetry, 126, 128,
132, 198n.39. *See also* Conservatism: as nationalism
National socialism, 3, 25, 125,
180n.9, 181n.18, 181–82n.19
Natural being. *See* Object
Natural sciences. *See* Science as
model of truth
Nazism. *See* National socialism
Negation, 141, 142, 150, 167,
200–201n.2
New Criticism, 137, 200n.1
Newmark, Kevin, 184n.1
Nietzsche, Friedrich, 192n.5,
194n.13; anti-historicism of,
75, 131; and Baudelaire, 81,
91; and Hegel, 102; and Heidegger, 102, 131, 194n.13;
revolutionary intent of, 119;
and sacrifice of consciousness,
81; and will to power, 91;
Also sprach Zarathustra, 102;
Untimely Meditations, 75
Nihilism, 70–72, 120, 121, 122,
132, 146, 185–86n.1
Noema, 149–51
Noematic correlative, 147, 149,
151, 157
Norris, Christopher, 192–93n.5,
200n.1, 202–3n.9
Noumenon, 112–13
Novel: classical (sociological),
7–10; as failure, 159; as genre,
206n.18; as merchandise, 159;
psychological, 7–10, 12, 18,
180n.5

Object: and consciousness, 31;
ontological superiority of, 56,
57, 64–65, 77–78, 90, 112–
13, 129, 150, 167, 168, 171–72,
184n.4, 202n.6; permanence
of, 56, 72–75, 165–67; sacrifice
of, 64, 82, 172. *See also* Separation (between consciousness
and object)
Oedipus, 189–90n.25
O'Hara, Daniel T., 205n.2
Ontico-ontological distinction, 58
Ontological question: and aesthetics, 121; as crisis, 121; and
existential categories, 70, 122,
146; and history, 122, 202–
3n.9; and politics, 121. *See also*
Resistance as repression: of
ontological question
Ontological superiority. *See* Consciousness: ontological superiority of; Object: ontological
superiority of
Ontologism, 47
Opiela, Stanislas, 193n.7
Origination: of flowers, 164–66;
of words, 164–67
Orpheus, 153, 204n.14

Parker, Andrew, 205n.3
Parmenides, 53–54, 118, 184n.3
Parousia, 95–97, 165
Pastoral convention: and Marx-
ism, 145; and separation,
140–41, 146
Patri, Aimé, 202n.7
Payne, Robert, 74, 186n.5,
199n.40
Pedagogy, 188n.19

Pels, Dick, 179n.1, 181n.11
Permanence: of intention, 76, 83; of object, 56, 72–75, 165–67; resistance to, 111; temptation of, 59, 69, 70–75, 111, 114, 129, 169, 177–78
Petit Larousse, 37–38
Phenomenon, 112
Philology, 199–200n.41
Pingaud, Bernard, 207n.20
Plato: *Parmenides,* 53–54
Poetry: as anti-historical act, 74–75; as distinct from poetics, 70, 134, 144; as historical act, 77, 132, 147, 175; and nationalism, 126, 128, 132, 198n.39; and philosophy, 104, 131, 188–89n.22, 190n.26; versus prose, 160, 195n.17. *See also* Literature; Language
Poetry of becoming, 56, 64, 69, 76–77, 87–89, 91; intentional structure of, 82–86
Poetry of being, 56, 60, 69, 89, 91; intentional structure of, 80–82
Politics: and literature (*see* Commitment and literature); and the ontological question, 121; and universal consciousness, 190n.26, 206n.19
Poster, Mark, 184n.4
Pound, Ezra, 120, 185n.1
Pour soi, 157
Prayer, 97, 98, 101, 103
Préau, André, 210n.40
Presence of the present, 94, 98, 109–10, 116
Prose versus poetry, 160, 195n.17
Proust, Marcel, 34, 35, 120, 156,

206nn.14, 18; *Du côté de chez Swann,* 7
Psychoanalysis, 203–4n.14
Psychology. *See* Science; Novel

Race. *See* Nationalism
Raval, Suresh, 205n.3
Reading and understanding, 195n.17
Redfield, Marc, 193n.5, 203n.10
Referentiality, 138–39
Renunciation, 90, 93, 171, 172, 209n.30. *See also* Sacrifice
Repetition, 194–95, 274n.14
Resistance as repression: of history, 71, 72–75, 122–24; of ontological question, 70–71, 122–23, 125
Resistance as revolt: against aberrations, 33, 34, 39–40; against sterility, 119; against stupidity, 34, 39
Resistance as vigilance: against mysticism and scientism, 199–200n.41; against temptation of permanence, 111, 115, 132, 158
Revue internationale de philosophie, 209n.37
Rhetoric: and analysis of figural language, 204–5n.2; and existential categories, xi, 61, 139. *See also* Death: as figure
Riccomini, Donald Roy, 203n.11
Richard, Jean-Pierre, 144
Richards, I. A., 137–40, 143, 200n.1; *Practical Criticism,* 139
Richardson, William J., 210n.40
Rilke, Rainer Maria, 120; and Heidegger, 94, 174, 209n.33;

as representative of complementary nationalism, 25; revolutionary intent of, 119
Rimbaud, Arthur, 31, 119
Romanticism, 68, 101, 121, 148, 155, 158, 159, 163, 167, 168, 206n.19, 208n.27
Roth, Michael S., 184n.4
Rousseau, Jean-Jacques, 155; and interiority, 170, 176; as Romantic, 121, 208n.27; *Julie,* 168, 178

Sacrifice: of consciousness, 31, 59–60, 62, 64, 81, 103; of hope, 101–2; and mediation, 102–3; of object, 64, 82, 172. *See also* Renunication
Salvation: and criticism, 142–43; and poetry, 92, 101
Sarraute, Nathalie: *L'Ere du soupçon,* 159
Sartre, Jean-Paul, 123, 172; compared to de Man, 156, 157–62; and concept of intentionality, 149; and conflict with Heidegger, 205n.9; influenced by Hegel 205n.8; and Mallarmé, 206–7n.20; and Merleau-Ponty, 182n.2; 'Une idée fondamentale de la phénoménologie de Husserl,' 159, 203n.12; *L'Imaginaire,* 157, 160, 203n.12; *L'Imagination,* 159, 203n.12; *Qu'est-ce que la littérature?* 158, 160, 161, 200–201n.2, 206n.18; Review of *Moby Dick,* 206n.10;

Situations I, 158, 159; 'Structure intentionnelle de l'image,' 157, 158
Sattler, D. E., 192n.4
Schelling, F. W. J. von, 86, 103
Schiller, Friedrich, 189n.24
Schneider, Heinrich, 185n.1
Schor, Alexandre, 183n.14
Science as model of truth: and history, 11–12, 17–18, 75, 77; and ideology, 17–19; and literature, 6, 8–10, 18, 21–26, 199–200n.41; natural and social sciences, 6, 11–12, 17–18, 23–24, 180n.7; and political judgment, 12–15, 18–20; practical use of, 12–13; predictive power of, 17; psychology versus sociology, 7–10. *See also* Deduction; Induction; Technology
Separation (between consciousness and object), 49–50, 51, 56, 57–59, 60, 62–65, 98, 112, 121, 146, 149–50, 157–58, 164, 169; historical origin of, 67–68; and language (*see* Language: as mediation; Symbol: as mediation; Naming: of separation; Pastoral convention: and separation); linguistic origin of, 93, 97–100, 128, 160
Serenity: as escape from ontological question, 70–71, 80–81, 110, 122, 132, 175, 178; as lucidity, 41, 42, 86, 178
Shelley, Percy Bysshe: 'Mont Blanc,' 42
Shusterman, Richard, 200n.1

Sociology, 29, 68; and literature, 23–26, 180n.5. *See also* Science
Socrates, 37
Sophocles, 88
Spengler, Oswald, 197n.31
Spirit. *See* Consciousness
Staiger, Emil, 195n.17
Steinbeck, John, 159
Stoekl, Alan, 181n.17, 191n.3, 205n.3, 209nn.28, 29
Subject. *See* Consciousness
Sychrava, Juliet, 203n.11, 205n.3
Symbol, 51; as identification, 53, 56; as mediation, 63–64
Symbolism, 39, 41, 67–68, 101

Taylor, Mark, 184n.4
Technology, 41, 121, 174–75, 176. *See also* Science
Telos. See Dialectic: final term of
Temporality: authentic attitude toward, 68–69; of consciousness, 56. *See also* Eternalism; History; Object: permanence of
Tison-Braun, Micheline, 199n.40
Totalitarianism, 3, 25, 120, 181n.19
Totality. *See* Unity
Tour de France, 107
Transcendence: and aesthetics, 30, 34–35, 39; and epistemology, 31–32, 33, 39; and ethics, 30, 33, 39
Types: ideological function of, 14, 17 (*see also* Nationalism:

and national temperaments); of novelists, 9–10; in novels, 7–8, 9

Ulysses, 189–90n.25
Unhappy consciousness, 71, 103, 140, 188n.22, 193n.11, 193–94n.12
Unity, 50, 51–53, 56; and death, 54–55. *See also* Naming: and unity
Université Libre de Bruxelles. See Free University of Brussels

Valéry, Paul, 40–41
Vandervelden, Frida, 183n.14

Wager, 144, 202n.6
Wahl, Jean, 202n.6
Walschap, Gerard, 22
Warminski, Andrzej, 186n.7
Waters, Lindsay, 200n.1, 202n.7, 205n.7
Weber, Samuel, 209n.31
Weil, Eric: 'Le cas Heidegger,' 125, 197n.22
Wells, H. G., 180n.5
Wheelwright, Philip, 200n.1
Wordsworth, William: 83, 155, 176; and imagination, 168, 169; and interiority, 170; 'Essay Upon Epitaphs,' xii; *The Prelude,* 168, 169

Yeats, 119, 167, 185n.6, 186n.5

Other Volumes in the series *Texts and Contexts* include:

VOLUME 1
Inscribing the Other
Sander L. Gilman

VOLUME 2
Crack Wars: Literature,
Addiction, Mania
Avital Ronell

VOLUME 3
Madness and Art:
The Life and Works of
Adolf Wölfli
Walter Morgenthaler
Translated by
Aaron H. Esman